THE RADICAL
REFORM
OF
CHRISTIANITY:
A Focus on
Catholicism

THE RADICAL REFORM OF CHRISTIANITY: A Focus on Catholicism

by

EDWARD P. BRENNAN, Ph.D.

Volume VII: The Church and The World Series
Cyriac K. Pullapilly, Saint Mary's College, Notre Dame, Indiana, General Editor
George H. Williams, Harvard University, Consulting Editor

Cross Cultural Publications, Inc.
CrossRoads Books

THE CHURCH AND THE WORLD SERIES

Dedicated to the scholarly investigation of Christianity's interaction with the non-Christian world. This includes the Church's initial encounters with the civilizations of the ancient world, its influence on the various tribal nationalities of the medieval times and its missionary impact in more modern times. Included also are Christianity's ideological and institutional impacts on the secular worlds of science, technology, politics, economics and the arts.

Authors who wish to pulish in the series are requested to contact the General Editor at the address below.

Editorial Board:

Cyriac K. Pullapilly, Saint Mary's College, Notre Dame, General Editor
George H. Williams, Harvard University, Consulting Editor

Published by **CROSS CULTURAL PUBLICATIONS, INC.**
CROSS ROADS BOOKS
Post Office Box 506
Notre Dame, Indiana, 46556, U.S.A.
Phone: (219) 273-6526, 1-800-561-6526
FAX: (219) 273-5973

TABLE OF CONTENTS

I

Lying to the young is wrong.
Proving to them that lies are true is wrong.
Telling them that God's in his heaven and all's well with the world
is wrong.

Yevgeny Yevtushenko

JIMMY

When I was a very young boy, in fact the youngest in a family of nine children, two parents and an aged grandmother, I had to share an attic bedroom with a brother several years older. I think everyone knows how night harbors a fullness and a mystery that go far beyond the mere absence of light. The dark becomes filled with anything and everything that we can imagine. It happens that the nights of my attic bedroom were inhabited by an unsavory, dangerous presence named Jimmy. The creator of Jimmy was, as I discovered in time, my roommate-brother. Jimmy's reality and overshadowing presence pervade the earliest memories of my childhood. I had to pay fealty to Jimmy. I had to behave in certain ways to serve the good pleasure of Jimmy. Bounty was exacted of me at times just to keep Jimmy content. Of course the very worst aspect of Jimmy was bedtime. I was greatly troubled to have to ascend to the dark recess of the attic alone at night and try to sleep there in Jimmy's domain.

I remember well my mother's logic when she tried to coax me out of the idea of Jimmy. I was able to come to the obvious logical conclusion that Jimmy could not possibly exist, much less live in our attic. However, Jimmy was not based in my logical mind, but in the fear of my heart. What could or could not be in this world was too big an issue for me to be certain about in my heart. So, turn out the lights and begin the ascent, and Jimmy became as perceptible to me as the creaking of the stairs.

It took me years of reflection to realize why my mother's logic could not dispel my illusion of Jimmy. The mysterious environment of my heart had been invaded by his presence, and logic alone cannot dispel this kind of presence. For value and meaning are not born in the mind; they take their origin in the desire of the heart. We are not threatened at the level of mind; we are threatened, vulnerable, only in the heart, in our emotional being. Logical arguments do not even approach this central place in the heart where we first create our world of meaning and value. It was necessary for me, on my own and in my own time, to struggle with and ultimately to conquer this illusion, this nothing-at-all-ness that inhabited my heart and its playground, my imagination, as Jimmy.

At a vulnerable moment in my life, when I needed an honest communication about our attic at night, I was lied to. Whatever valuable lesson in life I may have learned from my struggle with Jimmy—and this book will reveal an important one—to create an illusion like this in the life of another person is a cruel and unconscionable hoax that no one should ever perpetrate. Yet it happens. Happily, Jimmy's influence was limited to the realm of night, in fact only early night, since Jimmy vanished with sleep.

The symbolic significance of Jimmy is clear to me now. It tells me this: All of us are exceedingly vulnerable at that place in our heart where we sense life as both important and mysterious. In our heart we feel powerless because we really do not know how things ultimately are, and yet we feel the need to know.

This brings to mind a later time and the many chats I would have with a fine gentleman who was considerably older than myself. This man was quite talented and successful by ordinary worldly standards. He was also, without question, a pillar of the Church. I enjoyed talking with him because of his worldly wisdom, but also because of his openness to and enthusiasm about ideas. Now that he is dead, I remember a question he had framed many times in our chats: "Eddie, what's it all about?" I now regret that I could never relate to his question. Because of his advancing years this man was necessarily facing death, and he knew it. It was clear to me that he was afraid of death. So he posed the Great Question—"What's it all about?"—but I was unable to hear him.

Looking back, I know my own presumption at that time. It kept me from conversing seriously about his question. I felt that this man's worldly wisdom would have to suffice for him. I must now confess that I was mistaken. My presumption stemmed from the fact that I knew the framework upon which this man's religious thinking was built. It was the same as my own. I also realized how many years of formal study and personal pondering it had taken for me to go beyond narrow interpretations of religious symbols. Mistakenly, as I now believe, I thought my elderly friend was not prepared for this kind of work.

I could not bring myself to tell my friend that his mind was burdened with childish ideas. When the religious issue was first brought to him at a vulnerable age, it had been intruded into his life as a Jimmy. He was given an overpowering set of answers to all questions. They were the kind of answers that precluded further growth in spiritual understanding by foreclosing further questioning. As my friend's mental powers and worldly experience expanded beyond the symbols and ideas that befit a child's mind, he would now have to face the whole point of life, "What's it all about," as a man—on his own. In retrospect, I feel he was somehow asking for permission to do just that. He wanted someone he trusted to tell him that it is all right to suspend belief in anything that is merely told us, in everything that is not shown directly to our own intelligence. He needed leave to do the kind of *radical* thinking that could take him to the *root* of his own spiritual question, his quest. I failed an honest response. I will not make this mistake in the future, for every person has the right to our honest answer. And it is never too late to offer it.

Conversely, a person also has the right not to ask the Great Question and, above all, to be spared our answer. Some may well feel that the stakes are too high to allow that their view of the great matter might be inadequate, not to say mistaken. Having already made a large investment, they could insist that their stock is good. They might opt to live with what I am suggesting is the unreality of their Jimmy. To open the Great Question afresh could be more than they wish to bear.

But I know that there is a good and growing number of people who are anxious to move beyond their inherited presumptions— beyond Jimmy. They are prepared to give up their security-blanket ideas and ask themselves some hard questions. They are not afraid to seriously ask, "What is it all about?" This is the question at the core of spirituality. I want to foster this kind of inner dialogue in such religiously serious people. That, in a nutshell, is the purpose of this book.

II

Because they love mystery and not the bare truth, religions pamper them, only finally to bring them round to the truth.

Ramana Maharshi

AUTHENTIC RELIGION AND
THE HISTORICAL CHURCH

You take proper care of the things you value. It is not hard to guess the value you place on some particular thing by the kind of care you give it. If you value your new car, you keep it clean, oiled, tuned. It receives the right maintenance. When it malfunctions, you do not throw it away. On the contrary, you attend to it. You look into the problem and do what it takes to restore the car to its fully functional condition.

What is more valuable to us than the whole of our life? "Religion" is how we name the force within us which prompts us to pay attention to our life as a whole. Religion is not just one among many aspects of life. It is not even the most important aspect. Rather, religion relates to every dimension of our life. It draws them together and puts each element of life in its right place so that it might serve our life's ultimate purpose. For the task of religion is to orient our entire life toward its true goal. To say this much, however, does not answer the very large question of just what that goal is. Nevertheless, it suggests that religion is vitally important. It is as valuable as the purpose of our life. It deserves our greatest care, our unflagging attention.

Religion itself must not be confused with any particular religious form or organization. A religious organization is only an instrument for doing the work of religion. The organization is useful only to the extent that it actually serves the purpose of religion. It is worthwhile only to the degree that it draws our entire life together in the light of life's purpose. No one with any sense of history will argue that a religious organization, a church, cannot go awry and lose its connection to authentic religion. In the case

4

of the Catholic Church in particular, Pope John XXIII spoke of this fact with the telling, originally Protestant, phrase, *ecclesia semper reformanda*, "the church ever to be reformed." If a church is to be kept right (reformed) so as to serve the purpose of religion, and thus the purpose of life itself, then it is the responsibility of its members to correct everything about it that is not right. Its members are the ones who are cheated by its infidelity. They are misled when its ways become twisted. They are the ones who have the need and, therefore, the interest in preserving their church in its integrity. Thus it is first and foremost the members who are charged always to reform their church.

How do we determine what is not right in a church? To answer this question we have to get some sense of what religion is. We can give a simple description of religion by returning to the original Latin meaning of the word. *Religion* is supposed to derive from the Latin word, *re-ligare*, which means re-connect. As a simple description, religion pertains to whatever it is that might reconnect us.

Religion exists because people feel a disconnectedness. Our disconnectedness creates in us a pain more profound and more total than mere bodily ailments. I call it "the pain in the heart." We experience reverberations of this core pain of our heart when we feel fear in the face of death. Or when hard conditions cause us to question the meaning and value of life. Our core pain is felt as bewilderment when we experience life's reversals: the failure of love, the physical pains and mental stresses that beset us, our losses and frustrations. Our suffering of these experiences is all spawned from a center, from a heart which, as St. Augustine expressed it, is "disquiet."

Our restlessness of heart and the religious impulse it generates leave us vulnerable. For our need is urgent and comprehensive. We embrace one or another religious tradition as a means to reconnect. At the same time, however, we do not feel expert in the matter of our heart and of our destiny. It is a very profound matter. So we have to ask the obvious question: What is it that religion would reconnect us to?

Since we are the ones who feel the religious impulse as coming from a sense of loss or disconnectedness, we can say at least this much: Religion is what helps reconnect us to our Source. At this point we need not say much more about it. The religious impulse itself—our drive toward wholeness—already tacitly acknowledges and readily confesses an inherent value, a sacred quality, to human life. We try to act upon this recognition of the sacredness and therefore of the inherent rights of every person.[1] We feel guilty when we fail to do this. We are deeply offended at people who flagrantly abuse the sacred character of other persons. We know that every person is somehow related to a realm of the Sacred, even if the poignancy of separation is our present experience. At the same time we might be cautious about saying more about this until we are actually reconnected and know firsthand what we are talking about. But even the vague recognition of our sacred Source enables us to ask of any church the discriminating question: In what way do you help, and in what way may you be hindering, our reconnecting to our Source?

Does our church serve religion well, or does she serve poorly? The direct way to answer this question is to find out if we are actually reconnecting to our Source or not? How effectively does the church help make this happen for us? Is the service of the church working? Is our religious life one of a continuing strengthening of our reconnection? We surely feel our disconnectedness as a kind of thirst that is never quenched by the waters of ordinary life. So if a religious organization really works, then we ought to feel the reconnection and not just be assured by somebody else that we are all right. If we had a serious physical pain that prompted us to visit a medical doctor, we would certainly not be content with the doctor's reassurance that we are healthy. At some point we need to feel better.

In the final analysis, what do we have other than our own feeling for determining what is right or what is wrong in our life? Were we ever correct when, based only on the logic of our mind, we made a decision that ran contrary to our true feelings about a matter? A particular pair of shoes might be grand for someone else's feet. But if they do not feel right on our feet, those shoes are not for us. Our own feelings tell us just how we are in this moment and what is in our best interest right now. Our feelings express our sense of our own inner self; they are our ultimate criterion.

Our arm, for example, rises spontaneously to protect our face from a physical danger. In a sudden fall our body automatically turns its strongest part to take the brunt of the fall. Similarly, our body perceives if it is off balance even to the slightest degree. Is our psyche less intelligent than our body? I have to say No. Just as our body senses its own true condition, so our inner self has the capacity to sense its own condition and its needs best. Feeling is the wisdom that inheres in the very consciousness of both our body and our psyche. This does not, of course, suggest a simplistic appeal to our present feelings about something in order to come to an accurate judgement about what is right for us. As if the advice of the moment, "If it feels good, do it!", is a sensible guide. In order to give us an accurate report of our situation, our feelings must not be confused. They must be clear. In modern parlance, we must be in touch with our actual feelings. Sages invariably advise us to trust and follow our own heart. But we must first be clear about our heart. In other words, through our feelings we possess the natural power to know for ourselves what is right for us. But we must contact our own feelings directly and clearly. We make this power ineffective when we put too much emphasis on figuring things out mentally or logically. This is especially true when we use the thinking of others to come to conclusions about ourselves. We might say that the path to the Path (*i.e.*, our personal starting point for embracing a genuinely spiritual way of life) is to become clear about our actual feeling-state. This first step we must take by ourselves. No one can do it for us, for we alone feel what we feel. Until we take this first step into genuine spirituality, we are at best blind and being lead by others. At worst, we remain adrift in confusion, moved by ever-changing and impersonal currents.

Authentic religion is as personally intimate to our total life as our health is to our physical life. Religious traditions, like medicine, take on a social, institutional form, since they are designed to help many people. But the ultimate issue is very individual, very personal. Are you being restored to health through this medical assistance? This is the test each person must apply to medicine. Similarly, Are you being reconnected to the Source? is the test that judges religious traditions. Our own natural feelings, if we can get in direct touch with them, can advise us well about both these matters.

If only a real, a felt, effect validates a particular religious organization or church, then the evidence of the vast majority of people stands out. They are not being reconnected. They are not growing in happiness and wholeness. Even people who give great heed to a particular religious tradition live for the most part in hopes and promises, dreams of better things to come. Right now they experience dissatisfaction. They are searching for something much better. Perhaps we should be put on alert by this present and very real experience.

We all know many instances where a person was advised to live out an unwholesome condition: "It is just the way things are and must be," s/he was told. It can happen, for example, that a doctor out of sheer ignorance will relinquish a patient to unnecessary chronic suffering "because nothing can be done about this condition." Often a counselor or lawyer will consign a person to a destructive marriage relationship, again out of disregard for how the person feels about it and of ignorance of that person's need and willingness to take effective action. Submitting to bad counsel, many people have lived a life of hell. Instances of this kind could be recounted endlessly. Even the slaves in early America were told by their Christian preachers that the bitter, subhuman condition of slavery was willed for them by God, and that they were actually lucky to have been saved from their heathenish life in Africa by being captured and brought to their condition of slavery. They were told that their new circumstance was a positive good, "sanctioned by Scripture and capable of producing a Christian social order."[2] While slaveholders and missionaries were thus able to convince themselves that slavery provided an advantage for Negroes, namely enabling them to learn about the Christianity of their masters, it should be mentioned that the slaves themselves did not feel that way.

So how does the evidence read? Do we feel a reconnection? Or are we merely assured by somebody that we are indeed reconnecting? Are we asked to *believe* that this most important fact of our life is happening? Or do we know it for ourselves because we experience it?

The evidence I see is that religious life, true spiritual life, is at a stunningly low ebb at present. It barely exists. Most religious folk only believe and hope that something spiritual is happening in their lives. They have little evidence of it in their actual experience, in their feeling of life. They suffer the rounds of daily existence much as people do who make no pretence of being religious. The spiritual part of their life consists in little more than belonging to a religious organization, attending church services more or less regularly, offering financial support for the organization, and perhaps occasionally trying, too often unsuccessfully, to *pray*.

What is it that obstructs a full, experienced spiritual life for most people? Spiritual life is not for just a few, saintly people. Everybody who experiences disconnectedness needs to reconnect. True spiritual life is nothing other than this reconnecting and full participation in life. To continue our analogy with physical health, if all of us were physically ill, we would all have the same need to be restored to health. There would not be merely a few of us who should become healthy, and the rest of us honor those few. It would be everyone's task to be restored to health. By the same token we are all responsible for fulfilling our human destiny.

It is an understatement to say that Christianity is not spiritually effective for many [most?] Christians today. Although I will focus in a special way on the Catholic Church, by implication the entire tradition of Christianity must be considered by the same standards. *The Church* is the term I shall use to refer both to the Catholic Church and to Christian churches generally. For most of what is said here directly about Catholicism easily applies to other Christian churches. Much of it pertains also to religious traditions beyond Christendom.

Clearly, the Church needs to be put right by cleansing it of everything that does not serve its true purpose. Anything that does not serve its true purpose does not really belong to it at all. To take an example from our relationship with objects, if we own something that no longer serves its purpose we are wise to simplify our life and throw it away. However, cleaning up is much harder in matters associated with our life and destiny than it is with things. In politics, for example, when we become dissatisfied with a civic leader or a social situation, we have to wait for another election and then convince enough voters about our views. The Church, however, is not democratic; it has never allowed the vote. So purification in the Church cannot be brought about through an election. As I see it, the Church can be reformed most effectively through criticism, when we bring discriminating judgment to bear on the religious elements of our lives. In this book I hope to bring discriminating judgment to bear on the Church's fulfillment of her spiritual responsibility.

Criticism, especially as I create it in these pages, is a kind of diagnosis. In the present context, criticism is the first step in determining what belongs to spiritual health and what creates the spiritual malaise so common among us. Criticism is undoubtedly also a dangerous thing. It needs to be done carefully and humbly, and by a heart that is without rancor. Purifying criticism is done best when it comes from within, from someone who knows the whole range out of personal experience. Concerning criticism of the Catholic Church the noted Jesuit scholar John L. McKenzie had this to say:

> "...it should also be remembered that members of
> a church are able to criticize it in ways and in depth
> which the outsider cannot match."[3]

McKenzie's point is well taken. Who but an inside participant is environmentally aware—aware not only of facts and interpretations, but aware as one who has breathed the very atmosphere in which these facts and interpretations have been bred and nurtured?

Consequently, my special focus is on the Roman Catholic Church because I know it best, from the inside out. Born, raised, and schooled a Roman Catholic, having studied theology and been ordained a priest in Rome, I am a thoroughbred. I was privileged to meet the watershed personality of the modern Catholic reformation, Pope John XXIII. Later I was to stand vigil for a half hour or so, alone and unbeknownst, with his lifeless remains at the high altar of St Peter's. This has remained a precious and thought-provoking memory to me. Another privilege I was given straight from the spiritual heart of the Catholic Church was a personal visit with Padre Pio, an imposing yet unassuming spiritual personality who was in psychic and bodily alignment with the sufferings of Jesus.

A yet more profound reason recommends a special focus on Catholicism. This reason was articulated best by a Methodist, the insightful journalist and thoughtful writer Kenneth Briggs, who considered the central place of Catholicism within Christianity to be "self-evident":

> "The Catholic Church, in my opinion, is an essential point of reference for all other branches of Christianity unlike any other church, not because it is rooted in a divine or infallible blueprint, but because it is, rather, the trunk line bearing the whole legacy, good and bad, from which the rest take their points of departure... Protestantism is uniquely contingent on Catholicism."[4]

Coming from within the very embrace of Christianity, it is both difficult and necessary for me to measure her spiritual performance against the demands of authentic religion. This means, the Church must become accountable before, not a Christian god of her own fashioning, but reality. In other words, as a religion, Christianity must always be measured by the standard of authentic religion, by how faithfully and effectively she helps reconnect us to our Source. Further, it is not only the Christian experience of religion that must be measured against the standard of authentic religion. The many religious forms and institutions outside Christianity, which purport to serve our religious need, are all implicated in this questioning.

I must indicate what I see to be possibly our greatest obstacle to appreciating the validity and usefulness of a broad criticism. This obstacle is the categorical mentality that sees only in terms of black or white, of good or evil. It is for this reason that people sometimes cannot allow any criticism of their children. They know that their child is not bad, so they presume that any criticism is mistaken. Yet I have hardly met anything in life that is either completely good and wholesome or totally bad with no redeeming value. Our discriminating intelligence is what allows us to discern what is wholesome and valuable in mixed, but real, situations. This holds also for a church or any religious organization that exists to serve our religious impulse. A church is not necessarily completely good. And, since a church is there to promote the very purpose of our life, does it not deserve at least as much attention as, say, the health of our body?

In reviewing many aspects and dimensions of the Church in a critical way, I have hopes and expectations similar to those of the journalist and political commentator, David Broder, when he wrote a backstage book on journalism and living journalists. Not everything was complimentary in Mr. Broder's *Behind the Front Page: A Candid Look at How the News Is Made*. About its effect on his colleagues Mr. Broder said this to a reviewer:

> "I hope it stirs up some fights. I hope I've said some things that are going to make some people in our business mad. If it does that, it would please me a lot, particularly if it gets them thinking as well as gets them angry."

I have learned, however, that as dependent as American politics is on journalistic criticism, that service is not extended to the Church. In American politics we know that journalistic criticism is not only the respected but the expected order of the day. We agree that the truth should come out. Nobody is sacrosanct; nobody is even safe. Let everyone beware the truth.

Strangely somehow, journalism's demand for truth, which works somewhat well as applied to our American political system, is suspended when public attention turns to religion. My long-standing observation has been confirmed lately by historian-journalist Elinor Burkett and reporter Frank Bruni. In discussing notorious instances of child sexual abuse by priests, these authors write,

> "Reporters and their editors have been skittish about shining the same harsh investigatory light on priests and the Church that they do on other individuals in positions of community and trust...It was a more subtle collusion borne of respect

bordering on awe for an institution whose power
seems to transcend the temporal."[5]

Journalists tend to treat established religious bodies and their
leaders with a stunning deference. In the winter of 1987, for
example, the Vatican issued a document condemning many of
society's practices regarding human conception (surrogate moth-
erhood, in vitro fertilization and the like). The document appeared
quite dogmatic in regard to many issues that are still open for
discussion in the American mind. Moreover, the Vatican asked
the governments of the world to put into law many of its views on
these matters, a request that is alien to the American way of doing
things. Pluralism in thought is inherent in American society. Our
decision-making process reflects and even benefits from this
pluralism. Furthermore, our methods in science and technology
have opened our minds to the many possibilities that may reside
in new areas of investigation such as medical technology. Given
this American experience, therefore, the Vatican's preemptive
instruction, following its backroom deliberations, no doubt appeared ignorant and in parts preposterous to intelligent American
journalists. Yet shortly after the Vatican declaration, I happened
to see on national television some of the most respected journalists
of our country interviewing Vatican representatives concerning
views contained in their document. These hardnosed journalists
pussyfooted around a number of crucial social issues. They
showed traits I never notice in them except when they are in
discussion with Church leaders. Journalists do not hesitate to ask
the President of the United States if he is not indeed a liar. A
frontrunning presidential contender can be asked if he has ever in
fact committed adultery. But an Archbishop espousing views that
I feel many of the journalists would dismiss out of hand was
accorded their thoughtful attention.

It seems that the persons and institutions associated with
religion often cast a spell over otherwise intelligent and experienced men and women. Where does this sacred aura come from?
I suggest that it is a *cultic* appreciation of religion. Jesus, you will
remember, railed against the religious figures of his day. He
accused them of doing great harm to unwitting folk in the name of
God. He likened these religious personalities to painted coffins,
attractive on the outside but "full of dead men's bones."[6] From the
example of Jesus I insist that criticism in the matter of religion is
a very Christian thing. But who is going to do it?

Very few have the spiritual insight to offer so penetrating a criticism as that of Jesus and other prophets. But we all have some degree of intelligence, as well as some interest in truth and in our own destiny. We have a rightful need for clarity and good sense about things traditionally associated with religion. In this book I am appealing only to our ordinary discriminating intelligence.

In this spirit I neither expect nor desire anyone to accept from the present discussion a view that is merely mine. I want all readers to reflect on their own experience and to allow their own native intelligence to shine. This is an option that has only recently been given to Catholics, and even then only within certain limitations.[7] But I suggest that just as we human beings have shown ourselves to be masterful in scientific inquiry, so should we be capable of exceptional insight when we apply our intelligence to our inner experience. We can become clear about our impulse toward wholeness that we rightly call religious. For in the last analysis it is we who are responsible for bringing this impulse to realization. We are the ones charged with the responsibility for our own spiritual well-being. While the general notion of individual responsibility is supported by nearly everyone, I am here saying that the notion of responsibility is frighteningly absolute: each of us is finally responsible for our own ultimate destiny. This is daunting.

A final word must be said about using the idea of *cult* in the critique I am making. I do not use this term lightly. I will set out a clear definition of what I mean by cult in due time. In a preliminary way I can suggest something of the importance of the idea of cult in this entire critique.

We have identified authentic religion as that which responds to our sense of separation and which helps reconnect us to our sacred Source. All too often our intelligence is blinded by imaginary solutions offered to our spiritual problem, which is the core pain in our heart. One such imaginary solution is the ordinary person's idea of *heaven*, a *New Jerusalem* with streets lined with gold. Of course this particular biblical symbol of heaven as the New Jerusalem[8] is not expected to be taken literally. Still the reality it symbolizes is imagined to be quite like it. This is an instance of what one spiritual author has called "spiritual materialism."[9] Spiritual materialism amounts to thinking of and pursuing absolute reality in terms of the highest kind of experience we know from our life in the world. Spiritual materialism is the highest aspiration of people who have not yet seen very deeply into their actual life-experience. They look for a heaven of the same kind of experience, only upgraded to a heavenly degree—an eternity of creature comforts. "Visions of sugarplums dance in their heads."

Authentic religion knows that no conceivable extension of the life we know reconnects us to our Source. This is why authentic religion remains wary of turning our religious impulse to serve the restless purposes of our life in this world, even trying to extend it forever into an imagined heaven. As I will explain in some detail, the greatest challenge to authentic religion, *i.e.* to our spiritual impulse, is our clinging to this world of our present experience.

By *cultic religion* I mean simply the distortion of authentic religion, the twisting of true spiritual instruction to serve the purposes of what is finally only a worldly life. It is a very common thing. But it is also the worst possible thing. In the words of the famous Latin phrase, *corruptio optimi pessima* [the corruption of what is the finest is the worst sort of corruption]. Cult, as I use the word, signals the corruption of religion.

When I speak of the Cult, then, I am not referring to the Catholic Church or to any Christian Church as such. Rather, I am inquiring into cultic aspects of the Church. Every dimension or aspect of the Church that does not rightly belong to the simple but profound matter of authentic religion is cultic. Moreover, I am consciously including all cultic religion in the Christian example. The mere fact that cultic aspects are numerous in religious organizations does not invalidate what we can call a True Church. It just means that a True Church, always a living instrument of authentic religion, will be discovered only with effort, through acute discrimination. Perhaps this is a good thing. The effort itself might prepare the individual person for the daunting responsibility and work that authentic religion requires of all of us.

Before we examine the Cult, however, we will first consider something of the Catholic experience. We will see how cultic aspects have weakened the spiritual work of the Church. We will begin, then, by considering what it has been like for many Catholics to feel the loss of the Sacred in their lives.

NOTES

[1] The noted philosopher Immanuel Kant, although not religious in the conventional sense, based his ethics on the inherent sacredness of personhood which he expressed in a magnificent paragraph, almost poetic in quality, which describes the nobility of the human soul in terms of its responsibility or "duty." *Cf. Kant's Critique of Practical Reason and Other Works*, trans. T.K. Abbott

(Longmans Green and Co., 1873), p. 71.

2 Albert J. Raboteau, *Slave Religion*, (Oxford University Press, 1978), pp. 152ff.

3 McKenzie, John L., *The Roman Catholic Church*, (Holt, Rinehart and Winston, 1969), p. xiv.

4 Kenneth A. Briggs, *Holy Siege: The Year That Shook Catholic America*, (Harper San Francisco, 1992), p. 2.

5 *A Gospel of Shame: Children, Sexual Abuse, and the Catholic Church*, (Viking Penguin, 1993), p. 178.

6 *Matthew* XXIII, 27.

7 See "Dogmatic Constitution on Divine Revelation" of Vatican Council II. Pope Pius XII had made an opening in this regard particularly in his 1943 Encyclical *Divino afflante spiritu*, which allowed Catholic Scripture scholars considerably greater latitude in their study and interpretation of Old and New Testament texts. Catholic scholars made headway rather quickly in recovering much of the ground lost to their Protestant counterparts who had not suffered authoritarian, dogmatic strictures from their religious bodies.

8 *Revelations* XXI.

9 Chogyam Trungpa, *Cutting Through Spiritual Materialism*, (Shambhala Publications, Inc., 1973).

III

We share the opinion of those who consider an extensive and thorough reformation of the Church to be necessary and inevitable, however long it may be postponed.

Ignaz von Dollinger

THE CATHOLIC EXPERIENCE

How has religion reached such crisis proportions in the everyday lives of so many people? What has been their down-to-earth experience that has brought more than a few people, Christian people in particular, to spiritual confusion, even to an impasse?

A great number have experienced a religious crisis as members of the Roman Catholic Church. While I see the roots of this Catholic crisis extending way down into the foundation of religion itself, it will not hurt to consider the earthy way in which individual Catholics have come to sense a dislocation in their spiritual heritage. Sociologist Father Andrew Greeley has documented some aspects of a tremendous fallout among American Catholics during the decade following Vatican Council II.[1] Protestant theology had already taken serious note of the inadequacy of much of the Christian heritage in the face of modern life and thought.[2]

Nearly every Catholic I know who is spiritually serious experiences some degree of confusion about her or his Church. "What is happening?" they ask. "Are there no absolutes left? What will be changed next? Is there anything there that I can rely on? Is the ritual of the Church, particularly the Mass and Sacraments, what it purports to be? Is Jesus for real? Is he God? Is God there, and can I know this for myself? What do I finally believe? What must I believe? What is prayer, really? Is it appropriate to ask God to intervene in my affairs? Is the Catholic Church the One True Church, or is it just one more among the many religious organizations of the world? Is it just another human attempt to reach beyond our obvious, born condition? But on the other hand, how can I drop the Sacred from my life? I know, in my heart of hearts

I truly know, that my existence is founded in the Sacred. The restlessness of my own heart is proof to me of a Sacred domain. A brief sojourn on planet earth is not what my life is ultimately about. This I know and feel as strongly as I know and feel my heart's true desire." What a dilemma!

Before considering Catholics in crisis, however, we should take note of those Roman Catholics, and Christians generally, who adhere to their Church simply as it has been given to them. It appears that they are relatively satisfied with what their Church means to them. They do not seem to feel a need to think about its exact place in their life, not to mention its place in the great matter of universal existence. I should confess that when I attend Mass I sometimes observe what appear to me to be unreflective Catholics. They look like they are practicing their religion the best they know how, although it may well be without much spiritual content or demand. Observing people who appear spiritually satisfied makes me reluctant to offer a critique that might trouble them. But what I feel to be my better judgment tends to catch up with me. First of all, are these people really satisfied and unquestioning? And even if they are, is it not condescending to treat intelligent adults as spiritually naive and tender just because they have not yet been struck by what others find problematic? Authentic religion is necessary for everyone, for the simple as well as the complex, for the centrists as well as the left or right wingers, for the extraverted as well as the introspective, for the layperson as well as the professional. In any case, if there are satisfied Catholics who may be offended by the conversation I initiate here, I believe their need of protection is outbalanced by numerous others' need of serious reflection. My own experience gives me the sense that a great majority of seemingly satisfied Christians suffer, in novelist Iris Murdoch's pointed words,

> "...sentimental gushings of a ridiculous familiarity offered to a deity devoid of dignity, devoid of austerity, devoid even of mystery, but now just proving horribly hard to get rid of."[3]

In the Catholic fold we find numerous displaced men and women who range from dismayed Church members to embittered former Catholics. Most of them feel they have been betrayed by the Church in one way or another. Many had taken the Church's beliefs and practices as absolute. They were led to believe that their pipeline to heaven was intact. Now they feel deceived in discovering that many of their Catholic beliefs and practices were quite arbitrary, and that a good number of these beliefs and practices are no longer even in force.[4]

We might begin with a simple example, one concerned not with basic beliefs of the Church, but with long-standing practice. I speak of the awe with which Catholics once approached the Eucharist, Holy Communion. Communion had been their tangible as well as spiritual communication with their Lord through the bread and wine of Mass. This awe had long been expressed ritually in the requirement to abstain from food and drink prior to reception of this sacrament. The awe that was expressed through ritual, as well as the Eucharistic mystery itself, was lessened considerably when the abstinence period was shortened, first to three hours, then to one hour before receiving Communion. Finally the requirement to abstain was abandoned altogether, which significantly lessened for many Catholics the aura that had surrounded their Holy Communion. They were not impressed by the argument that more people would receive the Eucharist now that the fast was abolished. This sounded too much like cheap grace. In like manner, the sense of worship that was symbolized by kneeling to receive Communion was diminished for many Catholics with the adoption of the standing position. The old practice of a kneeling submission to Christ as God seemed to give way, with a loss, to equality with Jesus as brother.

A similar sense of loss accompanied the revision of the Lenten fast, the basic expression of this season of penance. The traditional fast had reduced food intake to only one full meal per day, two minor meals, and no eating between meals. This fast, combined with several abstinence-from-meat days, made Lent an occasion for spiritual reckoning. It gave meaning to the ritual of *Mardi Gras*, which is French for Fat Tuesday. This Tuesday is called fat because at one time it was the last fling before the rigors of Lent which would begin the following day, Ash Wednesday. It was a celebratory anticipation of the strong spiritual discipline of fasting. The entire sense of personal sacrifice and spiritual reflection that were symbolized, and to an extent enabled, by the full Lenten practice were essentially abandoned by the new self-indulgent legislation. The average Catholic would be hard-pressed to say what today's Lenten responsibilities regarding fast and abstinence are. I venture to add that maintaining this kind of discipline is relatively obsolete in the modern Church. When Lent as a season of penance was in this way denatured or *de-penanced*, Catholics were left with a sole regular reminder of their Catholicity: abstaining from meat on Friday. New Church legislation soon abolished this. The surface of traditional Catholic culture, however one may have looked upon it, was at last dissolved into mainstream American Christian religiosity.

Yet these very practical indulgences are not the most important, nor even the most striking, changes that have recently confronted Catholics. More embittered, because touched more profoundly at the level of life-experience, are those Catholics and former Catholics who have suffered terrible guilt because they were unable to meet the demands of the Church law, taught as divine law, against divorce. Many of these men and women came to discover that present-day unhappy marriages, marriages that seem to be very much like their own, are now annulled by the Church. Church annulment is a declaration that these unions were never real marriages in the first place. Never mind that often the *seeming* marriage involved two Catholic adults, that it took place in a church before a priest at Mass, and that it resulted in a large family. We can easily sympathize with guilty divorced Catholics who witness the Church's modern handling of unhappy unions that were entered into with full Catholic formality. If you go to the right priest and answer questions in the right way, the Church is now willing to consider your union to be only an apparent marriage and not a real one. Yet divorced Catholics of an earlier day see today's Catholics delivered from their marriage mistake, and free to marry new partners, without the pangs of conscience that they themselves were forced to undergo—pangs which all too often persist. This holds for those Catholics who, in spite of the Church's law, decided to break their, shall we say, "real" marriages and secure an unauthorized divorce. Then what about the many Catholics who paid the heavy price of living a destructive life with an incompatible spouse just to uphold the marriage law! They too are bothered by the easy annulment that the Church declares for modern unhappy marriages which for one or another odd reason are judged only apparent and not real.

Equally embittering to many more Catholics is the practical change in the Church's opposition to artificial contraception. Every priest who has counselled both within and without the confessional has his own horror stories relative to the Church's ban on artificial contraception. Many priests, active as well as those no longer active, feel remorse in having been a party to this insanity—imposing foolish rules into the consciences of decent people, rules that created untold conflict in their intimate, marital lives. What is it like to have insisted to a mother of four or five little ones that God will be seriously offended by sexual intimacy with her husband if such intimacy is not "open to life," *i.e.* subject to still another pregnancy and birth?

When priests began to recognize that gerrymandering the sexual nature of married people around a "safe" period—the so-called rhythm method of contraception—is itself hardly "natural," practical change began to happen. The party line on artificial contraception has not changed, to be sure. And this line still pretends to communicate the Will of God. God is declared to be offended by artificial contraception, and the official Church says she knows this for sure, more or less. I say "more or less" to reflect the irony in Pope Paul VI's tacit communication that he was not speaking infallibly [*ex cathedra*—"from the seat" of authority] when he formulated his condemnation of artificial contraception in his 1968 Encyclical, *Humanae Vitae*. In this Encyclical Paul VI rejected the overwhelming majority advice of the Commission he had established to study the issue, a Commission that undertook their study with the strong presumption that no change would result. However, after reviewing the Scriptural arguments, the Natural Law arguments, and the historical background of this ban, the vast majority of this sixty-some member Commission, with forceful theological and historical reasoning, recommended lifting the ban.[5] Meanwhile Catholics had come to learn that the morality of contraception was being reconsidered by a Commission of professionals and laypersons at the request of the Pope. It is true that during those years of study Pope Pius VI continued to insist that the question was not an open one—in the face of daring speeches and articles coming from renowned members of the hierarchy.[6] But this illogical insistence simply did not wash with most Catholics. The question did become open to the majority of them, and they discontinued looking for guidance for their family planning from celibate Roman authorities. Catholics' relationship to the entire matter of artificial contraception changed radically. The naive thing was that Pope Paul VI, who was in many ways aware of the modern cultural mentality, thought he could get this cat back into the traditional bag, that Catholics would adhere to his opinion on such a serious personal matter.[7] It was with such a mindset that he lent his authority to the very small minority of the Commission and issued the Encyclical that banned artificial contraception.

Not long ago nearly all priests and bishops both believed and delivered this party line. Today it is difficult to determine which priests and bishops, if any, truly believe this line, although all too many still deliver it. Where once artificial birth control was condemned regularly and vehemently from the pulpits—the pastor of my boyhood church called contraceptive practice "legalized prostitution"—today the issue is most often muted. For artificial contraception has become by far the majority practice among Catholics, and this with the blessing of many priests and some bishops who have no further ambitions. Still, betrayal and confusion are felt by many Catholics who submitted to having families much larger than they wanted, often at ruinous psychological and financial costs, because this burden was laid upon them as the Will of God.

Father Andrew Greeley has confirmed that the overwhelming percentage of American Catholics disagree with the Church's ban on contraception. He has noted that American parish churches suffered a serious decline in devotion and practice immediately following Pope Paul VI's Encyclical.[8] It is true that Pope John Paul II's more recent attempts to revitalize this ban on artificial contraception[9] has increased the official clerical lipservice. The politics of the situation requires this of those ecclesiastical spokespersons who must act as Church politicians. It is common knowledge that clear support of the Vatican ban on contraception is presently a litmus test for promotion to the office of bishop.[10] But as far as a practical effect among Catholic people goes, I would make this comparison: when the small Old-order Amish community persuades the rest of Americans to abandon our use of electricity and automobiles, then the Vatican just might persuade the Catholics of the world to abandon the use of artificial contraception. Of course neither of these will happen. It is perplexing that the official Church pays such exaggerated attention to the single issue of contraception in the face of so many pressing issues of an obviously moral character. She squanders her moral authority on a matter which is practically—I should say utterly—without moral significance. Yet such is the fact. To me it demonstrates a weakness in spiritual understanding when a religious organization becomes so preoccupied with a single and in any case minor concern. Where, we must ask, might we find the truly spiritual influence of the Church?

This is the question that struck me with considerable force when a decade or so ago I attended a gathering of long-standing friends. It was a relatively small group that included laypersons, nuns, and priests. Some years earlier this group of ours had exerted a lot of effort to bring about changes in the Catholic Church. We worked for the kind of renovation that we thought would make the Church more responsive to present needs. What I found most interesting at this reunion was that, in the religious sense, not a single person present that evening believes today what s/he believed back then. In my estimation nearly all of them would be hard pressed to say exactly what they believe today. I think of most of them as *threshold Catholics*, Catholics at the brink. These were the people whom the highly respected British priest-theologian, Charles Davis, seemed most to identify with when he dissociated from the Catholic Church:

> "I remain a Christian, but I have come to see that
> the Church as it exists and works at present is an
> obstacle in the lives of the committed Christians I
> know and admire. It is not the source of the values
> they cherish and promote. On the contrary, they
> live and work in a constant tension and opposition
> to it. Many can remain Roman Catholics only
> because they live their Christian lives on the fringe
> of the institutional Church and largely ignore
> it."[11]

Perhaps a story can communicate what I observed. One of the women in this group told of her husband's heart attack. She had already indicated to our group that at present she is not affiliated with a Church—I would say she feels disenfranchised. Someone in our gathering asked her what religion category she assigned to her husband on the hospital form. "Well, Roman Catholic of course," was her terse reply, as if the question itself was out of place. She went on to describe how she had also summoned a priest to her husband's bedside, a gesture her husband indicated he did not appreciate.

It puzzles me how people can have such a reflex Catholic identity without a corresponding connection to the Church. This kind of automatic Catholic identity was equally pronounced in the case of a nun who was present. Some issue arose concerning Church doctrine. This nun said emphatically, "I don't believe what the Pope says; I believe what I choose to believe." This comment may seem exceptional until we hear from England's Cardinal John Heenan. In *The Tablet* of May 18, 1968 this Church dignitary wrote:

> "Today what the pope says is by no means ac-
> cepted as authoritative by all Catholic
> theologians...The decline of the magisterium is
> one of the most significant developments in the
> post-Conciliar Church."

American theologian Richard McCormick expressed just as strongly the American experience:

> "I believe it is safe to say that the hierarchical magisterium is in deep trouble. For many of the educated faithful it has ceased to be truly credible."[12]

This raises the interesting question as to just how Catholics conceive of the teaching function of the Church. Does it only supply ideas from which any person is free to choose, what has come to be called "smorgasbord Catholicism?" This would make the Church quite like the media and other social institutions which supply ideas and views that everyone is free to accept or reject. How this relates to the traditional understanding of the Church's function as spiritual teacher is problematic indeed. This important issue will be discussed in a later chapter when we reflect on the essence and purpose of spiritual doctrine.

Here I should add that nearly everyone else who was present at our gathering suffers a similarly estranged relationship to the Church. The whole occasion created a wonderment in me as to what they actually think about the matter of religion. When I tried to talk about this issue explicitly, two of the persons present took great exception and inquired why I insisted on preaching at them. I then saw that even raising the issue of religion was too touchy a subject to discuss. Everyone is familiar with the old adage "Never argue religion or politics." However, it seemed odd to me that this caution against discussing religion was relevant to our long-standing group of once motivated Catholics, even though they might now be better described as non-motivated threshold Catholics.

While this particular group may not be typical of Catholics generally, it does represent a prominent mood within the Church. Moreover, this mood increases with advanced education and awareness among Catholics. There are too many Catholics whose concerns about the gut issues of life and death and afterlife are not intelligently addressed by the Church they know. Often this kind of person needs a critical appraisal of the Catholic Church, but does not feel he or she has sufficient background or ability to make the appraisal himself or herself. This book is offered also to such threshold Catholics.

Then I would address those who are simply disgusted former Catholics. In this group one can find those who feel their minds were fed childish ideas, such as Adam and Eve and the forbidden fruit, and much else that hindered for a time their open-minded, intelligent, wholesome approach to the world they live in. Of course certain beliefs such as Adam and Eve came to be revised by the Church for many Catholics when they came of age. Sophisticated teachers accommodated the thinking minds of their students to a modern interpretation of biblical texts. The modern interpretation of the bible, while accepting its divine inspiration, still recognizes various literary forms in these texts, including the form of myth. So today the story of Adam and Eve, although taught to be a profoundly meaningful story, is also usually taught to be a myth. But for many Catholics a kind of domino theory came into play—the entire belief-system became questionable. Somewhere between the nuclear destruction of Hiroshima and the first human moonwalk, the pre-Copernican and pre-Einsteinian cosmologies of the Church tradition became essentially obsolete for Catholic intellectuals, even for the aware Catholic-in-the-pew. Not only did virgin-births and one-true-churches cease to make sense. A Trinity in God, a God-Manhood for Jesus, and Transubstantiation of bread and wine into the flesh and blood of Jesus became questionable.[13] Certainly the dogma of papal infallibility has been roundly rejected.[14] The issue was no longer whether or not these kinds of things could possibly be true. The issue was raised to a higher level: do ideas such as these even have spiritual significance? If they have spiritual significance, who can know about their factuality, whether these things are actually so? Who would know how to get at such real facts? If it is all a matter of interpretation, then who is doing the interpreting? How dependable is this interpretation? Even further, are not all these myopic belief-systems an insult to intelligence? Has not the modern sense of the greatness of the universe, both macrocosm and microcosm, relativized puny human thinking about our entire existence, not to mention about God? In effect, the entire Catholic belief-system came into question. In the minds of many it is unacceptable. To some it is even childish.

This obsolescence of belief-systems was for many Catholics accompanied by an obsolescence of the Church, and even of religion itself. However, the question might fairly be asked: Does a belief-system belong to the essence of religion? Does it even belong to the Church at all? Is the Church really about mere beliefs? Are beliefs anything more than products of our terribly limited minds, our myopic assessment of things? Is it possible that beliefs themselves belong to the cultic aspect and only adhere leechlike to the Church?

One of the most harmful as well as pervasive influences of the entire Christian tradition has been the anti-sex attitude that developed in the earliest days of the Church. The self-alienation and general psychic disturbance in the personal lives of Catholics that was created by the official Church's superficial and ignorant views on human sexuality is impossible to exaggerate. Many, if not most, Church authorities have not shown a wisp of spiritual understanding regarding the sexual dimension of human life. The barbaric war the institutional Church has waged against our sexual nature has hurt us deeply. A distorted, shamed sense of sexuality has worked its way into the cultural psyche that will probably take generations to purge. Everyone, almost to a person, has been negatively affected by this outrage. Some, to be sure, have been damaged far more than others. They have a moral, although not legal, claim against the Church for what is known clinically as severe mental abuse. The young adolescent, condemned to a writhing guilt over his discovery of masturbation, is given a false and ugly communication to meet the awakening of his sexual energy. Persons of a homosexual disposition, whose inmost emotional sense of themselves is declared degraded and abhorrent by the Church's teaching authority, are among those who have suffered most. It is no wonder that when sexual unease brings a person to seek professional help, one of the first questions many therapists ask is: "Is your religious background Catholic?"

Ironically, many of those who claim to represent the Church's teaching authority are themselves victims of the same miasmic anti-sexual atmosphere. So we need not be astonished when we read, as in the case of Cardinal Danielou and a little later of the Archbishop of Paris, of a cardinal or archbishop dying in the arms of a prostitute. Nor should it surprise us to learn that some bishops, pastors, and other priests have surrendered and made peace with their own sexual nature. At times overtly, more often surreptitiously, many clerics maintain, for however long a period of time, a heterosexual or homosexual liaison. The thorough research of Richard Sipe, conducted over a quarter century, has come to the thoughtful conclusion that at any given moment about one-half of American priests are sexually active.[15] Apart from the many instances of seduction, abuse, and dishonesty, this fact often speaks to me not so much of hypocrisy as of courage, when men claim their just and natural due after suffering the ravaging consequences of an unnatural, imposed celibacy.[16]

What I have suggested so far is only a modest representation of the kinds of difficulties modern Catholics and former Catholics have with their Church. Yet it is enough to show that there is something fundamentally wrong. The Church is not meeting the true spiritual needs of many of its members, and certainly not of its former members. It fails to perform satisfactorily. There must be a reason for this; indeed, there is a reason for this. Yet the failures and occasional stupidities in one or another aspect of Church teaching and practice do not add up to the basic reason. They are only symptoms.

I think I recognize what is fundamentally wrong with the Church. And it is fundamental indeed. But the same thing is fundamentally wrong with nearly all alternative churches that, despite their many differences, share the same overall condition. So disgruntled Catholics have a bigger problem on their hands than they may want. But like any other ailment in life, the only real solution is to get to the heart of the matter, as painful and painstaking as this may prove to be.

My analysis of the fundamental problem, the Cult within the Church, the Cult within every particular religious body, will not be easy to confront or to reflect upon. But it is fundamental. It is not about some mere fault which can be identified and then be either healed or eliminated. Rather, it has to do with the relationship of church, and here I include every religious form, to authentic religion. This is the most challenging issue that we must face in these pages. It requires us to ask of ourselves just how religious, how truly spiritual, we ourselves really are. In Jesus' words, are we really in service of God or, rather, of mammon? Although the present critique applies to every form of religion, since they all need to be tested, my focus remains on Christianity, the Roman Catholic Church in particular.

The Catholic Church once had a way of escaping accountability on this score by pretending to be the sole instance of true religion. She is now required to prove this if she can. It should be acknowledged that her more recent response indicates that she has become less and less smug about her place in the spiritual life of humankind. So here we are not talking about a crisis within Christianity. Rather, we are exemplifying Christianity and the Catholic Church as a crisis within religion. With many contemporary Catholic theologians we admit that the Catholic Church is by no means the sole instance of true religion. It is not the One True Church, an issue that will be given attention in this work. This gives us a certain freedom, a freedom acknowledged by Catholic theologians, to look into the form of the Catholic Church to discover what is wheat and what is chaff, what is authentic and what may be merely cultic. While I surmise that my reflections will be a threat, perhaps an insult, to many solid citizens of the Catholic Church, it will also prove surprising to an equal and opposite number of confused Catholics and disenchanted former Catholics to find that there may be wheat there after all—wheat, however, that needs and deserves to be winnowed through critical reflection.

To pursue this simile, there surely is wheat in the Catholic Church. She has not persisted for two millennia as a spiritual hoax, notwithstanding the many horrendous actions and entire eras in her history. She has not served as the nourishing mother of saints by offering nothing more than chaff. Nor has she inspired the highest forms of art, music, poetry, and architecture by wandering wholly adrift from the Sacred. She has not permeated western culture because we are stupid and foolish, but because we aspire to the gods, to God. It is true that many in our culture cannot live with the Church as she is. But what would western culture and history be like in her absence? This question may be momentarily provocative. Ultimately it is not even useful. The fact is that Christianity, and the Catholic Church in particular, have formed the backbone of western culture and history and continues to have a prevailing influence. The important issue now concerns her connection to the Sacred. How can she become more effective in reconnecting us to our Source? How can her spiritual authenticity be more fully restored? Any intelligent person should be able to recognize and admit that great cleansing and attunement are required if the Church is to serve her real purpose. No one would put up with an automobile or dishwasher that performed so poorly.

In modern times increasing numbers of persons are not putting up with the Church either. Yet many people do not know where to turn. With automobiles and dishwashers, we can turn from one brand to another, or from American made to foreign made and vice-versa. But alas! Alternative church prospects rarely offer Catholics, for example, greater promise than their own Catholic experience. This does not say that many former Catholics have not settled for an alternative. Yet, a careful look might show that they have often given up as much or even more than they got in return. And some seem to know this, at least implicitly. My own limited experience with once-Catholics-now-something-else tells me that many of them are gnawed ones. There is something not quite right in their gut. In this book I will speak to these gnawed ones. I will speak also to disgruntled Catholics who know they cannot become something else. They have been forced to remain nominal Catholics, Catholics by default we might say. What is this Catholic thing that maintains such a powerful embrace around so wide and so diversified a circle of both present and past members? As we look into this matter we must remember that we are raising up for critical inspection an ancient and enormous institution.

This alone makes the task formidable. Even more importantly, however, the Church is a religious, moral, cultural, historical, sociological, political, and extremely personal reality. Monumental wars have been fought by, because of, for, against, and about it. It is primarily because Christianity belongs to the religious, moral, and personal realm that it has a marked connection to me. And it is this very personal connection to me that both allows and necessitates this critique.

Is this call to personal examination a challenge to faith itself? Is it not infidelity even to question faith? Such is the Catch-22 that had bound the minds of many Catholics for centuries. They were not even allowed to question their faith. In fact, we have been told that we are basically incapacitated to do so because of Original Sin. We are supposedly deprived of the competence to judge for ourselves.

We will challenge this view that envisions humankind as under the sign of Original Sin. The myth of Original Sin has usurped a place in Christian thinking that it does not deserve. Does not the idea of Original Sin burden us with a false sense of ourselves? Might we not be originally pure as well as originally intelligent? Why should we believe that "our minds are darkened through Original Sin?" We already experience our intelligence. We can use it to understand what faith is. I will suggest that faith is *not* belief, although in common thinking it has come to mean the same thing as belief. Many religious people cannot imagine religious faith except as believing something. But is there a necessary link between authentic religious faith and belief of some kind? Believing seems to be a misuse of, or I might say a failure to use, one's own intelligence. The people of Missouri say: "Show me." Why is this not the proper religious attitude? We have a right to find out for ourselves. After all, it is *our* existence that is at stake. I think it is important for all of us to come to terms with this matter of faith and belief. If we let go of a believing attitude and insist on *knowing*, then we might well expect that our belief-system itself will begin to seep through. We will be forced to ask the purpose of doctrine. What, after all, is the purpose of spiritual teaching? Is it to provide our minds with a foundation or floor of dogmas, of "truths that must be believed in order to be saved?" Just how does a dogmatic clinging to some particular idea as true serve our spiritual interest? Perhaps we will come to see that religious doctrine is not a set of mental ideas at all. Could it be so simple that religious doctrine is practical *instruction* about our reconnecting to our Source? The plain idea of religion suggests as much.

But what does this reconnecting amount to? Is religion supposed to bring an entirely different life to us at some future time? Or can religion be looked at as affecting our life profoundly in the present? May it be that religion is to reestablish us *now* in the natural ease and happiness we already instinctually know but are not yet able to feel? Many persons who experience their religious need are firmly committed to a belief in unhappiness now and happiness later. They think happiness can be achieved only at the end of life when life itself is abandoned in death. They believe that they will be given an entirely different life because of their servile accommodation to the whims of a divine will in this life. It will be a challenge for such future-oriented persons to think of religion as something *present* rather than something promised in the past that is supposed to happen in the future. The future-oriented view makes religion seem wholly irrelevant to now, at least for many persons.

Making religion a matter of the present demands an entirely different understanding of revelation. Is revelation only something that was shown long ago to others? Can we not think of revelation as a present event? Must we think of truth as remote from ourselves? Perhaps genuine revelation happens to each of us when we enjoy a heartfelt understanding of instruction about The Kingdom of God and about The World [to use Jesus' metaphors]. There is no biblical demand that revelation applies only to others and not to ourselves. The Gospel suggests the contrary: revelation is addressed to our fundamental unhappiness. It follows that when we truly hear spiritual instruction, revelation happens. And when we are willing to implement spiritual instruction fully, we will mature to the point of being set free of our unhappiness in that moment. Does this not sound more like what the Gospel's promise and demands are about: "You will know the Truth and the Truth will set you free!"[17] Those who are willing to apply their intelligence can ponder all these issues with great profit.

If authentic religion is about the simple but profound matter of becoming a mature, genuine human being, a person who at last has within her\himself the freedom and its consequent wisdom to judge about and relate properly to others, to the world, and to life in its entirety, then what is to be said of the Church when it does something other than teach and foster such growth? To the extent that a religious body does not serve our human growth by instructing us into mature freedom and wisdom, it makes us servants of the world. It promotes The Cult. It is to that degree inauthentic; it is cultic. We will now do well to look at the essence of *cult*.

NOTES

[1] See *The American Catholic*, (Basic Books, Inc., 1977).

[2] See Langdon Gilkey, *Naming the Whirlwind*, (The Bobbs-Merrill Co., Inc., 1969).

[3] Iris Murdoch, *The Sacred and Profane Love Machine*, (The Viking Press, Inc., 1974), p. 5.

[4] This modern contention is insightfully described in Eugene Kennedy's *Tomorrow's Catholics - Yesterday's Church: The Two Cultures of American Catholicism*, (Harper & Row, 1988).

[5] The history of this Commission's work is reviewed in William H. Shannon, *The Lively Debate: Response to 'Humanae Vitae'*, (Sheed & Ward, 1970), pp. 90-98. A more descriptive history that supports Pope Paul's Encyclical is found in Janet E. Smith's *'Humanae Vitae': A Generation Later*, (The Catholic University of America Press, 1991). An extended study of the contraceptive issue in the Catholic Church, published prior to the Encyclical, is John T. Noonan's *Contraception*, (Harvard University Press, 1966).

[6] *The Lvely Debate*, "The Widening of the Birth Control Debate," pp. 56-73.

[7] The common assessment of the Encyclical's status in respect to "infallible teaching" is that it did not intend an infallible declaration, by far the most common assessment of theologians. But there has been insistence on its infallible character on the part of some theologians, particularly those Commission members who wrote the minority report, which the Encyclical supports. See Janet E. Smith, *Humanae Vitae: A Generation Later*, pp. 155-160.

[8] *The American Catholic*, (Basic Books, Inc., 1977), p. 138.

[9] Pope John Paul II has formalized his anti-contraceptive stance in his Encyclical on various moral themes, *"Splendor Veritatis,"* August 6, 1993. See *The Splendor of Truth: Regarding Certain Fundamental Questions of the Church's Moral Teaching*, (Office for Publishing and Promotion Services, United States Catholic Conference, Washington, D.C., 1993).

[10] See Patrick Granfield, *The Limits of the Papacy: Authority and Autonomy in the Church*, (The Crossroad Publishing Company, 1987), pp. 27f & p. 31.

[11] *A Question of Conscience*, (Harper & Row, 1967), pp. 6-7.

[12] *Proceedings of the Catholic Theological Society of America*, vol. 24, 1970, p. 251.

[13] The recent work of Uta Ranke-Heinemann, *Putting Away Childish Things*, (Harper San Francisco, 1994), speaks challengingly to certain traditional beliefs of this kind.

[14] See *The American Catholic*, p. 128: Only thirty-two percent of American Catholics think that it is "certainly true" that the pope is infallible when he speaks on matters of faith and morals.

[15] *A Secret World: Sexuality and the Search for Celibacy*, (Brunner-Mazel, Inc., 1990).

[16] In addition to Sipe's book mentioned above, there are a plethora of books that discuss priests' and nuns' struggles with celibacy. Mentioning only certain titles is unavoidably subjective. But only a representative sampling of relevant titles can be mentioned here. Although certain of the works I cite may surprise and disturb some persons, I do not view them as being published for shock value. They speak to an actual condition. Some relevant titles are: *The Celibacy Myth: Loving for Life*, Charles A. Gallagher and Thomas L. Vandenberg, (Crossroad, 1987), *Lesbian Nuns: Breaking Silence*, Rosemary Curb & Nancy Manahan, (The Naiad Press, Inc., 1985), *Sex in the Parish*, Karen Lebacqz & Ronald G. Barton, (John Knox Press, 1991), *Shattered Vows: Priests Who Leave*, David Rice, (William Morrow and Company, Inc., 1990), *Lead Us Not Into Temptation: Catholic Priests and the Sexual Abuse of Children*, Jason Berry, (Doubleday, 1992), *What God Hath Joined: The Real-Life Love Story that Shook the Catholic Church*, Terrance A. Sweeney and Pamela Shoop Sweeney, (Ballantine Books, 1993). In addition to these popular titles, the monumental historical work that should be added here is *The History of Sacerdotal Celibacy in the Christian Church*, Henry C. Lea, (Russell & Russell, Inc., 1957).

[17] *John* VIII, 32.

IV

They changed the method [of authentic Christianity]...and naturally the world conquered.

Soren Kierkegaard

THE CULT OF THIS WORLD

Cult has become a distasteful and even dangerous word in our time. This is partly because we have lost the root meaning of the word and rely on a meaning that comes from recent experience. At its worst *cult* brings to our mind the image of Satan and a weird gathering of people joined in a bizarre activity. Worse yet, it makes us remember the 1978 Jonestown tragedy. Modern times have seen western culture confronted by an array of religious beliefs and practices that are totally unfamiliar. An insidious idea of cult has entered our common mentality.[1] While we might be unable to give a precise definition of the word *cult*, most of us feel that we know one when we see one.[2] For the most part we do not like what we see. It does not jibe with our idea of what religion should be.

This modern, negative sense of cult stands in contrast to the traditional meaning of the word. *Cult* originally had a positive rather than a negative meaning. Our word *culture* is related to this positive meaning of the word. In ancient times cult described the worshipful action of a spiritual community, an action that nurtured or *cult*ivated a living relationship to the spiritual principle of existence. In our own time scholars sometimes use the word *cult* in a positive sense. In his book *Black Sects and Cults*, the scholar of Black religion, Joseph Washington, has attempted to identify those elements that characterize a cult, as distinct from a *church* or *sect*, in the religious communities of African-Americans. He quotes Milton Yinger's description of cults as characterized by "small size, search for a mystical experience, lack of structure, and presence of a charismatic leader." Similar to sects, cults nevertheless represent a "sharper break, in religious terms, from the prevailing tradition of a society."[3]

The early Christian community was precisely a *cult* in Joseph Washington's terms. Nothing negative is implied in defining early Christianity this way. Those early Christians we now call martyrs paid a heavy price for their non-traditional religious form. As the word *cult* is applied today with negative overtones to small religious groups, it stands in contrast to the publicly more legitimate sense of *church*. St. Paul, it is true, used the word *Church* to refer to the early Christian community. But St. Paul's understanding of Church is not the same as the sociological meaning implicit in the word church today. For St. Paul *Church* was the community of those who adhered to the person and teaching of Jesus. However, we now accept the designation church for any social body that decides to call itself this. Sociology, which studies this kind of social body, does not have theological views when it looks at religious communities. Thus sociology will call any socially acceptable religious body a church, however valid or invalid its theology is thought to be. It is important to note that the ordinary meaning of church for the average Christian tends toward the sociological meaning. That is why Christians are willing to call some particular religious community a church even when they feel that this community is unfaithful to the teachings of Christ. They call it a *false* church. The main point is that the early Christian community did not become a church in today's sense of the word until it made peace with the Roman state under the emperor Constantine in the early fourth century. Because of Constantine Christianity came to be the religious establishment of the Roman Empire. This church-state unity is what is called *Christendom*. In the context of this book the capitalized word *Church* will simply mean the historical Christian Church, both Catholic and Protestant, eastern and western, without theological consideration about fidelity to the teaching of Jesus. But I am giving a distinctive meaning to the word *Cult* in these pages. More in line with the modern sense, and clearly breaking from the traditional understanding, Cult here denotes something negative. However, the negative factor I will try to identify by this word is not the qualities that have created the modern cult scare.[4] Despite a few demonically harmful little groups, most modern cults are not harmful, despite their bad press. Still the modern sense of the word *cult* does express the danger of a religious body when it fails to serve the genuine purpose of religion.

Is it not unfair, reckless perhaps, to apply the negative meaning of the word *cult* to small religious groups just because they are unfamiliar to us and maybe frighten us? Perhaps we would do better to examine the dangerous, irreligious quality itself that is presumed to lie at the heart of cults. We know very well that many religious organizations and churches have not been fully faithful to the true purpose of religion. I am using the word Cult here to identify and name the principal factor in any religious form that causes it to deviate from the only valid purpose of religion.

A careful study of the ancient Church shows something unique in the community, a trait that belongs to its essence. That unique trait is the early Christian community's radical departure from the life and values and ideals of ordinary society. Jesus' words were remembered and kept: "My kingdom is not of this world."[5] This raises an important question: When the early Church in St. Paul's theological sense became a church in the sociological sense, that is, when under Constantine it went to bed with the state, so to speak, did it lose its purity? Did it lose something essential to its character? There can be no doubt that the Church began to relate to ordinary society in a new way, eventually even to dominate it. But is this new way compatible with the essence of the Church, with the teaching of Jesus? Did not Jesus teach and recommend a clean break from the concerns, the values, the ways, and the ideals of ordinary life?

We can ask this question in another, more telling way: Has the Church as Christendom pursued singlemindedly its only true purpose, to cultivate our relationship to the Divine Source of our existence, to God? Recalling Jesus' assertion that "No person can serve two masters...A person cannot serve both God and mammon [*i.e., money* or *the world*],"[6] we can ask whether the worldly, socially accepted Church tends to give full service to God. Putting the question this way suggests a negative answer.

I can now give the precise meaning of the word *Cult* that I intend in speaking of cultic aspects of the Church. Cult is that dimension in any religious church or group that deflects it away from its true purpose of reorienting and reconnecting us to the Source of our existence. Some religious bodies, perhaps, are a Cult and nothing besides. But what is *cultic* can exist as an element in a religious body which in many respects does serve our spiritual purpose. Any element in any religious organization that does not promote our reconnection to our Source is cultic. It certainly has no valid place in the Church. But all too often it is there.

We can examine the essence of cult with further precision: Is there anything that by its very nature tends to turn people away from our Source? Spiritual traditions have always identified a three-fold danger to spiritual life: the world, the flesh, and the devil. If we will understand this triad at any depth, we easily see how our higher aspirations tend to be overcome by enticements or concerns generated by our external life (the world), by our bodily needs and desires (the flesh), and by ideas and plans for life that are clearly contrary to human truth and well-being (projected as the devil). While we necessarily bring our unruly body and aberrant mind (flesh and devil) into the Church—for it is there precisely to help us become free relative to these, we surely do not expect to find "The World" in the Church. But alas we do! It is, then, this latter factor that I shall name Cult in these pages.

It is not the world as such, but worldliness in the sense of *belonging to the world*, that stands in competition with religion for the human heart. The gospel shows that Jesus made a stark contrast between the world and the Kingdom of God. In Christian Scripture there is a certain ambiguity in the idea of world. For example, in St. John's gospel we are acknowledged to be *in* the world. But we are told not to be *of* it. In this Gospel there are two senses of world. In one sense, "The world hates you, but know that it has hated me [Christ] before you."[7] But on the other hand, "God so loved the world that he sent his only-begotten son to save it."[8]

St. John's gospel is not in the final analysis ambiguous about the world. For it is not the world as such, our temporary abode, that stands in opposition to the spiritual conduct of life that Jesus taught. It is our belonging to the world, being possessed by it, that obstructs our connection to our Source. If we are to take Jesus' criticism seriously, we must become discriminating in our understanding of his instruction about the world. It is evident that the same world can, spiritually, be either positive or negative. How? It clearly depends upon how we relate to it. Jesus' own communication about this is uncomplicated: If we *belong* to the world, we are separated from the Kingdom, from God, from reality. But Jesus never suggested that we cannot live here in this world. We must. Just as clearly, he taught that we can live in this world without belonging to it. We can be masters of our life in the world rather than slaves. In a word, we can be *free*. Authentic religion is about freedom, about our becoming truly free. Is our happiness really different from our freedom?

The important thing to see clearly is what *belonging* to the world amounts to. The religious issue of belonging has to do with what the world means to us. The world becomes negative only when it captures and limits the human heart, when the world becomes our primary preoccupation. If a person's horizon and goal, the efforts of all his seeking, are the transitory accomplishments of a fast-moving life in this world, only then is he outside the pale of authentic religion. His worldly condition has become his *goal*. He no longer sees the circumstances of his life to be only a *means* for being fully alive, even as he lives in the world. We can create a simple analogy to describe how, while we need the things of the world, we do not have to make them the center of our attention: Consider our home and our livelihood. Obviously we have to have both a place as well as the wherewithal to live. If, however, a person's house or job becomes his or her top priority, the very center of attention, while spouse and family are relegated to a lesser place, then the marriage and family relationship is essentially finished. It becomes a story of human failure. The home and job themselves become meaningless. While house and job must be attended to, they must not take priority, or else the life they are meant to support becomes a failure. This exemplifies the spiritual story of the person who *belongs* to This World in the sense that the worldly condition has assumed top priority in his or her life. This person is, in the final analysis, a member of the only religious cult there is, namely The Cult of This World. In this book such belonging to the world is the exact meaning of *cult*: *Cult* means The Cult of This World. It applies first to any religious organization that serves only a worldly purpose. But it also applies to every element in every religious body that does not help orient us toward reconnecting to our Source.

Over time, as theology began to replace Jesus' spiritual teaching, his instruction concerning the world became both diluted and complicated. Eventually it was lost by his followers. As a consequence Christianity was forced to wrestle with the problem of how to relate to this world, a problem that it has never really resolved. It attempts to figure out an answer to this issue theologically. However, if genuine spiritual understanding were to prevail, this issue would not even exist. The world is not our problem; it is not even part of our problem. For this world is clearly the only place we have where we can live our lives. The question is whether we live in truth or in delusion. Are we, in delusion, submitted one hundred percent to the confusing, ever-changing demands of life as it appears on the surface? Do these ever-changing conditions of our life take priority? Or, do we enjoy an essential sense of peace and are we instructed in a genuine spiritual practice. Are we able to accept, and work with, and stay free in the midst of any and all conditions that life brings us? Staying free in the midst of worldly concerns pertains to the essence of spiritual work. If we do not apply ourselves to this kind of work, then we will never understand the life we have, nor will we experience freedom even while we live. In that case we are possessed by the world. We *belong* to it in the sense Jesus chided.

The Church in the Modern World is an issue only because spiritual understanding is weak. It is not surprising, then, to see this issue raised again as a problem in theological thinking at the Second Vatican Council of the Catholic Church in the 1960's. The Council discussed the Church in the modern world as the essential theme in one of its sixteen official documents.[9] But the world is a problem for the Church only to the extent that the Church has become a part of the world. As a *worldly* force the Church has no choice but to get along well and use its power most effectively in the world. Yet all of this marks the Church as just another political force. Historically the Church has often shown itself to be an abominable political force, while at other times she has promoted justice and humaneness within the arena of world politics. But authentic religion is not a worldly political force. In fact it relates to the world only indirectly, through the transformation of its members by instructing and supporting genuine spiritual practice. Moreover, spiritual practitioners are able to relate to the world only as unproblematically and helpfully as the maturity of their practice enables them to. Without the strong presence of authentic religion through actual spiritual *practice*, people have little choice but to content themselves with much that is cultic in religion. They are not sufficiently challenged about their commitment to this world. The fact is, many people who consider themselves religious unwittingly belong in great measure to This World. Their religious inheritance does not give them adequate instruction nor does it challenge them to live in this world in freedom. It does not show them how to put spiritual understanding to work as a way of life. Jesus spoke to this condition of ours. He spoke of humankind as *orphans,*[10] his word to describe people bereft of a spiritual inheritance. Most of us probably have parents, as well as food, clothing, and shelter. Jesus nevertheless saw us as *orphans*. What do food and clothing and shelter amount to if we are bereft of the one thing that is essential? That is, when we lack instruction about *the point of it all* and how to deal with it properly?

As time passes and personal life ebbs people increasingly realize they are losing this world. It is then that the promises of salvation and an afterlife take on a special importance. For many this becomes the mood with which they approach religion in their advancing years. They need to hear about salvation and heaven. They hope it is true. They are drawn to religious preachers and religious systems that support their hopes for an eternal life. From the viewpoint of authentic religion this grasping approach toward a heaven of human imaginings leaves us quite vulnerable to deception. We create in our mind some image of an eternal heaven. But a good look at any human image of heaven shows that it is made of this-worldly stuff. Cultic religion offers the promise of an eternity of life as we already know it. Such religion does not really demand an actual reconnection to the Source now. It does not direct the true Gospel against our present unhappiness. Its promises are futuristic. It is cultic in attempting to cultivate the best of this world and try to make it eternal. Its imagined god is not Real God, but an anthropomorphic (human-form) god, a creator-father who is supposed to make sure that his children do not get hurt too badly in their worldly games. Then he is to provide an eternal resting place for them after they have been reasonably good during their little day on earth.

It is no wonder that this immature view of human existence has generally been abandoned by a good number of modern intellectuals. But not surprisingly, what replaced it for many of them is an adolescent rejection of every type of religious instruction. They stand smugly above the childish imagination, but in place of it they hang on to their own imagined views, or non-views as the case may be. They are not about to be told anything. In rebound from exploding their childish imagination, they become unavailable to mature instruction about the essence and purpose of their life. They content themselves with their own views, as adolescents are wont to do. Many people who belong totally to This World are bemused at others who look to another world as if to a kind of dreamy heaven. They figure that if on the odd chance an afterlife comes up, they will deal with it then. They consider it neurotic to worry about a questionable future when there is an obvious present that must be lived. The fact is, of course, such persons are not usually mature, happy human beings. They do not live their present life with great intelligence and unbounded happiness. Their negative reaction to cultic, futuristic religion is understandable. But the energy of resistance and scorn is not a sufficient substitute for true peace. It skirts the trouble of genuine questioning. As secularists they look upon themselves simply as worldlings, which is what *secularist* means. But I feel there is another, inescapable aspect to their situation. They are not merely worldlings. For their form of adherence to This World refuses to be tested. They will not face directly the poignant question of their existence. They, too, blindly presume an answer, a secular one, without submitting to the work of the real question. So secularists are not automatically adult citizens of this world. Rather, in blind commitment to their secularist views, they too may be members, albeit adolescent members, of The Cult of This World.

Because my critique focusses in a special way on Catholicism, I will refer often to what is cultic within the Catholic Church. It reflects everything in the Church that weakens her connection to her own spiritual principle. It criticizes adaptation to the world on the world's terms. The Church in fact made this kind of peace with the world when, through Constantine, she became Christendom at considerable cost to her own essence. The Cult made a serious infiltration into the Church at that time.

The Cult of This World is particularly perverse because it distorts what is absolutely important to human beings. It misdirects our spiritual impulse and saps our spiritual potential. It deflects the spiritual possibility of humankind away from our authentic spiritual goal, away from the Real, and toward what is actually only this world.

The Cult of This World is especially insidious. Unlike the small modern cults that are always kept on the defensive, The Cult of This World tends to attain political predominance and thus escape the need for accountability. This is why I call it *Of* This World. It is not merely a bedfellow *with* or *in* this world, and therefore something the world might keep an eye on. Rather it is a major figure, indeed a formidable one, *of* this world. The Cult has achieved a prominent seat in the inner circle.

This perversion of authentic religion has been noted by certain modern theologians who have actually called for the abolition of religion. The famous and highly respected German theologian Dietrich Bonhoeffer, who was an heroic stalwart against the Nazi outrage and was even put to death by them, called for a "religionless Christianity."[11] A century earlier the Danish religious thinker Soren Kierkegaard wrote a scathing criticism of this-worldly Christianity in his *Attack Upon Christendom*: "...for Christ's judgment after all is surely decisive, inopportune as it must seem to the clerical gang of swindlers who have taken forcible possession of the firm 'Jesus Christ' and done a flourishing business under the name of Christianity."[12] He summed up the essential problem in terms not unlike those I am using: "They changed the method [*i.e.* of Christianity]—and naturally the world conquered."[13] Bonhoeffer and Kierkegaard were certainly not condemning authentic religion or true Christianity. Rather their attack was against what I am calling The Cult of This World. Karl Barth and Paul Tillich likewise have made clear and pointed criticism of cultic religion in modern times. There are contemporary voices that continue to rail against The Cult of This World. One might read Jacques Ellul's *The Subversion of Christianity*[14] for a contemporary and poignant criticism of much that passes for the Christian Church today.

Naturally The Cult of This World cannot *appear* to be that. It has to appear as authentic religion. The Cult expresses its antiquated philosophy or worldview as dogma, and holds this dogma to be truth itself which everyone must accept as coming from the mouth of God. The Cult communicates its thinking as theology, as if this thinking is a meditation on God's Word. And finally, The Cult issues its behavioral commands as morality, as if it alone knows the right and righteous way to live. As if it alone possesses the only way of life that is founded in the Revelation and Will of God. To support these very heavy claims The Cult has recourse to a spiritual figure whose authority it claims to represent. In the case of Christianity in general, and Catholicism in particular, that figure is obviously Jesus and, for Catholics, his surrogate, the pope together with the considerable Vatican machine in which the pope is enveloped.

We will have the opportunity to review some of the more exaggerated expressions of this identification of Christ with the great Vatican machine when we come to reflect on the fact that even a True Church necessarily has a political character since it takes shape in this world.

The trait of cultic religion that is most offensive and of greatest concern to people is the absolute devotion to the charismatic leader. Cult members seem to abandon personal responsibility for their own lives when they dedicate themselves to the interests and directives of their leader. Most of us are offended at cultic devotion to a fellow human being because of our instinctive feeling that each individual person must remain responsible for her or his own life. Indeed we feel that such personal responsibility is inalienable. We are responsible for ourselves, whether we like it or not. It is therefore true that mere attachment to a leader or teacher is cultic when it does not entail our own responsibility in actually doing the spiritual work. This marks the essential difference between cultic and authentic religion. Cultic religion does not instruct; it tells. Cultic religion does not support true learning and understanding and personal growth. Rather it demands assent and acquiescence and conformity. Small modern groups we call cults might well be tested by these standards as to their worth. Parents are wisely alarmed when their children associate with cults that do not promote personal responsibility in their adherents. Cults that keep members in submissive alignment to the leadership. But these same parents ought to look at their own spiritual lives as well. Does their more traditional version of religion instruct and nurture them in mature spiritual responsibility? Or are they likewise being maintained in childish dependency on a tradition and leadership that only tells rather than teaches? Are they properly instructed, and do they feel responsible for their own reconnecting? Do they exercise themselves in this responsibility and make the reconnection happen? Is it actually happening for them? Are they leading an authentic spiritual life? Or do they hope to be saved by somebody else? We must consider in detail this matter of our own spiritual responsibility.

NOTES

[1] See Bryan Wilson, "Sect Development," in B. Wilson, ed., *Religion in Sociological Perspective*, (Oxford University Press, 1982), p.88: "...a movement committed to heretical belief and often to ritual acts and practices that departed from orthodox religious procedures." An example of a book that helps promote the cult scare is *Strange Gods: The Great American Cult Scare*, David G. Bromley and Anson D. Shupe, Jr., (Beacon Press, 1981). Informed and unprejudiced research into small spiritual communities that are commonly thought of as cults has been done by J. Gordon Melton and Robert L. Moore, *The Cult Experience*, (The Pilgrim Press, 1982).

[2] A fine study of an individual sect that is commonly thought of as a cult is Eileen Barker's *The Making of a Moonie*, (Basil Blackwell, 1984).

[3] *Black Sects and Cults*, (Doubleday, 1973), p. 6. See also J. Milton Yinger, *The Scientific Study of Religion*, (The Macmillan Company, 1956), p. 330.

[4] The Jonestown tragedy and the more recent cult-related murders in Switzerland and Canada are not alone in creating a public fear of cults. Accusations of child abuse in connection with cult activity such as Satan worship surface from time to time.

[5] *John* XVIII, 36.

[6] *Matthew* VI, 24.

[7] *John* XV, 18.

[8] *John* III, 16.

[9] See *The Documents of Vatican II*, ed. Walter M. Abbott, S.J., (The America

Press, 1966), "Pastoral Constitution on the Church in the Modern World" [*Gaudium et Spes*], pp. 199-308.

10 *John* XIV, 18.

11 *Letters and Papers from Prison*, (Macmillan, 1972), pp. 280-287.

12 *Kierkegaard's Attack Upon "Christendom" 1854-1855*, tr. Walter Lowrie, (Princeton University Press, 1944), p. 117.

13 Walter Lowrie, *A Short Life of Kierkegaard*, (Princeton University Press, 1942), p. 234.

14 (William B. Eerdmans Publishing Company, 1986).

V

He seemed to feel his soul in devotion pressing like fingers the keyboard of a great cash register and to see the amount of his purchase start forth immediately in heaven.

James Joyce

OUR SPIRITUAL RESPONSIBILITY

It does not require much experience for us to realize that we are held responsible for our life in this world. We notice that our daily performance is somehow scrutinized by others. We are held accountable for it. The intelligent person sees that this is how the world works. He knows that his success in life will be measured according to his degree of responsibility. This holds no less for our spiritual maturity than it does for our cultivation and development of our worldly skills. Any religious form we may use to help us in meeting our spiritual task can be evaluated by the spiritual responsibility it helps foster in us. One of the earmarks of cultic religion, as I have described it, is that it does not put the demand for personal spiritual maturity on its members. Following the leader is more prominent than the spiritual growth of each member.

The Cult has become very powerful in many religious bodies today, including the Catholic Church. Alas, there is no one to blame. We are all equally innocent/guilty of it. Like any other society the Church necessarily evolves a leadership structure, from pope and bishops on down through parish nuns and priests. These various personalities are only expressions of the way the Church has happened to develop. They alone do not make the Church what it is at any particular moment. By tacit agreement the non-leadership or lay members of the Church have created the leadership who, in turn, teach or form these same lay members. All the factors and factions of the Church have worked together to create its actual condition. We must now deal with the situation we have created. There are no merely passive members of the Church.

43

In a marriage we know that the seemingly passive partner contributes a great deal to what kind of marriage it is. Similarly with the Church, all Catholics are to some degree responsible for the kind of Church they have created. Disgruntled Catholics who tend to point their accusatory finger at their Church leadership might usefully reflect more directly on the fact that this leadership arose out of their own ranks. Since the process of just how this happens is not obvious, they do not notice that they, *the People*, have put their leadership in place. Laypersons strengthen the system by their acceptance and quiet support of it. Many Catholics could come more quickly to the heart of their own problem of alienation if they would share the blame, or, better yet, drop the whole issue of blame. The Pope and bishops, the *Magisterium* as it is called, are simply expressing their own version of Catholicism through their words and actions. Perhaps they are ignorant; at times they have been nasty and pigheaded. But for the most part they just hand on the Catholic tradition as they feel they have received it. They employ the structure of the Church as it has in fact developed.

In the official tradition and structure of the Church, the actual living or *practicing* of spiritual life is implicitly assigned to the Church as an institution, with an authority class and a subservient class. The First Vatican Council could not have been clearer about this. Following its dogmatic pronouncement regarding infallibility it went on to insist, "Christ's Church is not a society of equals as if all the faithful in it had the same rights; but it is a society in which not all are equal."[1] It is the authority class in the Church that is supposed to update or clarify doctrine and theology. It is this same authority class that is to provide a meaningful form of worship. The authority class is to spell out how Catholics are to approach other religions and ways of life. More importantly, this class determines "what's naughty or nice," the righteous or the sinful actions that save or damn us. These established authorities presume to know exactly what is just or sinful even in the personal and relational lives of the people. Nor do these authorities hesitate to burden their people with demands regarding intimate matters of personal life. The basis of these demands is nothing more than how they, as authorities, happen to understand and judge of such matters at the moment. Yet they propose as the Mind and Will of God their own judgments that were formed from a horribly narrow viewpoint, which is all that any particular moment in human history allows any of us. While the Second Vatican Council did indeed amend the mood of the First Vatican Council's statements, it did not fundamentally change the implicit structure of authority and subservience.[2]

To put this in concrete terms, innumerable Catholics have often waited years, and I mean five, ten, and fifteen years, for elderly men in the Vatican to arrive at the conclusion that their previous marriage was not valid and thus they may enter a new marriage. Innumerable priests and nuns, again, have waited months and years to be released from their vows. Concerning the matter of contraception, marriage intimacy of an untold number of Catholics was regulated, often at unbearable cost, by these same authorities. The Church's demand in respect to contraception is excusable, if at all, only because of her ignorance and fear regarding sexuality itself that has somehow made this morally inconsequential matter central to her present understanding of moral life.

The individual Catholic, the person in the pew, is supposed to remain a spiritual child, the recipient of either the benign or the tyrannical directives, advice, and overall treatment of Mother Church coming through the authority class.

What underlies this common acceptance of the Church is the presumption that the leadership of the Church actually *knows* about God and eternity and all these things, and that it is this leadership's job to cue the rest of us in, to tell us what to think and say and do, so that our life might somehow mesh with our salvation. On the other hand, however, and ironically, Catholics neither demand nor expect profound religious knowledge and spiritual accomplishment of the teachers they accept and ordain. So when our leaders prove to be incompetent, and sometimes morally amiss, well, we chalk that up to the human face of our Church of sinners.

There is a reason for this. Traditionally it has been the Church *as a system* that was thought to be the holder of spiritual knowledge and the provider of salvation.[3] Mysteriously it is believed that this knowledge and salvation somehow comes to us even through unknowledgeable and spiritually inept authorities. Our own personal growth and transformation is expected to come about through such external and mechanical means.

This is not only a mistake, it is a large and serious mistake. It has created a false mission for the Church which tends to abort her true mission. Nevertheless, in the final analysis the responsibility for spiritual growth rests with us who must do the growing. And this for the basic reason that the religious problem exists only within each individual person. It is nothing other than his or her own felt disconnectedness. Reconnection obviously has to happen likewise *within the person.*

The Church is only a means, a help, for our personal work. When we understand spiritual life this way, it becomes clear that the Church as such does not practice religion. The Church can only serve (or dis-serve as the case may be) the practice of religion. It is only the individual person who can actually practice religion; only the individual person can reconnect. The first step of spiritual responsibility is to recognize that no person, no institution, no divinity, can do our spiritual work for us any more than someone else could learn our mathematics for us. It is a matter of change or transformation *in us.*

Hence there is no surrogate, no substitute, who can effect our reconnection to our Source, despite the endless doctrines and dogmas and theologies that describe how salvation (being reconnected) happens through mysterious external means: God, Jesus, Grace, Sacraments, and whatnot. Sadly, despite the validity of all these potential helps, they become denatured by magical notions of them promoted by cultic religion.

It is necessary for us as individuals to ask ourselves why we are so inclined to place the burden of our salvation outside ourselves. Why do we feel that spiritually we are and must remain at the level of childhood? Individual Catholics who become truly serious about their eternal destiny and wish to look profoundly into the matter of religion have no choice but to start with themselves. Although they are often in no position to fathom the complex of issues that the Church leadership, rightly or wrongly, decides to deal with, they can find access to themselves, to their own mind, and, perhaps, to their failure to mature spiritually. They might begin to recognize their implicit concession to live their lives as Catholic children. For it is individual Catholics who have unwittingly conspired to put themselves at the receiving end of the spoon, to make others superior to themselves in the matter of their own eternal destiny.

This matter needs to be considered carefully. For example, if we were to find a person who for some reason failed to grow physically, we would immediately recognize this condition as a deformity. So too, when we find a person who has not grown mentally, again we identify a malfunction, a mental deficiency. Similarly when we find persons who have not grown emotionally. We see a problem there. They are not just right. They are outside the norm. We recommend therapy.

But for some reason people consider the failure to develop

humanly or spiritually, being stuck in spiritual childhood, acceptable and normal. We allow the appearance of success according to worldly standards to substitute for human (spiritual) maturity. So the fact that the great mass of human beings are chronically dissatisfied, unhappy, confused, depressed, struggling with adverse inner (psychological/ emotional) and outer (livelihood, environment, *etc.*) forces of life, and destined to exist under the constant sign and fear of death, somehow we readily take this as just how life is. We accept this situation as normal. We even admire human failure when it is packaged in worldly wealth or power.

But as common as our condition is, it is not normal. It is human malfunction. It is spiritual malaise. It is profound suffering from which our small daily preoccupations and entertainments distract us only for the moment. The true object of religion is exactly this pervasive unhappy condition, and not fairy tales about some grand sin and salvation scheme that has enveloped us just because we had the misfortune to be born. As we will come to discuss, we have not in fact sinned, nor has anyone else like Adam and Eve sinned for us. Nevertheless we do find ourselves in a predicament that requires serious attention.

So we must find that place in ourselves where we tend to get stuck in spiritual childhood. I think it is not too hard to find. To look back to Chapter One, it has very much to do with Jimmy. It is about insecurity and fear. In that delicate moment of our development, when we should have been encouraged to face the world and grow to maturity, we were lied to about our basic situation. We were advised that there is a kind of Jimmy, an offended Jimmy at that, who must be appeased, pleased, and approached in fear and trembling. Our lives, we were advised, must be guided by the will, often a whimsical will, of Jimmy. Not that any of us has faced, seen, or even heard from this Jimmy personally. But we are told that he has made his expectations about our lives a little bit clear, and that there are persons who do know something about him and his will. They are charged, we are told, to communicate all that they know to us. We are not to be troubled by the small hitch that they themselves have not personally faced, seen, nor heard from Jimmy either. They *believe* that they have every reason to be somewhat certain that they nevertheless do know something about Jimmy and his expectations, and that this ought to be enough for us.

The catch is that, despite the absence of any direct contact with this Jimmy character, we are all nevertheless bound to accept a particular vision of reality because of Jimmy's supposed communication. We are required to live out a way of life based on Jimmy's presumed will. In fact, we are warned that if we take exception to this bondage, both of our minds and of our lifestyle, we become subject to the direst of possible consequences, ultimately to an eternity of hellfire.

Why are we inclined to accept this kind of nighttime ghost story? Why do we think that we can escape responsibility for our own lives and destiny?   The problem of our failure to become responsible for our human growth seems to have an overall reason. As I see it, progress in any area of endeavor is stymied for those who do not have an overview of the whole or who have a mistaken overview of the whole. We are unable to move without some sense of the whole and of our particular place within it. For example, a person finds it difficult to continue reading a book when he or she has no sense whatsoever of what the book as a whole is about. Nor can someone listen to a lecture or participate in a conversation when she stands outside the entire context. A person will fail to follow simple directions—he will not even get them straight—when he has no idea of what the whole program or recipe is about. In those situations where we lack such an overview, we become like children, totally dependent upon someone who does have the overview. Not seeing the whole, we need to be told step-by-step how to proceed. This seems to describe the childhood stage of development. Every step must be explained in detail.

But what about ourselves in the context of our life's final purpose? I am absolutely astonished by this single fact: people who recognize the tremendous time and effort it takes to develop and finally to master any field of expertise, such as physics, mathematics, art, music, and so on, feel they can know the essentials of the spiritual matter when they are seven or eight years old. They think that in some equivalent of Sunday School a human being can get an essential grasp of the whole matter of existence. Contrast this with our appreciation of what it takes to master a single area of human interest such as physics. Those, for example, who delve seriously into a science soon recognize that a profound transformation in thinking must take place just to relate to the subject in a truly scientific way. But it is assumed that a child's mind can be told about sin, salvation, God, heaven, *etc.*, and basically get the picture. It is my experience that intellectually cultivated adults often harbor childish pictures as their fundamental view of their existence. Their presumption that the great issue of their eternal destiny is conveyed in such simple imagery would be ludicrous, except that it does concern the serious matter of their very purpose in life.

When children ask about gravity, or heat, or the sun and stars, of course we have to answer their questions. But we know that the answers we give them are only a modest beginning. Our answers are *not* the literal scientific truth about these matters. When children grow to be adults and still think of scientific issues in terms of the images we gave them so long ago, they simply stay outside the realm of scientific knowledge. It is not that we lied to them when they first asked us about those things. It is that a child's mind is undeveloped and not capable of the depth of thinking that such difficult matters require.

Genuine spiritual knowledge, which has been available through the Great Spiritual Tradition for thousands of years, is not less profound, nor is it less difficult, than science, mathematics, and other subjects of human interest. Moreover, the *kind* of knowledge that spirituality requires puts it in a special category. Sacred writings (scriptures) are only a modest beginning for spiritual interest. The real work starts when the books have been sufficiently grasped that a person is able to engage an effective practice, to actually step onto the spiritual path. Let me put this comparison between ordinary knowledge and spiritual knowledge: it is easier, through intellectual work, to become par with Einstein than, through spiritual knowledge and practice, to become par with Christ.

The knowledge required for the spiritual task is not contained in the mere stories about life, sin, and salvation that can be narrated to and understood by children. Furthermore, coming to terms with our total existence is something each of us must do for himself or herself. Nobody did it for you; nobody will do it for you; nobody can do it for you. Creating the childish vision of a sin/salvation scheme simply defers the spiritual task to which each person must finally submit. In the words of Jesus, "You will not get out of it until you have paid the last penny."

Spiritual growth has many parallels with ordinary human growth. In general there is the obvious overall structure to our growth: childhood, adolescence, and adulthood. And, of course, there are numerous grades within each of these stages. The notable thing about the childhood stage of development is that it aims to get beyond itself. We give our children step-by-step directions precisely so that they can learn the matter themselves and be on their own. I as a parent, and most parents generally, welcome enthusiastically self-sufficiency when it appears in children. It is pathological for parents to try to retard this necessary growth in their children. The transition to adolescence, as clumsy and erratic and rebellious as it appears in the small picture, is known to be a wholesome stage of personal growth. Parents who are ignorant of the process and do not know how to honor the fact of adolescence, as well as how to fulfill their own responsibility in relating properly to their adolescent children, will tend to foster either a perpetual childhood or a traumatized, stuck, ever-rebellious adolescence in their children.

The adolescent stage of growth, growth beyond the child's step-by-step dependency, is always marked by some kind of apprenticeship, whether we call it that or not. When we start to learn something for ourselves, we are in a seemingly paradoxical situation. We are neither children who must follow the step-by-step directives of someone else, nor do we yet enjoy a full overview of the area that would allow us to proceed on our own in complete independence. The successful apprentice moves quickly beyond adolescent rebellion. He already enjoys a beginning wisdom, an internal confidence that he is truly on the way, as well as an increasing respect for the full vision which belongs to the master of the trade, her or his teacher. The wise and successful apprentice knows what s/he is doing, yet listens carefully and appreciatively to the master.

It might appear to be a harsh criticism to suggest that almost everyone is at the childhood level of spiritual development. But it is my experience with people, including highly skilled, well cultivated, humanly sophisticated people, that such may be the case. Most of them have apprenticed with considerable success in one or another area of human interest. But they have not yet taken in hand the reins of their own spiritual growth. And spiritual growth will not happen on its own.

It seems that we usually associate the idea of apprenticeship with only a particular area of accomplishment, some kind of job or artistic endeavor. But we ought to see that the same dynamic holds true of life as a whole, which is the mission of religion. Why are we inclined to think that life as a whole will be taken care of with less effort and less attention on our part than we put into piano or stone masonry or sculpting or journalism?

It should come as a surprise that a culture as sophisticated as ours in nearly every branch of human endeavor is content to remain a spiritual embryo. Would anyone deny our attainment in a vast array of interests! Consider mathematics, science and technology. Look at the wizardry behind computers. Watch the space launchings. Study the pictures of Saturn that were taken on the spot. Do we not enjoy Mozart, Bach, Beethoven? And the Beatles for that matter? Are we not elevated by the likes of a Michelangelo, a van Gogh? Do we not take pride in Socrates, in Plato, in Nietzsche, in Shakespeare and Goethe?

Given this tremendous sophistication that is our cultural inheritance, we must still confess that spiritually we are religious primitives, barely out of the trees. But what astonishes me most is our naivete about it. Not to have a state of the art knowledge of something is perfectly understandable. But for an otherwise sophisticated person to be inattentive to what is absolutely central to her or his life perplexes me. I do not know how people satisfy themselves with childish views relative to the very point and purpose of their existence. It would be like a New York businessperson remaining at the level of pony express in connecting with, say, counterparts in San Francisco. Of course this could not happen. S/he would long since have failed in business. But, perhaps because it does not impact immediately on their daily lives, people persist in naive, simplistic views concerning the very point of their life, as well as of their eternal destiny.

We might well ask how this could be so, how we came to be so childish, so ignorant, regarding spiritual understanding. The answer as I see it is that we have been born into a religiously arid environment. We live in a spiritually vapid culture, a culture that has lost the means of handing spiritual instruction on to us. I recall a newspaper report about the discovery of a tribal culture which had no scientific tradition as we know it. The tribal chief was a humanly sophisticated person. Yet when he was asked about the airplanes that occasionally flew over his island, he answered in terms of "the gods." He viewed the airplanes as some kind of divine observation and potential intervention in his peoples' lives. Why did such an intelligent and wise man have such naive views about airplanes? The answer is easy: he was without a scientific culture. Four-year-olds of our culture know more than this tribal chieftain does about airplanes. But this superior knowledge is inherited. It is not a personal achievement.

I use this story only as an example. For developing a scientific culture is not essential to authentic human living. But the same cannot be said about spiritual knowledge within a culture. For spiritual knowledge and practice is the one essential to authentic human life. While our culture does offer us a decent apprenticeship in particular areas of interest—schools, colleges, and universities provide this—a considered reflection on the purpose and cultivation of life as a whole is not our cultural inheritance. This failure of culture has not, however, eclipsed our need for just such instruction, such apprenticeship.

What we suffer in our culture is a dichotomy between our sense of the totality of life and the many competitors for our everyday attention, which come in terms of money, style, education, power and position, skills, entertainment, and so on indefinitely. The competitors have won hands down. Our culture is dedicated to these interests. There are limitless apprenticeships available to us when we are determined to become competent in any particular area of life. A recent self-help book spells out five dimensions of life that should be cultivated and integrated for successful living: health, wealth, relationship, recreation, and career. Let us say a person does all of this superbly for eighty years or so. Then what? Does it not occur to people that we are going to be dead a lot longer than we are alive, no matter how old we get to be! The literature built upon the legend of Dr. Faust is exactly a reflection of the shortsightedness, the foolishness, of total dedication to mere worldly interests. Those who have the fortune to live to be eighty or so often become poignantly aware of the insufficiency of a lunch already digested. When This World has been their priority throughout life, how do they feel when at last they notice that their own particular experience of This World is fast disappearing?

People of experience do realize that life as a whole is an issue that must be handled. For eventually everybody dies. Yet, distracted and coopted by everyday concerns, they feel that the purpose of life as a whole is too large a matter to be dealt with fully by the individual person. It is a rare person for whom the point of life takes absolute priority. So the problem of life as a whole is commonly handed over to professional religionists who are to manage our spiritual lives for us. Nor is there any dearth of such professionals who are anxious for the business.

But clearly this is a faulty conception. Spiritual life is more like learning or bodily healing than it is like having some external function of our life—like our plumbing—taken care of. While teachers, for example, can assist us in our learning, they do not learn for us. We learn. Similarly, while medical professionals can assist in our bodily healing, they do not heal us. Our bodies heal— or sometimes do not. And so with true spiritual growth: *we* grow—or we do not.

The Church has deviated seriously from her spiritual function. The deviation is by no means total. The tradition endures, with a body of literature and human teachers who both take this literature seriously and are competent to teach others. My criticism is that these are not the prevailing influence in the Church, although they should be. As *magisterium* or teaching authority, the Church does not instruct us at a high level about our spiritual growth. She has replaced this very concrete and practical function with a kind of intellectual mission. She tries to tell us how it is in the great picture. She gives us only an idea, a vision of our spiritual condition, as if religion is primarily a matter of believing particular views concerning our life and destiny. To the degree that someone submits to religion in these terms, as a belief-system, that person is bereft of a spiritual practice and might well be relegated to a childhood stage of spiritual development.

This is a tragic squandering of human life, perhaps the only real tragedy there is. Worse yet, this is the norm rather than an anomaly. Physically and mentally, with rare exception, we do grow. Humanly, however, except for all too rare exceptions, we do not grow. Confronted by the whole of life, by death and infinity, we allow ourselves to be protected like children and to have the matter supposedly taken care of by others, by those who are purportedly stronger and more knowledgeable than ourselves. We agree to set such persons up as our leaders. We put a system in place, we call it the Church, that will handle the communications network that is implicit in this childish view of existence. And this entire setup we call, blasphemously I am tempted to say, our *faith*.

This is not faith. Spiritual responsibility demands real faith as well as a life that unfolds out of this faith. The first priority of our life is to identify true faith, to awaken to it, and then to submit to the way of life that it reveals. It behooves us now to ponder the meaning of *faith*.

NOTES

[1] *The Church Teaches: Documents of the Church in English Translation*, selections translated and prepared by John F. Clarkson, S.J., John H. Edwards, S.J., William J. Kelly, S.J., and John J. Welch, S.J., (B.Herder Book Co., 1955), p. 93.

[2] See *The Documents of Vatican II*, "Decree on the Apostolate of the Laity," especially Ch. V.

[3] See *The Church Teaches*, pp. 87-94.

VI

When all self-centered striving ceases, doubts and irresolutions vanish and life in true faith is possible.

Sengstan

FAITH OR BELIEF

Everyone who is highly sensitive to his or her mortality, and therefore to the great question of existence, has the potential to be spiritually serious. Spiritually serious persons rightly regard faith as the essential spiritual factor in their life. Faith is thus, without question, the pivotal matter of this book. Nearly every major religion asserts that faith is the quality which marks the awakening of spiritual life within a person. This gives us a common ground for examining faith. In relation to religion as I have described it above, we can say that faith is what strikes the initial connection between us and our Source.

But it is here that the common agreement ends. We are far from common agreement about just *what faith is.* A longstanding tradition of the Catholic Church has always understood faith as an intellectual assent to truths revealed by God.[1] This intellectualistic understanding of faith was already the implicit teaching of many of the Fathers of the Church in the early centuries of Christianity.[2]

But within Christianity Catholics and Protestants have a fundamental difference in their theoretical understanding of what religious faith is. When Martin Luther and other reformers were trying to rehabilitate the basis of the Christian religion out of the foolery to which it had been degraded—the hawking of indulgences was only a more pronounced instance of the general corruption—they came to see faith in experiential terms. In Luther's view we can actually feel our trust in the saving work of Christ. Faith puts us in a new, felt disposition in relationship to God.

This new Protestant view of faith as trust was rejected in the sixteenth century by the Council of Trent. In contrast, the Council emphasized the intellectual character of faith.[3] It held further that

54

genuine faith continues to exist in a person even if s/he cuts her/
himself off from God through sin.[4]

The Protestant tradition started with a decidedly clearer appreciation of what real faith is. Martin Luther saw faith as our
bonding with the Divine. It is "keeping oneself candidly and
openly in God." "Faith beholds nothing. It is the way of
darkness." "Faith has to leap from the secure bank of this life to
the abyss where there is no feeling or sight, no footings or props."[5]
Luther was at his most succinct when he declared, "Faith is prayer
and nothing but prayer." Here, however, the meaning of prayer
must exceed the superficiality of a mind-lip exercise, which
unfortunately is about all that our spiritually vapid culture offers
us. However, the Protestant trusting faith was soon established in
an underlying belief-system about God and us. The nineteenth-
century Lutheran religious thinker, Kiergekaard, revitalized
Luther's insight into the true nature of faith and heavily criticized
theological interest in mental "what" questions. "How!"
Kierkegaard insisted, is the only issue. He saw as his task "to
revise the definition of a Christian."[6] He rightly observed, "It is
clear that in my writings I have given a more precise determination
to the concept of faith."[7]

But Kierkegaard was not able to fully extinguish the mental
mode which became essential also to Protestant theology. As the
Protestant view of faith took shape in history, it has not been much
more successful than Catholicism in maintaining and supporting
the notion of faith in its spiritual purity. Despite its insistence that
faith is of the heart rather than of the mind, The Protestantism that
developed after Luther and Calvin turned out to be as dogmatic or
creedal as the Catholic Church ever was.[8] In spite of Kierkegaard,
the "What?" questions won out. That is to say, mental attachment
through belief in how things [supposedly] are is about as strong
among Protestant clergy and laity as it is among Catholic. And,
of course, Protestant belief-systems are likewise misrepresented
as the faith.

This factual distortion of faith can be seen, for example, even
in the theology of the modern Protestant theologian, Paul Tillich
[d. 1965]. Tillich was an astute observer and interpreter of
modernity. He recognized that a new era has opened for us and
that the simplicity of our past is gone for good. Being a thinker
rather than a mere expositor of beliefs, Tillich attempted to come
to terms with the reality of faith, particularly as a possibility for
modern persons. Can a modern person, knowing what we know
about the universe and about ourselves, be a person of religious

faith without being medieval or even silly? This question has been felt by many people today. It surely deserved the attention Tillich gave it.

Tillich went straight to the heart of our religious impulse, our felt need to be reconnected. It is the same experience that St. Augustine had confessed on the opening page of his *Confessions*, "*inquietum est cor nostrum*—restless is our heart," a phrase that has become a spiritual classic as "the restlessness of the heart." It is a reality that we all know firsthand.

But Tillich spoke of this religious impulse as "ultimate concern."[9] Many people have recognized their own sense of life in these terms. From their own experience they know what Tillich was talking about. They recognize concern as the basic disposition of their own heart. "Ultimate," for Tillich, identifies the central concern of our heart as it becomes the single focus of all our energy and effort to resolve.

Ultimate concern is perhaps a useful way of understanding and articulating the basic human experience. Strangely, however, Tillich understood this concern to be faith.[10] But concern is precisely *not* faith. Concern is the feeling of the religious impulse prior to the awakening of faith, when faith itself is still obstructed. Ultimate concern might very well be the majority experience, even of believers. But concern is the troubled disposition of the heart that is not yet strong in faith.

Tillich rightly placed ultimate concern beyond the mind. He called it "a centered act of the total personality." But his language is quite vague here. He does not say what the whole personality is, nor does he see clearly what the mind is. While he separates himself from the view that makes faith a merely intellectual assent, Tillich finally falls into the long-standing tradition that theologizes about faith in terms of beliefs: for him our ultimate concern has an object; our relationship to this object takes place through our mind. This makes beliefs of some sort—he calls them "creedal statements"—an essential part of faith. Tillich insists, "At this point it must be stated as sharply and insistently as possible that in every act of faith there is cognitive affirmation..."

What holds for Tillich in regard to faith holds for Protestant theologians generally. Without abandoning their initial insight that saw faith as a disposition of the heart, "prayer and nothing but prayer," the spiritual environment of Protestantism was likewise too arid for a sustained cultivation of living faith. The interest in how things are was too strong, and the understanding of religion as a belief-system that answered this interest was too entrenched, for mainline Protestantism to highlight sufficiently the need for spiritual practice to shape peoples' lives. So as a practical matter Protestantism too has continued to promote belief as belonging to the essence of faith.[11]

In going into the issue of faith, we touch upon something that is obviously close to the heart of many of us. It lies at the foundation of our life. People are quite naturally reluctant to tamper with something this fundamental. There are many reasons for such reluctance. Sometimes we are afraid to look deeply into something important to us because we suspect that things might not prove to be what we want them to be. Or at times we may feel that talking about something might interrupt it—just as gamblers become mum when they have a run going, or baseball team members stay quiet when their pitcher has a no-hitter going. I think that more often we just do not feel that we ourselves are adequate to investigate something profound.

This reluctance must not hold in the case of faith. Faith is too important a matter to be left to others. It will not be hurt by looking at it, when we become clear within ourselves as to exactly what belongs to true faith and what does not. We are not inadequate to the issue of faith. For real faith, although profound, is also very simple. It is within us. It is our own condition, our beginning reconnection to our Source. So we certainly are able to look into it. In fact, if we want to become spiritually responsible, we must look into it.

No one should deny that a religious problem pervades contemporary culture. But this religious problem is not a problem of faith at all. It is not even a spiritual problem. In fact it is said to be a "religious problem" only because it creates an obstacle to spiritual awareness. Near the heart of today's religious problem, as I see it, lies the confusion of faith with belief. It is the view, made dogmatic in the Catholic Church, that religious faith *is* belief. But I insist that *faith is not belief.* Clarity about the two may resolve many of the problems that contemporary people have in coming to terms with the place of religion in their lives.

To separate religious faith from belief is not to deny the naturalness of having beliefs as our outlook on many things. We do have minds. We ponder both the universe and our own lives. There is one meaning of *believe* that is natural and wholesome. Beliefs arise as views in our mind when we ponder the things of our experience. This simply means that we mentally envision ourselves and our world in certain ways. Generally we adhere to our views until more effective views replace them. So to discuss religious beliefs we must make a clear distinction between these natural beliefs and *the absolute commitment to a view* which is commonly taken to be the believing that is religious faith.

When we approach our life in the world with an open, curious mind, we are essentially believers in a basic sense. It is as believers that we begin to absorb the world. As believers we engage the great process of learning and knowing. When we are students, for example, we are dependent upon the findings and teachings of others. We bring what they tell us into our own life as a kind of belief. It is here, however, that a great difference must be noted. The believing of the ordinary learning process does not imply any *absolute commitment* to what is told us. We allow ourselves to be tutored by what others know, or think they know, without having to commit ourselves. We do not feel the need to deny things either. We simply consider something possible, or even probable, until we can find out for ourselves, if we are interested. This is the natural and wholesome meaning of *believe*. Budding scientists, the genuine students of science, are believers in this sense. They apply themselves to the vision of reality that the current scientific view gives them. But at the same time they hold fast to their own personal, intellectual integrity. They adhere to the Missourian "Show me." Science advances exactly because scientists are able to appreciate and use one another's findings without being committed to them in an absolute, dogmatic way.

To take another homely example, we know that the tables in the back of a mathematics book are usually accurate. We exercise belief when we use them. But on that rare occasion when an error has crept into the tables, we do not feel betrayed. For we were not committed to the tables. It is just that they were there, they are usually accurate, and we used them.

The answers others offer us always reflect particular views, whether of themselves or of the world about us. These answers often entail a vision that allows us to move on and to question further. Sharing views of this kind, tentative answers that encourage further questions, can rightly be called believing. But this kind of believing is just an openmindedness that does not despise the views that come from the experience of others. Actually, views such as these are necessary for us to function in the world without having to start out at the very beginning. We do not have to reinvent the wheel for ourselves, so to speak.

It is not a mistake, either, to look to others even regarding the profound issues of life—with questions about our happiness and our destiny. It is with this kind of openness that we might approach the spiritual tradition, which has accumulated a tremendous store of wisdom to instruct us about our life's purpose. It is possible to receive these views and test them for ourselves without submitting to a mind-freezing, dogmatic absoluteness.

However, only a heart that is confident in real faith can accept religious views in this uncommitted sense. Only real faith enables us to have an open believing that can both receive and use a spiritual heritage and still maintain personal responsibility for our own path to our destiny.

It is another sense of believing that is more commonly and, I am saying, erroneously associated with religious faith. The quality of this believing is not that of simply having a view which, if used in the right way, could enable us to grow beyond it and find out for ourselves. Rather, religious believing involves a *commitment* of the heart and mind to a passing view. It is a commitment that takes a mere idea in our mind to be the truth. It takes as a true fact what is only a mental view. This kind of religious believing commits our mind to something in an absolute way without our having the evidence for it within us. Ironically, this distortion of our intellectual integrity is called a virtue —as if *god* is somehow pleased when we hold firmly that something is true even though we ourselves do not have the evidence for it. What is virtuous about that? It lacks human integrity. God would not play such games with our intellectual and moral nature.

Believing of this kind falsifies faith into a mental picture and firm commitment to a particular picture of *how it is* in the grand scale of things—in respect to God and creation and the like—despite the absence of evidence. Moreover, while our mind does not and cannot reach beyond the world that is familiar to us, committed beliefs imply the pretense that our mind does exactly this, that somehow we can speak truly of things that we do not experience or know, things like God, heaven and hell, and so on. It takes a severe jolt to show us how insufficient to our religious need, how extrinsic to real faith, is our commitment to a belief-system.

This fact came home to me most poignantly when my ninety-year old mother, a staunch Irish-Catholic mother of nine, approached the close of her life in 1986. Some two months before she died my mother spoke directly and pensively to my sister: "I'm not ready to go. I know what *this* is [finger pointing downward to the earthly reality of the room]; I don't know what *that* is [finger pointing up]." Her beliefs, of course, had supposedly given her knowledge of *that* throughout her entire life. While she surely was not a woman without faith, believing had been too prominent in her life. It stifled for her the cultivation and strengthening of her real faith. In my view it was after this confession of, dare I call it *disbelief?*, that her real faith began to wax strong in her. Then, just a few weeks later, shortly before she died, my mother spoke again to my sister. This time, still speaking directly but no longer pensively, she declared: "I want to go home." My sister understood the beautiful thing our mother was saying.

The views that are offered by any religious form either support real faith or become solidified into a belief-system that substitutes for real faith. Only the deft instruction of a teacher who understands spiritual matters through experience can use religious views rightly: to show us how to turn directly to ourselves and to begin to look profoundly into ourselves as we actually are. Similarly, only the person already confident at heart, a person of real faith, is able to submit to such spiritual instruction and use it properly.

In the absence of a spiritual culture and without teachers of genuine spiritual experience and knowledge, that is, when religion is heavily cultic, the views that are handed down to us pretend to be the truth itself. Such views attract our eyes outward toward themselves as objects of our faith. But they are only beliefs, and, taken together, comprise only a belief-system. Sadly, they leave our heart in its problematic, painful state. Such views are no longer used or even useful for turning our attention inward, which is the work of authentic religion. They do not instruct us spiritually. They become doctrines that purport to tell us what is so and dogmas that demand our strict mental adherence. And this at the same time that we admit not knowing the matter for ourselves! Such is the obstacle that cultic religion places against our spiritual maturation.

The simplicity of real faith has been travestied in our culture with beliefs of every kind. Faith is wrongly made into belief-systems, conflicting belief-systems at that. During the entire history of Christianity, people have been at one another's throats over whether some doctrine is true or how some dogma is to be understood. Such conflict has been the long, painful experience between Roman Catholicism and Protestantism until recent times. As one author has remarked, "...while the sheer number of philosophical and religious options in society serves to weaken the credibility of them all, how can we know which one is really true?" In this conflict it is wrongly assumed that faith itself is at issue. The fact is, only the mentalisms of belief are at issue.

As modern experience provides an expanded view of the world, many people have grown beyond myopic beliefs. They feel that antiquated beliefs are cloying and untrue to life. Many who have felt tethered to their particular religion as a belief-system have chosen to break that rope and breathe fresh air. Unfortunately for some of them, their identification of the profound reality of faith with beliefs has caused them to think that they have abandoned faith itself, as if faith is just a myopic fixation in a belief-system. While real faith might be very much alive in these persons' lives, they experience a certain emptiness in not being able to enjoy their faith in simplicity and clarity because they confuse it with unprovable, improbable, and even nonsensical beliefs.

To clarify faith by distinguishing it completely from belief can be a spiritual watershed. It could mark the moment of liberation for those who have already sensed that an absolute commitment to beliefs is not particularly true or even relevant to life, but who still feel religion in the marrow of their bones. They may recognize that real faith is in their hearts, even if the stories or doctrines as promoted by one or another religious form have lost all significance for them. When they are liberated from the mentality of mere beliefs, such persons might become sensitive to the reality of genuine faith in their lives. They may also become available to their need for instruction in an effective spiritual practice.

At the same time, however, to separate faith from belief could be a threat to others. This is understandable, and also crucial. It marks the very point where authentic religion makes a break from merely cultic religion. For it must be admitted that all beliefs, all doctrines and dogmas, in a word all our visions and views of life, belong to our minds. They are, therefore, *of this world*. It is necessary for a spiritually serious person to acknowledge that our mind belongs to this world. As products of our mind, beliefs are only this-worldly stuff. Separating real faith from belief forces us to face the issue whether this world is our primary concern. Many religious beliefs appeal to people precisely because they appear to explain this life, as well as promise an afterlife made up of the best that we know of this life. They give us a vision of heaven that is comprised of the best of our worldly experience. This entire mentality represents The Cult of This World pure and simple.

Alas, it is also a dominant religious force in contemporary culture.

Of course it is not enough merely to assert that faith is not belief, particularly when much of the tradition of Christendom either identifies faith as belief or at least intertwines faith inextricably with belief. A demanding and thoughtful consideration is required to appreciate the simplicity of faith as independent of any and all beliefs and belief-systems.

We will begin this reflection by a preliminary, down-to-earth description of the experience of faith. Deep within us we are already connected to reality, before we mentally project or imagine any problems about life. We do exist. *We stand here.* We are *firmly* here already, without being propped up. We are *consciously* here already. We definitely can take heart in the undeniable reality of our existence. Consciously and courageously *taking heart* in this reality marks the awakening of real faith. Faith is a matter of feeling rather than of intellectual conviction. Its feeling-tone is a happiness that suffuses and exceeds every type of experience. No one can take this happiness away from us because it is the feeling of reality itself. It is not a quality limited to the mere comings and goings of our experiences.

If the image of a great banquet would be useful for understanding faith, I suggest this: faith is *not* that we find ourselves at a wonderful banquet where we have no inherent right to be because of our unworthiness; rather, faith is finding that we are at our own wonderful banquet, where we have every right to be precisely because of who we are.

To face squarely the difficult question where belief has substituted for faith, we must look at both sides of believing. There is the objective side, what we believe. This is referred to as the Word of God or divine revelation. Then, of course, there is the subjective side, what goes on within us when we commit ourselves as believers.

Why does any Christian hold a particular belief? The answer, I think, is that he feels he is believing God: "God has revealed this to us." Here is the point where the notion of divine revelation is brought in. Yes, it is admitted, our darkened minds cannot fathom the depth of existence. However, God has revealed to us the great picture and our place within it. However, revelation understood this way is not revelation in the literal sense of "pulling the veil back" [*re-velare* in Latin]. While revelation in its literal sense means an actual *showing*, the divine revelation of the Christian tradition is defined as "God's spoken *testimony* to us." God supposedly reassures us about the big picture, but without showing it to us. This amounts to giving us a second-hand knowledge that we are to believe. Faith, then, came to be defined by Thomas Aquinas as "A habit of the mind by which eternal life begins in us making our intellects assent to things that we do not see."[12] This understanding of divine revelation and faith does have a strong logic. For if indeed God chooses to tell us something, we are well advised to believe it with an absolute commitment, even if we have no evidence of our own about the matter.

But the real issue concerning divine revelation has to do with facts. *Did* God speak to humankind? Just how did human beings experience this "speaking?" *What* did God say? Exactly *who* has heard God speak? I do not know of a priest, bishop or pope who claims he has heard God speak. And even if you hear the claim that God has spoken to someone, how do *you* know that it was God whom this person has heard? When we bring this matter of divine revelation back to earth—where it is said to happen—it becomes a touchy matter. No wonder its details are kept enigmatic. We are not told how the earthly image of one person speaking to another applies to God speaking to us.

If the metaphor of God speaking seems enigmatic, exactly what God has said is ambiguous beyond enigma. Where once the Word of God was either precisely or at least roughly equivalent to Sacred Scripture, the Old and New Testaments, modern ways of thinking have put Scripture to the test. It is not possible to telescope two centuries of intense investigation of Scripture into a few paragraphs. But there are significant principles that have come to be commonly accepted. Scripture is no longer taken as divine dictation.

The original Protestant movement insisted on scripture alone as the bearer of God's Word, against the Roman Church which included her own tradition as well. Yet the Catholic position did not assert absolutely that there is some particular divinely revealed truth found only in tradition with no presence in scripture. The general Catholic consensus runs counter to this. However, the wrenching of the words of those ancient texts in order to make them somehow contain certain doctrines and dogmas that grew up in the Catholic Church is Orwellian. To cite the more blatant examples, try to find the Immaculate Conception of Mary, or her Bodily Assumption into Heaven, in the scriptural texts. Try to discern Papal Infallibility in the words of Jesus, "Thou art Peter, and upon this rock I will build my Church."[13] The Church in her long tradition of teaching simply made herself the authority over God's Word. However, the Protestants and their scripture-alone understanding of God's revelation has hardly fared better. The idea that every person in his own armchair is guided by the Holy Spirit as he reads scripture has produced mass disarray. Such sheer ambiguity about what God actually said is a natural consequence of a revelation that comes indirectly, through other persons and worldly means, even if it be a sacred text. If you do not hear God speaking his Word yourself, then you are at the mercy of human, all-too-human, mediators.

Modern thought has complicated even this tenuous situation. Karl Barth, a renowned Protestant theologians of the twentieth century, articulated the conclusion that God's Word is *not* identical to scripture. How could something so limited as a text be equated with the Word of God![14] But Barth still saw scripture as a foremost carrier of God's Word. A further difficulty is that the text of scripture itself has come to be acknowledged as a human work by human authors. Cardinal Koenig of Vienna spoke to the assembled Second Vatican Council regarding our current understanding of Scripture: "In Holy Scripture the historical and scientific accounts sometimes diverge from the truth." In other words, the merely historical or scientific information that is also present in scripture is not part of God's revelation that is contained in it.

What is spiritually reliable in this vague situation? Revelation as an intangible testimony, spoken somewhere by God but mediated to us so humanly and ambiguously, lacks spiritual effectiveness. True revelation is an *unveiling*, a real showing, not a testimony. Revelation comes directly to the heart of the individual. By all means, listen and listen with all your heart. Such is your spiritual responsibility. But when you truly *hear*, you will *know*, and not merely believe. And when you say to another what you truly know, you will speak with the power of a prophet. If someone hears you, then he too will know. The transmission of spiritual knowledge is thus heart to heart, and each person must realize it by his or her own effort. This fact belongs to the very essence of spiritual life.

Karl Barth was right about scripture. Scriptures are valuable. They are sacred to the extent that they carry spiritual knowledge. But only a person of *realized spiritual knowledge* is an authentic interpreter of sacred texts. There is no divine magic that draws spiritual knowledge from the ignorant. The culture of spiritual knowledge, as well as the community of earnest spiritual practitioners (the *true* Church), is compromised and degraded by pretenders who assume spiritual authority by the magic of office rather than through the actualization of wisdom within themselves.

Revelation as the spoken testimony of God is based on a circular argument. We are told that "God has revealed this" without our ever being allowed to investigate the matter for ourselves. We are not given a direct connection to God, so that we ourselves might hear and *believe God*. What really happens is that we find ourselves believing what somebody else has alleged about God, namely that "God said this." And there is no end to the number of people who insist on telling us "what God wants" and the like. Our belief, however, is in this somebody else, someone in the world who does not deserve an absolute commitment from us. We are told further that we would be unfaithful to God if we were to question what they tell us. In Catholic doctrine it is said to be a sin to doubt, or even to question, this supposed faith. There seems to be a Catch-22 here. The only solution, as I see it, is to make clear the reality and simplicity of true faith. The absolute commitment of belief is a commitment, not to God, but to a figment within our own minds that is founded on hearsay.

If the Catholic belief-system is not the simple revelation of God it has claimed to be, it is nevertheless a very powerful reality in the world. It is no easy matter for any individual person to stand up to such a powerful force in her or his life. Yet as particular beliefs of the system are called into question, together with the authority that demands mental assent, many persons are moved to ask some very basic religious questions about faith.

I do not come to this question of faith without a personal history. I have been a strong believer. This does not embarrass me. It means that I took my life seriously, as best I knew how. So I took religion seriously—religion as our reconnection to our Source. In my upbringing, the only thing I had for addressing our religious problem was a belief-system. I was committed to it. But my fidelity to myself was stronger than my commitment to my belief-system. I can now see I held my beliefs as a security, a defense. I kept this defense alert, however. The belief-system had constantly to show that it was doing its job, that it was true to me. After all, it was my life that was at stake. As I look back, I can say this about myself: perhaps I would have given my earthly life for things that seemed like they deserved it; but I would never have surrendered my existence, my destiny, for anything at all. Some-how I realized that my responsibility for my own destiny was something inalienable. Pursuing this became the obvious point of my life. In fact it is the point of everyone's life as far as I could tell. So I was not inclined to make my life a faithful servant of any particular belief-system just because I happened to inherit this system. So when one or another belief of the system began to seem implausible, it would just fall away. But I never felt that faith itself was affected. Even when I began to notice that believing itself no longer made sense, my faith remained the same. It even became stronger as it became simpler and clearer.

We must now look carefully at our own willingness to believe. This entails a very difficult work of introspection, of looking into ourselves to see why we so readily sacrifice the natural character of our minds by an absolute commitment to believe what has not been shown us. What is it in us that prompts us to sacrifice our own intellectual integrity? One of the greatest ironies is that believing betrays a weakness or even the absence of real faith. Belief is just the mind presuming that the foundation of our existence lies outside ourselves, and that we ourselves are weak and vulnerable and in need of salvation. Faith as belief, then, looks for salvation. Its main purpose is to secure things; it must always check the locks. However, history has shown that the security of beliefs is about as strong as the securities of Wall Street. Every revolution in our cultural thinking reverberates throughout the belief-system. So of course Tillich was right in making doubt intrinsic to faith—as he understood faith. But it is faith *as belief,* and not real faith, that is flawed in its essence by doubt.[15] Psychoanalyst Carl Jung had already noted the connection of doubt to belief: "Wherever belief reigns, doubt lurks in the background."[16] Genuine faith, on the contrary, establishes us in an openness, a freedom, and a clarity of mind to which doubt is not relevant.

We will begin to inspect our confusion of faith and belief with a story. A preacher, the story goes, announced that he would reveal on television his discovery of the ultimate foundation of the world. His promise attracted a wide viewing audience. At the awaited moment, the preacher approached the podium and solemnly proclaimed: "The world rests on the back of a great turtle!" A dissatisfied viewer called in demanding to know, "And upon what does this great turtle rest?" Taken aback, the preacher replied, "On the back of another turtle." But the caller insisted, "And upon what does this second turtle rest?" "Sir," came the terse reply, "it's turtles all the way down."

We all have some sense of the tremendous work that is required to grasp an ultimate foundation, either of the world or even of our own selves. Still, it is easy to see the flimsiness of "all the way down" as a satisfactory answer to the question about the ultimate foundation of the world. This kind of answer feathers the issue into obscurity.

Believing has to do with turtles. As in the turtle explanation, believing always has to do with explanations, with saying how things are. Believing belongs to the mind. What many consider religious believing is only a mental attachment to some vision about the great picture, a vision that has indeed entered someone's mentality, but which that person insists has come from a divinity, from God. A normally intelligent person of our culture will smile at the turtles story. But too often this same person does not recognize that his or her own story about existence and religion is just a slightly more sophisticated version of the turtles story. S/he could easily fail to see herself/himself in the turtles story. We are more honest when we acknowledge that our mind has no capacity for, no grasp or vision of "all the way down." Our mind, as well as any view within it, is a very limited thing. It enables us to tie our shoes, to drive our car, to make and use computers, even to theorize about the universe. In a word, our mind enables us to proceed with our life. But it goes no further than this. Our mind is not adequate, it is barely relevant, to the great totality of existence and our relationship to it.

Relating to this great totality, what I have called reconnecting to our Source, is a practical matter in the finest sense of the word practical. It is not a matter of theorizing, and no kind or amount of theorizing strikes the reconnection. For the problem of disconnection is felt in the heart; it is not a mental mistake of some sort. Its real solution will likewise be a felt matter, not a theory in our mind.

We should question why we tend to displace our basic problem into our mind and then intellectualize about it. Why should we presume that we have to know the foundation of our existence in order to exist properly? I should mention here that the knowledge problem (What is knowledge? How do we come to know? How can we be certain about what we know?) has taken over the philosophical interest of western culture almost from the beginning of our recording of philosophy. A person could, of course, spend his/her lifetime studying this problem and the ten thousand supposedly philosophical views that have been proposed to answer it. There are always many philosophers who do exactly this. But any person could take another tack. S/he could allow her/his own intelligence to see through the whole knowledge-game at a stroke. Ask yourself: If I *knew* everything (whatever that would be like), would that make a real and profound difference to me? For myself the answer is No. The whole universe exists, and, aside from human beings, nothing else claims or tries to know this existence. Bugs and trees and stars do not create a problem for themselves by trying to figure out their existence. They simply exist, and very competently. Moreover, the very idea of knowing the foundation of our existence implies a kind of stepping back from it and sizing it up and figuring it out, as if we were merchants looking over an object of some kind. But we are not objects to ourselves, as if knowing ourselves objectively could make any sense at all. We are self-aware already. This is not problematic in itself.

Religious belief amounts to setting up a knowledge relationship to the great totality of existence, but without having the basis for this knowledge within ourselves. Thus we conceive of a God who created a universe; we conceive of the appearance of human beings who are somehow inveterate sinners; we conceive of the birth and life of a savior; we conceive of the human death of this savior as having a sacrificial quality that has a positive effect on the inherent sinfulness of humankind; we conceive of the saving work of this savior taking place over the centuries in a community of people whose main connection to the savior is through believing the whole story.

Attempting this knowledge stance is itself the misstep. It is an unnecessary mistake. We exist properly and competently without possessing the ultimate foundation of our existence through some kind of knowledge. Interestingly, the mere fact that our minds are limited and will always be unclear about the big picture does not change anything real in the big picture at all. Rather it tells us something important about our minds: we are obviously not connected to what is ultimate through our minds.

As I see it, our tendency to believe with absolute commitment is the disposition of the traumatized child within us. The wonder that is natural to our childhood has not been nourished in an atmosphere of wisdom which could lay open to us the way to our own nature. Our cultural environment has been without such wisdom and is hostile to truth. Our culture (our own take on the World) tells us, implicitly at least, that the restlessness of our heart will be settled by a certain amount of worldly goods and experiences. We put our minds to work and go for it. Sooner or later, however, we get some taste of our mortality. The wonder of our childhood, already jaded by worldly pursuits, then becomes traumatized by fear. The sense of our mortality gives religion a fresh hue. Awareness of the fact that we will definitely die puts everything in a serious perspective. It impresses upon us that we do not have forever to figure things out, a seemingly infinite task. Yet this same awareness of death makes us susceptible to the easy answers that are offered by one or another religious form, answers that pretend to explain our whole situation to us and demand that we accept this explanation. We may too readily fall in line. For who are we, we may feel, to question the matter! Thus we approach a religious form poised to believe with the commitment which that particular form or organization demands. We become, as Eric Hoffer has described it in his book by this name, *The True Believer.*[17]

Real faith is obstructed when our natural confidence becomes displaced by a religious view or belief-system. That vision of the whole is taken as literal truth. But since the object of this belief lies outside us as a hopeful object of our minds, the belief itself has to be held. And since it concerns nothing less than the fundamental meaning of our life, as well as our eternal destiny, *it must be held tenaciously.* It is the tenacity of the commitment that marks the true believer as Eric Hoffer has described this mentality. There is no need to wonder at the fanaticism of the true believer. For fanaticism is the psychic equivalent of a nuclear explosion. When we are not strong in real faith, the core energy of our heart is alienated from its natural repose in self-confidence. It is as if the world has somehow penetrated to our heart and bombarded it out of its natural and stable condition. This unleashes the vast vital energy at our core. But at the same time we are weakened by this instability at our core. This gives us the feeling of vulnerability and actual threat. We spontaneously use our unleashed energy to defend ourselves. But rather than using our energy properly, to restore ourselves to balance and repose at our center, we make a package out of our chaos and tie it together, as it were, as a belief-system that we have determined is our salvation. The weaker we feel at the core of our existence, and therefore more vulnerable and more threatened, the stronger will be our defense of what we grasp at as our salvation. This is why the absolute commitment to believe what is outside ourselves tends toward true believing in Hoffer's chilling sense.

A spiritually empty culture leaves us all a legacy of weakness in genuine faith. When we are deficient in self-confidence, we are not apt to let our own intelligence move toward that place in us where all real questioning first arises, namely in our heart. So it is not so surprising that those who are spiritually disinherited must relate to the foundation of their existence by having the great question asked—*and answered*—by somebody else. Without genuine spiritual support, religious persons will use their religion, their church, as a means of escaping their responsibility to *really* ask the great question themselves. Dogmatic belief is the precise technique of the pseudo-religious escape. This is contrary to the ordinary worldly part of our lives which does not view believing to be worthy of our intelligence, and certainly not its goal. We constantly seek to know. Conventional religion has countered our natural instinct to know by giving a supposedly religious status to believing. It has even made believing a virtue by the Alice-in-Wonderland ploy of simple declaration. Believing is simply declared to be the essential religious act or disposition. What from the ordinary point of view is a prostitution of our natural intelligence shows that it has become the honorable establishment when people refer to themselves in a religious way as "believers." Enshrouding themselves this way in a belief-system, they then become impervious to all significant questioning, particularly to the question whether believing may not itself be a defrauding of their own intelligence.

A religious believer might feel every kind of negative emotion at this suggestion. One or another believer will become angry at the very idea of criticizing belief. Exactly. But let me speak to this angry one for a moment: Do yourself the favor of inspecting your feeling of anger. Anger is a strong emotion. It shows great energy. Why are *you* angry? Where does this energy come from? One of Christendom's most respected theologians, St. Thomas Aquinas, viewed anger as a defensive emotion aimed against a threat. Whom or what might you be defending? No one would think of defending something that is invulnerable, something that cannot be threatened. So no one needs to defend God. God is never endangered. What about the Church? Is the Church vulnerable? Catholic doctrine has always declared that the Church is invulnerable. Are you perhaps defending yourself? It does not take much pondering over one's own anger to come to recognize that anger is always a self-defense.

In what way are you threatened by the mere suggestion that believing is counter-intelligent? I have no guns, no ammunition of any kind. Physically you are all right, for only thoughts are at stake. At the very worst, all I could be is mistaken. And mistakes happen all over the world at all times. Do not be deceived that your concern, your anger, is on behalf of others who may be harmed in some way by these thoughts. The world has always been and remains full of harm to many persons. This fact rarely disturbs your equilibrium. So truthfully, what is your anger defending? What do you feel to be so vulnerable?

Consider this: Your fundamental belief-system is threatened. This means that your belief-system is not founded securely in your heart. As this system takes shape in your mind, it seems to offer security. So you get its logic down pat. You can argue it endlessly, and you love to do just that. But the root and dynamic of believing is not in the mind. It is in the heart. The insecure heart, which is the heart that does not rest in faith in the spiritual sense, holds onto beliefs to allay its gnawing emptiness, the absence of real faith. If you were to abandon your mere believing and make yourself available to truth, no matter what that might prove to be, you would find yourself in the *real* experience of the great question. Your own intelligence would begin to move. Ironically, your threatened feeling feels much worse than does a heart that is moved by the great question. Beliefs clearly do not provide the comfort we expect them to provide. The profound feeling of vulnerability, and its often accompanying anger, are sufficient evidence of that. Believing is a premature foreclosure of questioning. It represents infidelity to one's own intelligence. It is reason gone a'whoring.

Religious beliefs might be likened to a scab formation surrounding the great question. Perhaps, despite the momentary pain, we would do well to just let it all go. Simply admit that at this point you do not know. See that believing is not an honorable substitute for knowing for yourself. Then realize that you want to know. You want the foundation of your views within yourself. Nevertheless, to say only this much cannot do more than suggest something, perhaps arouse a suspicion about believing. It does not yet actually penetrate our confused disposition toward belief. Yet if suspicion is aroused, the reader may be moved to follow an analysis of belief, particularly as it stands in stark contrast to genuine faith. S/he might begin to see how the escape to belief is itself the fundamentalist attitude.

Let us see how confusion is a basic ingredient in committed believing. It is so because there comes a point in questioning where our imagination begins to flag. Our minds can go no further. In the turtles story the preacher was brought to this point and muttered, "Sir, it's turtles all the way down." If the man continued questioning, "Down where?" for example, his telephone line to the station would likely have been cut. We can grasp explanations like the Great Turtle in our imagination. But we tire of those further questions that try to fathom the ultimate. Our mind is not equipped for this. The mind, as I have already suggested, is an instrument for much more mundane, functional purposes. It is for this reason that authentic religion, the matter of the heart, simply exceeds the mind and all its products, all mentalisms.

Absolute beliefs are the dreams of those who spiritually tend to remain children. The spiritual path does not ask us to believe something about ourselves or our condition. On the contrary, it requires us first to discover and then to work with ourselves, our actual condition. This is a demanding task. The great Christian spiritual mentor, St. John of the Cross, called the period of this initial discovery and work "the Dark Night of the Soul." But until we acknowledge and accept this task, we remain spiritual children. True faith is the dawning of spiritual maturity. Its tenor of happiness makes our necessary task not only bearable but desirable. The saints are commonly known to be happy, whatever the circumstances or experiences that appear in their lives at any particular time. They are people in whom faith is strong.

Christians, and anyone else for that matter, who want to mature spiritually must come to the point where they can appreciate their faith in itself. They must *feel* their faith as a reality far more profound and far more significant than any religious belief. Awareness of real faith enables a person to discern the religious vision that supports and nurtures an effective spiritual practice, as distinct from mere intellectual views that only purport to tell how things are.

So we must attend to the nature of real faith, beyond the preliminary suggestions I offered above. In separating the reality of faith from belief, from being a mere product in our mind, we can no longer approach our faith as an inventory of what we believe. We will probably continue to believe many things, and wisely so. But we have to reckon with the fact that they do not comprise religious faith. Of course this does not mean that our faith is completely mysterious to us, something simply unfathomable. For surely we can relate to our own faith. It is a most precious element of our being. But at the same time we must realize that we cannot approach something which is so inward to us and know it as an object in the ordinary way that we are accustomed to know things. Faith is much more like what St. Augustine said about God, "more inward to me than I am to myself" [*intimior mihi meipso*].

If we want to inspect real faith we have to reach deeply into our life to that place where, unproblematically, we simply *are*. When we actually touch base and become aware of our own depth, the place where we exist before we make a problem out of living, then we can see that we exist in faith. Surely it is a profound realization in anyone.

I would make this analogy for showing how we must approach the reality of our faith: When a woman says to a man "I love you," it would be completely irrelevant to her real love for him by asking, "What is love?" An intellectual inquiry into the nature of love is neither necessary nor conducive to the real thing. Intellectualizing might well kill it. It would be a little like our biological inquiry into the nature of a frog. We kill a frog in order to inquire into it. I know this, because both in high school and in college I did this. Trying to know a frog, I studied, ironically, a dead frog, a no-longer-frog. While we do learn something about biology through dead frogs, we do not get to know real frogs through dead frogs. To learn real frogs, actually to know them, requires a much different approach. It demands an actual relationship to a living frog.

I speak of love and of frogs only to give a sense of what is required as we discuss real faith. The reality of love is realized only in the lover. The reality of a real frog is known only in a real relationship to a live frog. And the reality of faith is known only directly, that is, when real faith awakens. Even then faith is not known as an object, but directly.

The most valid reflection on faith for Catholics and all Christians must appeal to the sense of faith expressed by Jesus in the gospel stories. Yet, before I do this it is fair, and revealing, to relate an anecdote connected with my preparation to write this chapter.

As I thought to write this chapter I reviewed the textbook in a course on faith in my own theological training at the Gregorian University. The Jesuit author of this text proposed the thesis that "Faith is an act of intellectual assent." As was customary, he defended this thesis by citing the New Testament, which contains numerous references to faith. With incredible irony, however, this author explicitly cut out Jesus' references to faith because they do not support the idea that faith is intellectual assent. He allowed only two of the many passages where Jesus spoke of faith. These two he allowed because in them "the word 'believe' seems to mean 'accepting the Word of God.'" So, of course, this author's scriptural defense of faith as intellectual assent was based almost entirely on the letters of St. Paul.

In this context I feel it is important that we abandon the notion that a spiritual teacher is magically graced to be able to give what he himself does not have. Now to the obvious: St. Paul was not of the spiritual stature of Jesus; consequently his spiritual understanding\teaching was not of the quality of that of Jesus. And it is Jesus' communication about faith that should instruct a Christian, not St. Paul's.

When healings occurred in the presence of Jesus, he often turned to the healed person and attributed the healing to that person's faith: "Your faith has made you whole." Jesus spoke of faith in reference to the heart, not to beliefs of the mind. The single, touching gospel story I will cite is about the hemorrhaging woman. This woman thought to herself, "If I but touch the hem of his [Jesus'] garment, I will be healed." She subtly did touch his clothes. And, as the gospel tells it, Jesus "felt power go out of himself." This was true revelation to the woman, from the heart of Jesus to her heart. She did not have to hold onto it. What belonged to Jesus became also her own. Jesus, the Gospel continues, turned around and realized what the woman had done. Then he remarked to her, "Your *faith* healed you." The clarity of Jesus' revelation in her heart had flowed through and purified even her physical body.

Now what are we to suppose that this woman believed? It does not seem relevant to ask about her creed. She profoundly *faithed*, if we may so speak, but there is no reason to assign to her any particular belief. Certainly, as the gospel story narrates, she did say to herself, "If I but touch the hem of his garment I will be healed." But her entire action occurred at the real level. The mental components were most ordinary, merely functional—obviously she had to figure out how to get close enough to Jesus to touch his clothes. In faith she had already recognized Jesus and felt that some physical connection to him would make a healing difference in her life. But as far as the conventional religious sense of believing goes, I do not detect a trace of doctrinal belief or dogmatic commitment in this woman who had suffered a flow of blood. Yet her story is powerful enough to touch anyone. This woman's faith issued in a healing. But particular beliefs were not a part of it. I think we can agree that when Jesus spoke of faith he was referring to *our very participation in the great reality*. He was not speaking of belief-figments that do no more than shape and limit our minds.

Faith is simply the awakening of self-confidence in the heart, when the heart, no longer overwhelmed by the many problems created by the mind, is able to rest in its own nature in fundamental peace. In monumental faith we are able to stand firm even in the midst of birth and death, including our own. For faith is our heart's true nature when that nature emerges with an awareness that is stronger and more intense than our chaotic, fear-inducing mentality. Faith is our own self-confident heart in wonder at and enjoyment of the unshakable existence that we already know directly because it is what we *are*.

NOTES

[1] The intellectual character of faith was declared dogmatically in the Council of Trent and in the First and Second Vatican Councils. See [Denzinger's *Enchiridion Symbolorum*] Roy J Deferrari, tr. *The Sources of Catholic Dogma*, (B. Herder Book Co., 1957), pp. 243 & 445, and *The Documents of Vatican II*, p. 113.

[2] The Early Fathers of the Church concerned themselves directly with the substance of belief rather than with the "act of faith" itself. Yet their indirect references clearly indicate that they understood the essence of faith primarily in intellectual terms of believing. This matter is amply discussed in Roger Aubert, *Le Probleme de l'Acte de Foi: donnees traditionnelles et resultats des controverses recentes* ["The Problem of the Act of Faith: the received tradition and the results of recent controversies"], (Louvain: E. Warny, 1958), esp. pp. 13-20 *et al.*

[3] Aubert, *op. cit.*, pp. 77f, clarifies the intention of the Council to contradict the Protestant "trusting faith" [*fides fiducialis*] by asserting that through faith we "believe to be true the things divinely revealed and promised." Aubert even quotes the bishop of Porto who wished to make the Council's declaration more explicit by adding that "faith is not trustingness [*fiducia*] as the Lutherans say."

[4] See *The Sources of Catholic Dogma*, p. 256.

[5] See Friedrich Gogarten, *The Reality of Faith: The Problem of Subjectivism in Theology*, "Luther's War Against Free Will," (The Westminster Press, 1957).

[6] *Kierkegaard's Attack upon "Christendom" 1854-1855*, p. 284.

[7] *The Journals of Soren Kierkegaard*, trans. Alexander Dru, (Oxford University Press, 1938), No. 1117.

[8] See John Hick, *Faith and Knowledge*, (Cornell University Press, 1966), esp. p. 30.

[9] Paul Tillich, *Dynamics of Faith*, (Harper & Brothers, Publishers, 1957), pp. 1ff.

[10] Ibid., "What Faith Is." Unless otherwise noted, the quotations from Tillich can be found in this chapter.

[11] John Hick's *Faith and Knowledge* gives an historical profile of both the

Catholic and the Protestant identification of faith with belief, which Hick likewise acknowledges to be true.

[12] *Summa Theologiae, IIa IIae*, q. 4, a. 1.

[13] *Matthew* XVI, 18.

[14] See *Church Dogmatics I, 1*, (Charles Scribner's Sons, 1963), esp. p. 150.

[15] *Dynamics of Faith*, p. 18, "If faith is understood as being ultimately concerned, doubt is a necessary element in it. It is a consequence of the risk of faith." Tillich departed radically from Kierkegaard, for example, in connecting doubt with faith. While agreeing with Kierkegaard that faith is not of the mind but of the self, he did not follow Kierkegaard in emphasizing the inverse correlate of faith as despair.

[16] C.G. Jung, *Psychology and Western Religion*, (Princeton University Press, 1984), p. 6.

[17] *The True Believer: Thoughts on the Nature of Mass Movements*, (Time Incorporated, 1963).

VII

In the end men may discover that religion shines all the brighter for the loss of all its doctrinal wrappings.

H.G.Wells

DOGMA OR INSTRUCTION

"God said it! I believe it! And that settles it!" This bumper sticker say-so is a brief but accurate expression of the dogmatic mentality. A belief-system reportedly dictated by God becomes our unshakable faith. The dogmatic attitude assumes that the matter of our very existence, our purpose and destiny, is settled without further ado on our part. We have only to believe. End of questioning. In providing ready answers to all our important questions about a life that transcends this world, dogma enables us to devote full attention to this world. We do not have to actually involve ourselves in the great question about life itself. We dogmatically declare the answer. And we assure ourselves that no less than *god* is the guarantee of our answer. What a wonderful, consoling *faith* we have!

In contrast to their own dogmatic security, many people, Catholics and other Christians among them, are bemused when they learn of various mythologies that have fed the religious imagination of other peoples around the world. Many of the famous Greek and Roman myths have filtered into our own cultural heritage. We are not strangers to the names Zeus and Jupiter, and numerous other names as well. Visitors to modern Rome rarely fail to visit the Pantheon, a church that was once an ancient temple dedicated to "all the gods," as the word *pan-theon* itself signifies. We are tempted to puzzle, "Did those civilized and intelligent pre-Christian Greek and Roman people really believe those stories of their gods? Did they even think about whether the stories were true or not? Did they ever try to discover what the truth in their stories was, if it was there at all?"

The status that most of us allow to the religious imagination of other peoples of the world is much less than the status we give to our own. In fact we consider this difference to be the difference

77

between fiction and truth, between fancy and fact. We comfort ourselves that we are the ones blessed with truth, with fact. The others are left with fiction, with fancy. They are, after all, *pagans*.

Perhaps we should turn our questioning mind to what we take to be divine revelation. Is it true? Did revelation really happen? Exactly what is the *it* that God told us in his revelation? Who heard God say it? How have *I* gotten the word? How do I know I got it right? Just whom am I believing? Why should I think I am believing God when I did not even hear God for myself, when I got it only second or third-hand at best?

Divine revelation, defined theologically as "God's spoken testimony to us,"[1] is taught to be our seal of truth and fact. Others, we are told, are left with their yarn-spun mythologies. In the previous chapter we have discussed the hard questions that face us when we take revelation to be an event in the distant past: How can we ourselves be certain about it? Why would God not speak directly to everyone? What is this divine information supposed to mean in our lives?

Part of the answer given to these questions is that God's purported revelation, as intangible and intractable as it seems to be, becomes available to us through dogmatic pronouncements of the Church. Moreover, we are told that the Church is guided personally by the Spirit of God. So we need not fear any error on the Church's part as she mediates God's information to us. Over time *dogma* for the Church has come to mean "defined, indisputable, and unchangeable [*irreformable*] truth."[2] Dogma lays out for us *how it is* in the great spiritual realm. It assures us of an accuracy, a firmness, and a security that are unknown to any other area of human experience. For our part we are advised that our faith compels us to an unwavering adherence to this belief-system, since it is God's spoken word to us.

Dogma did offer Catholics security in their beliefs for centuries. This made dogma appear to be the very watermark of the Church. In modern times, when many dogmas have become meaningless or even obsolete, a large number of Catholics have allowed their connection to the Church to vanish along with their beliefs. This is understandable. The Church leadership has not yet learned how to let a symbolic belief-system take a non-dogmatic shape. Most theologians have come to recognize that what are called "symbols of the faith" are not factual truths. They are not dogmas. Early in this century certain progressive theologians attempted to clarify the non-dogmatic nature of religious symbols. But the thoughtful reflections of those theologians were condemned as the heresy of *Modernism*. In this not so distant past the Church cast out some of her most brilliant religious thinkers as heretics. She called them *Modernists*.[3] This violent attack on new and creative thinking not only served to reinforce the dogmatic mentality within the Church, it also severely hampered Catholic thinking for half a century. During this period the Catholic Church fell almost hopelessly behind the times. She found herself in needless conflict with a world rapidly progressing on many fronts.

For the past three decades or so a number of theologians have been wrestling with many *irreformable* dogmatic statements of *the faith*. They face formidable problems in trying to relativize this system of absolutes. They know they must reform many dogmatic statements even while they must say that those same statements, being dogmas, are "irreformable." I appreciate the dilemma of these theologians. They remember all too well what happened to the modernists and other supposedly heretical forebears when these persons were subjected to investigation by the Vatican's Holy Office of the Inquisition. This Vatican entity has undergone name changes in modern times. But there has not been a wholesome, wholesale change in its forceful investigative spirit.

It is interesting to witness the ingenuity modern theologians demonstrate in their struggle to reform the irreformable and still make sense. They reformulate irreformable formulations of the faith in a way that makes these statements mean the opposite of what they once said and meant. At the same time they maintain that the dogmas as originally stated were *true*. Of course these theologians are required to explain such a sleight of hand.

One of the most striking examples of this kind of magic is found in a long-standing dogma of the Church. This dogma was defined by numerous ecumenical councils and popes over the centuries. I speak of the ancient maxim "Outside the Church there is no salvation," which dates back at least to St. Cyprian in the third century. Here we will cite only one of its many formulations. The famous decree *Unam Sanctam* of Pope Boniface VIII reads: "There is but one holy, Catholic and Apostolic Church outside of which there is no salvation or remission of sins...We declare, announce and define that it is altogether necessary for salvation for every creature to be subject to the Roman Pontiff."[4] The meaning and intention of Pope Boniface's declaration are not ambiguous. He certainly intended to express an irreformable dogma of the Church. But on the other hand, the noted theologian Gregory Baum has expressed a contrasting view that is common

to modern Catholic theologians and to Catholics generally. Baum
has stated that "According to the repeated teaching of Vatican
Council II there is plentiful salvation outside the Church."[5] An
older generation of American Catholics will remember the struggle
a certain Father Feeney engaged with Church superiors who
insisted that he not preach nor even personally hold that "Outside
the Church there is no salvation." Father Feeney was finally
excommunicated for asserting precisely what Pope Boniface VIII
"declared, announced, and defined."

In support of Father Baum the Jesuit theologian Father Avery
Dulles has correctly observed that "...the ancient understanding of
the formula [i.e. Outside the Church there is no salvation] is
repugnant to practically all Catholics."[6] Yet given the fact that
this maxim was a proclaimed dogma of the Church and therefore
presumably true, Father Dulles went on to assert, "The old
formula was not totally wrong. It was based on a valid insight into
the ecclesial [churchly] character of all Christian salvation..."

Father Dulles still thinks that it is important to find truth in a
dogma which he knows "practically all Catholics," including
himself, repudiate. An old device for finding truth in dogmas that
we now disavow is the idea of doctrinal development: over time
dogma does not change; it *develops*. Truth that has always been
there in seed form comes forth, over time, to flourish in a clearer
and more explicit form. While the notion of doctrinal development has had a brilliant expositor in the person of Cardinal John
Henry Newman,[7] I have always found this notion spiritually
troublesome. For meeting the needs of the modern era the notion
is simply untenable. In Dulles's words, "In order to bring out the
deeper and divinely intended meaning, which alone is inseparable
from faith, it may be necessary *to discard the human concepts as
well as the words* [emphasis mine] of those who first framed the
dogma."[8]

If we assume that Jesus was a Spiritual Master of the quality
that Christians presume he was, why did he not make his instruction clear at the beginning? Should people who are born later be
at a spiritual advantage compared to those born earlier simply
because of the mere passage of time? Moreover, is this supposed
"development" not a matter of human invention? Can we assign
it to God? Does God favor the latter-born over the earlier-born?
On the other hand, the notion of doctrinal development is utterly
reasonable if understood simply as the application of a principle
to new and unforeseen circumstances. This reasonable proposal,
however, is not how the notion is being employed, most notably

in the dogma under discussion.

To apply the idea of doctrinal development to the dogma "Outside the Church there is no salvation," we have to allow that "Outside the Church there is no salvation" is the seed form of the truth that "there is plentiful salvation outside the Church." But logic can hardly admit such a connection. Moreover, Father Dulles did not suggest this. Father Dulles's argument is more subtle. The kernel of truth ["valid insight" is Dulles's expression] in the dogma "Outside the Church there is no salvation" is this: all Christian salvation is related to the Church ["the ecclesial character of all Christian salvation" are his words]. On the face of it, to say that "Christian salvation" is "related to the Church" looks too much like a tautology to warrant dogmatic proclamation. It is definitely not what Pope Boniface VIII intended to proclaim, as we will see. For Father Dulles, the *truth* of the "no salvation outside the Church" dogma is not even related to our present view that there is plentiful salvation outside the Church, notwithstanding the words. Dulles's argument, moreover, runs exactly counter to the Church's own position as stated *dogmatically* in Vatican Council I and reiterated as recently as 1950 in Pope Pius XII's monumental Encyclical, *Humanae Generis*. Pius XII's Encyclical bolstered the Vatican Council's declaration by condemning "dogmatic relativism" and rejecting the position that "...the mysteries of faith can never be signified by adequately true notions, but only by what they call 'approximative' and always mutable notions..." Lest absolutists become gleeful, however, this same Pope Pius XII had taken a significant bow to the notion of doctrinal development in a major Encyclical of 1947, *Mediator Dei*:

> "Clearly no sincere Catholic can refuse to accept the formulation of Christian doctrine more recently elaborated and proclaimed as dogmas by the Church...because it pleases him to hark back to the old formulas."[9]

While Father Dulles is fully knowledgeable of the history of dogma, particularly this present point which he discusses in his book, I do not know how he can proceed logically with his own thesis if language is to have any meaning at all. We must simply acknowledge that Gregory Baum, together with "practically all Catholics," contradicts Pope Boniface VIII and many other popes and Church councils when he says "there is plentiful salvation outside the Church."

The renowned theologian Father Karl Rahner addressed this

difficulty concerning dogmas. Rahner explained that, although there is a truth in every dogma, this truth may be wrapped in a formulation that has considerable untruth. This is based on the plausible principle that the infinite Word of God cannot be contained in any finite formulation. Whatever is said in a dogmatic statement leaves much of the matter unsaid. Hence the need for an ongoing theology. Moreover, no one [including the pope] is ever able to determine with certainty the element of truth in a dogma at any particular point in time. Rahner's explanation of the development of doctrine fits with Dulles's reflections on the "Outside the Church" dogma. It works this way: the *truth* contained in this particular dogma is not related to the necessity of belonging to the Church in order to be saved, despite words that seem to say the contrary. We can even concede that Pope Boniface VIII thought he was saying as much. But in Rahner's view, no one has any way of identifying the core truth of any dogmatic statement.[10] So even as Father Dulles identifies a "valid insight" contained in that obnoxiously formulated dogma, no one, including the pope, can even now say for sure exactly what that truth is. What a position to be in! To possess the truth but have no way of getting at it. However, Rahner's full position is not that unambiguous. For in another place and with a more practical concern he also asserts, "There is an authoritative teaching office which is able to express the Church's faith in genuine human conceptuality as true and binding on everyone. It can reject a contrary affirmation and can command assent in saying that such an affirmation is contrary to the truth..."[11]

The example of dogma I have used, "Outside the Church there is no salvation," might be considered obsolete in our day. I did not choose an obsolete example in order to mock some absurdity of the past. I used it because it is a clear and straightforward example that can be used to look into the very principle of dogma.

The way I analyzed the arguments of Father Dulles and Father Rahner does not want to imply that their argument is foolish, although the "middle way" Rahner attempts to strike is quite questionable. Their argument has its own logic. In fact, in my view Rahner's understanding of the development of doctrine can be correctly applied to human inquiry in general.[12] It is easily applied to the development of modern science. The history of scientific theories does show one theory giving way to a succeeding theory on a regular basis. Although the expressions of the two theories may contradict one another, somehow the later theory is dependent upon the earlier one. It is not too much to suggest that a *truth* was contained in the earlier formulation, although no one at the time was able to say exactly what that truth was. The truth implicit in an earlier theory becomes more explicit in the later one, even when the formulations of the theories contradict one another. However, as science becomes increasingly aware of the nature of its own progress, the scientific attitude no longer closes the door and pretends to hold an absolute truth at any particular point in time.

Here I am saying that the idea of doctrinal development conflicts with the essential meaning of dogma. The Church's dogmatic proclamations were never thought to be *tentative* expressions of the faith. They were intended to say exactly how things are and to say it *irreformably*, to cite again the language of the dogmatic declaration of Vatican Council I. The Church's official understanding of her dogmatic proclamations would never allow the patent contradiction that "Outside the Church there is no salvation" contains an infallible truth that is compatible with "there is plentiful salvation outside the Church."

The central flaw in all of this is *dogma* itself. Dogma is a profound distortion of spiritual doctrine. It takes spiritual teaching in the wrong direction. It is important to study just how dogma disorients spiritual teaching. For it is here that dogma fails the Church in her primary spiritual function, to teach a way of life. Then we might look at the consequences that this basic distortion has brought to our own spiritual growth. Finally we can assess the problems that dogmatism poses when antiquated pronouncements are obviously in error or even make no sense at all in the world we have come to know.

Dogmatism, first of all, is unquestionably a distortion of spiritual teaching. Every religious body has considerable spiritual lore. This lore is often found written in what a religious community considers its Sacred Scriptures. We can be grateful for this. Most of us are grateful to have the scientific and medical lore that makes twentieth century life untellably superior to that, say, of the Middle Ages. In those days even the wealthiest lived precariously. If we are pleased to have a worldly tradition that informs us about our everyday life in the world, how much more might we be pleased to enjoy a tradition that advises us concerning our proper place in existence in respect to our ultimate destiny. The great spiritual tradition is what carries and communicates this knowledge.

What, then, is the precise function of spiritual teaching? What is Sacred Scripture meant to do for our life? What is the nature of its communication? No one will deny that all teachings arise to respond to our felt questions. But what kind of questions should we bring to spiritual teaching? Theoretical questions? Speculative questions? Is any Sacred Scripture there to answer our question, "What?" "What is this world? What is God? What is our purpose? What is our destiny?" Are these the kinds of questions we should bring to our spiritual heritage? Or does spiritual teaching respond to another kind of question altogether?

This issue pertains to the very nature of spiritual knowledge. Over the ages gifted persons have wrestled with issues that concern human knowledge and the place of knowledge in our life. It is a deep issue. However, we do not need to solve most of these questions before we can understand the place of *spiritual* knowledge in our life. For we already know the problem that brings us to spiritual teaching. It is the religious problem, our felt disconnectedness, the *pain in our heart*. The knowledge we seek is entirely practical: How can we reconnect and be free of this pain? The spiritual question is always a *how-to* question. This is easy to show. Every single question that comes about because of a practical problem is obviously asking for a practical answer. If, for example, a person is seriously injured, the questions are all practical: how best to deal with this injury. How to get the best and quickest medical help. In such a context anyone who would ask a question with no practical bearing on the problem would strike everyone as foolish. If, for example, someone were to inquire, "How tall is the doctor?," everyone would be puzzled and ask, "What difference does that make?"

We can take this point a step further. When we gain insight into the needs and interests of our own heart, we see that all our questions without exception are practical. Beyond religion, even the questions that science poses are ultimately practical. They are asked for the reason of serving human interests. It has been said that we have two basically different kinds of questions. That in addition to practical questions we also have theoretical questions. Many persons feel that there really exists *knowledge for the sake of knowledge*!

Although knowledge for the sake of knowledge, like art for the sake of art, is a commonly accepted shibboleth, I suggest that such is not the case. We do not in fact desire knowledge for its own sake, whatever bearing that might have on life. Would you, for example, want rocks in your pockets for their own sake? This would not make sense. If we were to chance upon a person who does carry rocks in his pockets, we might be interested in why he does this. We would never be satisfied with "rocks in the pockets for the sake of rocks in the pockets." We know too much about ourselves and about human nature to be content with such an absurd answer. Rocks in the pockets must somehow interest this person, and it might strike our fancy just what his interest is. If we do not find out just how rocks in his pockets serve a sensible interest of this person, then we tend to judge him as outside the norm. In any case, we feel certain that "rocks in the pockets for their own sake" is not the real reason for this person's exceptional behavior.

A careful look at our search for knowledge shows that knowledge for the sake of knowledge makes no more sense than rocks in the pockets for their own sake. We do not approach anything for its own sake. We are always moved toward things because of *our interest*. Every teacher knows well the hardship, indeed the near impossibility, of teaching a student when the student has no interest. Learning just does not happen in the absence of interest.

Exactly what is this thing that we call *interest*? What we might first notice is that we always experience interest as *a felt need*. For example, we experience interest in the things around us. Our interest is our need to be connected to them. *Interest expresses our felt connection to things and the connection of things to us.* The very word *interest*, according to its Latin source, means *being among* [things]. We can further note that interest is felt as a *problematic* connection. Interest prompts us to do something. Interest causes us to take action, to make right what we experience as problematic. That is why the special interest we have in knowledge takes shape as a question. A question about something arises in our mind because our mind is a tool to help us take appropriate action about a problem that we experience. Questions always arise as *the conscious intelligence of the problematic heart.* There is no other kind of question.

What needs to be underlined is that all human questioning arises from a problematic feeling. All human questioning is rooted in the heart. In this sense, all questions are personal. This holds even for questions that seem to be only academic or scientific. They too arise to solve a problem we feel. When I contrasted dogma with science, I did not want to suggest that science is a distinct kind of intellectual function. The contrast concerned only this difference: science, unlike spiritual teaching, progresses when one theory gives way to a succeeding theory. This makes science *appear* to be a theoretical enterprise. Science looks like a pure desire for knowledge—knowledge for the sake of knowledge. However, this does not prove to be the case. Science was born and lives in order to relate us properly to the world, in a word to serve our interests. There is no *disinterested* science. Science is very interested in results. Its results are ultimately practical. Bad results—results that do not prove to be effective—are what bring a scientific theory under suspicion. A scientific theory is overturned when its results prove to be ineffective. Science is always governed by our interest in relating effectively to our world by solving problems we feel. Science progresses because it is moved by our interests.

The difference between spiritual teaching and science is not that science is purely intellectual while spiritual teaching speaks to human problems. Both science and spiritual teaching are entirely problem-based. Both exist because of our felt needs. Spiritual teaching differs from science in one essential way. Spiritual teaching turns us directly inward toward where we feel our basic problem. But science rightly turns to the things of the world to help us meet the needs we have because we live in the world. Any confusion of the task of science with the task of religion comes from a fundamental misunderstanding of the purpose of religious teaching. The root of this misunderstanding is conceiving of spiritual teaching as dogma, as if it is there to tell us what is so. It is a mistake to think that spiritual teaching has the purpose of communicating God's views about certain worldly and otherworldly matters, and that we, in turn, are to accept these views in faith [belief]. This misconception of the function of spiritual teaching is what has put religion in the same field as science, orienting us toward what is outside us. It is this outward orientation that has often appeared to put religion in conflict with science: many times have religious dogmatic statements about *how it is* conflicted with scientific discoveries. The most notorious conflict between science and the dogmatic religious outlook concerns the origins of our universe and especially of humanity. I am speaking, of course, of the creationism/evolutionism debate which still refuses to die. The world, the origins of the world, and even our place among the things of the world are all external matters. Knowing about them has no relationship to the basic restlessness of our heart. Such knowledge, were it possible, would serve no spiritual function. That authentic religion is associated in the minds of intelligent people with such a spurious cousin as *creationism* is just one more instance of how dogmatic beliefs distract us from our sole spiritual interest, how to reconnect to our Source.

Pointing out its true nature does not intend to disparage human knowledge. Rather, it shows us the kind of thing that human knowledge is. Our knowledge does not aim at things for their own sake. On the contrary, knowledge is the know-how that enables our interests to make a connection to the things of the world and to the world itself. Human knowledge is only functional; it is only *know-how*; it is not theoretical. Even the knowledge that science provides is, in the final analysis, never *a knowledge of things* but always *know-how*. Through science we learn *how to* relate to things and *how to* deal with them.

We might best understand the nature of knowledge through the example of a map. A map is not a picture. It is not even a cloudy preview of one's trip. While a map's function is important, the map itself means nothing at all to us beyond the function it serves relative to actual places and actual travel on roads and paths. A map is entirely functional. It has no intrinsic substance other than the practical guidance it offers. This is what all knowledge amounts to; knowledge functions in our life. Knowledge enables us to find our way in the world. It shows us how to see the working relationships of things and how best to relate to things when we see how they actually work.

What is here being said about knowledge as such might be looked upon as revolutionary for western philosophy as a whole and for theology in particular. Theology, after all, takes not only its issues but its very bearings from secular philosophy rather than from spiritual masters. Hence the question of the validity of our knowing in general—How do we know things for certain? or On what basis do we judge among various "truth claims"?—have come to the fore in Christian theology. Taking its cues from philosophy, contemporary theology has become faced with justifying its own particular Christian beliefs in a "pluralistic" world, a world that enjoys a cornucopia of religious viewpoints and beliefs. How do we determine which among these many views of life are *true*? Or if any of them are true? In particular, how can we hold the Christian "faith" [understood as "belief-system"] to be true when many of its tenets seem to be contrary to the views of other "faiths"? These questions derive from the assumption that faith is knowing things and that knowledge is our grasp of what things are. This is why "pluralism" has become such an enormous problem for today's theology.[13]

Although this is hardly the place to digress into the philosophical discussion that could speak to the knowledge-issue in western philosophy, I can point out that all the issues associated with "pluralism" in religion dissipate in their entirety when spiritual knowledge is understood as *practical know-how* rather than as a theoretical knowledge of *what things are*. The implications of this distinction between theoretical and practical are not mysterious. Theoretically, for example, "turning left" is the contrary of "turning right." The one is incompatible with the other. As practical instruction, however, one person may be advised to "turn left" and another person advised to "turn right," so that they both arrive at the same destination. The seeming "pluralism" of "turn left" and "turn right" is simply not a problem in the practical order. So quite aside from the philosophical issue of whether *all* knowledge is know-how, it can still be affirmed that spiritual doctrine intends a practical function in our life. The truth of spiritual instruction is determined by its effect: does it move us toward our destination?

Surely religious doctrine is not meant to give us a picture or preview of God or heaven or afterlife or anything of the kind. It is not a deposit of faith as if faith consists of a warehouse of supposed truths. Rather, spiritual teaching addresses the problem of our heart as we presently experience it. It is practical instruction that shows us how to reconnect to our Source now. Spiritual teaching targets a real change in us, and now. It uses ideas, of course. But these ideas, just like the theories of science, are purely functional. They are to have an effect. As one ancient sage put it, "Truth is what works." The truth of spiritual instruction is tested and validated directly, by each person for herself or himself. It is recognized and experienced in the heart. The two disciples of Jesus who encountered him on the road to Emmaus gave eloquent testimony to the *heart-experience* of spiritual instruction: "Did our hearts not burn within us when he was talking to us on the way and opening the Scriptures to us!"[14] Similar words were used by the renowned third-century Doctor of the Church, St. Clement of Alexandria, to speak of the effect of his spiritual guide, Pantaenus, "that spirit full of grace whom I was privileged to hear." Clement looked upon his own words as "a mere image and outline of the vigorous and soul-shaking discourses of that man." "Vigorous and soul-shaking" words that "make our hearts burn within us" describe the truth-power of spiritual instruction.

Therefore, when our heart is fully at rest doctrine will be exhausted, just as when we arrive at our destination we no longer pore over a map. When we become unproblematic human beings, when our spiritual journey is finished, we will no longer consult doctrine because we will have no further need of it.

In summary, sacred teaching is carried on in a tradition under the name of *doctrine*. The word doctrine in itself is apt. It literally means *teaching*. But the idea of teaching can be taken in either of two directions, to "tell what things are" or to "instruct how to do something." This has lead us to ask directly about the nature of spiritual teaching: Is religious doctrine a *view* to be held in our mind through *belief*? Or is it an *instruction* that is to be validated in our life through putting it into effect, which is *practice*? In the religious context of our human mortality, our suffering, and our impulse to rise above these, spiritual teaching obviously comes from our *how-to* interest: how to rise above our condition of suffering and mortality. Religious doctrine is clearly *instruction* for practice and not *dogma* for belief.

To see spiritual doctrine as instruction rather than dogma is not to declare that it is untrue. Rather, it points to the kind of truth doctrine is, without having to settle the question whether or not all human truth is thus. Religious doctrine is not the truth of mere ideas. Our finite ideas are never ultimately true in any case. Why should reality be reduplicated through ideas in our minds? We do not need pictures, a reduplication of reality; we already participate actively in the real thing. The truth of doctrine is a higher truth. It is a truth that really works. When we apply instruction through actual spiritual practice, we *grow* in our participation in reality. That is, we become *more real* ourselves. This is what religion is about. For the suffering that impels us to religion is our disconnectedness from reality. Our healing, our *salvation* if you want, is our reconnection. Truth gets its start in our lives through instruction that is effective in reconnecting us to our Source. Truth is fulfilled when we become full participants in reality [*realized*]. It is then that our minds are at peace and our hearts come from restlessness to rest. It is then that our nature is relaxed into its uncomplicated self. This is no mean feat. It implies profound inner work. But we do not further our goal by committing ourselves to a head full of ideas, as if they themselves are truth, while our heart pines away in spiritual neglect.

NOTES

[1] See *The Documents of Vatican II*, "Revelation," together with Introduction and Response, pp. 107-132.

[2] *The Sources of Catholic Dogma*, p. 457. [The translator chose the acceptable English word 'unalterable' instead of the more common and more literal

translation 'irreformable' for the Latin *irreformabiles* in the Council document.]

[3] See *The Church Teaches*, pp. 52-55. Many of the condemned theologians are identified by the editor on p. 53.

[4] *The Church Teaches*, pp. 73-75.

[5] *Concilium 21*, "The Magisterium in a Changing Church," (Paulist Press, 1967), p. 69.

[6] *The Survival of Dogma*, (Doubleday & Company, Inc., 1971), p. 161.

[7] See *An Essay on the Development of Christian Doctrine*, (Doubleday & Company, Inc., 1960).

[8] *The Survival of Dogma*, p. 161.

[9] Para. 63.

[10] See *Theological Investigations V*, "What Is a Dogmatic Statement?" (Helicon Press, 1966).

[11] *Theological Investigations: IX*, "Theology and Teaching Authority," (The Seabury Press, 1969), p. 87.

[12] *See Theological Investigations IV*, "Considerations on the Development of Dogma," (Helicon Press, 1966), pp. 3-35.

[13] John Hick is perhaps foremost among theologians who have attempted to honor the many religious views in the world and still hold fast to the Christian "faith" [as cognitive beliefs]. In addition to his *Faith and Knowledge,* see *Problems of Religious Pluralism,* (St. Martin's Press, 1985), *The Experience of Religious Diversity,* (Gower Publishing Company Limited, 1985), and *An Interpretation of Religion* (Yale University Press, 1989). A recent work that takes issue with Hick by holding even more tenaciously to the "propositional validity" of Christian tenets is Brad Stetson's *Pluralism and Particularity in Religious Belief,* (Praeger, 1994).

[14] *Luke,* XXIV, 32.

VIII

We have not sinned, but we have been born.

Franklin Jones

ORIGINAL SIN OR ORIGINAL PURITY

The teachings of religion address our most basic human problem, what I have called our felt disconnectedness. The first step in dealing with any problem at all is to diagnose it. No one will question the need for an accurate diagnosis in order to address a problem properly. This holds likewise for our universal human problem, the condition that religion addresses. Our religious problem is profound and it seems to infect everybody. Perhaps we could think of it as a spiritual epidemic. But how shall we approach our fundamental problem?

To use again the example of a health problem, we know that a diagnosis should not be hasty. While any diagnosis might relieve our anxiety, what is important is that the diagnosis be accurate. Moreover, a diagnosis must do more than describe our symptoms. Symptoms show that we have a problem, but they do not show us what the problem is. Discovering the fundamental condition of health can thus be a profound, complex, and prolonged matter. For this reason a wise person is willing to submit to all the examining and pondering that a correct health diagnosis may require.

To turn to our spiritual problem, how, exactly, do we envision our fundamental condition? We know that our earthly life is a brief one, no matter how old we may get to be. We may not like the fact of our impending death. But even the fact of our mortality is not itself our fundamental problem. For our death is at a future time, while we can feel our spiritual problem right now.

Religion speaks to the basic condition that is with us now. It is the restlessness of our heart which is present whether things are going well or poorly at any particular moment in our life. Once we distinguish between all temporary conditions and this basic problem, we are prepared to inquire into our fundamental condition to diagnose it. How strange that we should be born, only to

91

live a little while and then die! What is our status as human beings in the great scheme of existence? While we are alive we desire happiness. Yet only temporary glimpses of happiness grace our lives. Every experience of happiness proves to be passing, so that we come to know our heart's desire, happiness itself, more in its absence than in its presence.

I have already made a strong criticism of the distortion of spiritual teaching when it is separated from its practical purpose and made into mental stuff as dogma. This criticism is nowhere more appropriate than when religion faces the fundamental problem we all experience in that we are suffering and dying human beings. There are relatively few people in the world who have enough resources to be able to distract themselves from this basic problem for any significant length of time. These few are usually gifted with health and wealth and other desirable things. But eventually even these people will lose their loved ones. Then they must face their own impending death, and often an illness that precedes it. In due time they too will come to know through experience the pervasive suffering that belongs to human life itself. They too have to face the fundamental human condition. So everyone without exception stands in need of a diagnosis of our basic human condition.

Yet we must diagnose our condition accurately if it is to stand as the starting point for the practical, healing work of religion. To apply proper healing measures, we have to know the condition we are seeking to heal. That our desire for happiness is so total while our experience of happiness is so sparse reveals how profound our human problem is. It is so pervasive and so total that it demands that we inquire into our place within the entire scheme of existence. We need a *vision of the totality*. What is this great matter into which we have been born? And what is our place within it, our relationship to it?

We have already noted the purely functional nature of all knowledge. We must now apply this fact to spiritual knowledge. The words and ideas that religion presents are symbols of something else. They are metaphors. They are guideposts meant to help us reach a practical goal. The philosopher Karl Jaspers did not exaggerate in saying that *all* words are metaphors. Words are not the reality toward which they point.

When we ask for a *vision of the totality* we should realize that we are asking for a metaphor. A vision of anything is not the thing itself. Moreover, we are not asking for only a simple metaphor. We are asking for a complex and structured metaphor. In a word, we are asking about our fundamental *myth*. *Myth* is a large issue. What I have already tried to suggest about the nature of human knowing can prepare us for looking into myth. We cannot remain naive in our thinking and hope to be equal to the challenge of myth that our religious imagination offers us. For myth, after all, is the language of the religious imagination.

The work of Joseph Campbell has made him the great master of myth for our time. Campbell's communication has demonstrated to his audience something of the *Power of Myth*, as a book of his conversations is titled. Through the work of Campbell and others, the people of our culture enjoy an increased awareness of the significance of myth for understanding various kinds of human experience as well as our very condition in the whole of existence.

Myth, however, for all its power and fascination, exists at the level of imagination. It does not pretend to represent spiritual understanding. Myth stands at the beginning of spiritual thinking. The spiritual function of myth is to open to us a vision, a context for instruction. It fleshes out in story form something of the structure of our existence. The story contained in a Great Myth places us in relationship to the whole of existence, to *the gods*. In this way a Great Myth, through the power of imagination, gives focus and orientation to our life in the total context of existence.

To appreciate the significance of myth, we must see just how myth functions as a complex metaphor. We can begin by letting ourselves be challenged by the poet-philosopher Goethe who declared that even *things* are metaphors. This seems like a strange thing to suggest: *Things* are metaphors! Yet if we ponder this thought, how a thing is a metaphor, we can ready ourselves to face the profound meaning of myth. We must reckon with the possibility that *myth may be truer than fact* as far as our mind is concerned.

Myth, to our mind, is indeed more true than fact. A fact is like a thing in Goethe's sense. A fact refers us only to some particular quality or aspect of reality. This does not deny that a fact is real. But what we call a fact offers our mind only a single instance, nothing more than a faint hint, of the fullness of reality. After all, how much either of ourselves or of the world comes to light in any particular fact? When we are confronted with a fact of any importance, our questions only begin. We question this fact in order to connect it with other facts. We try to uncover a fuller significance of this fact in terms of everything else. Indeed, we come to see that facts are not really isolated events at all. Each fact

is connected with everything else—with the totality of existence—in a web so complex that no particular fact can be fully
understood in itself without first understanding the whole. Scientists have come to recognize this interconnectedness of all things.

In contrast to a mere fact, a myth enables us to picture in our
imagination something of the structure of our reality in a clear and
proportioned way. This is what makes myth truer than any single
fact. Myths offer us a degree of clarity. They map out for us some
structure or quality of our existence. The drama that is expressed
by a myth gives focus and proportion to an underlying quality of
our life-experience. The proportion or balance of a myth is what
enables it to give orientation to our life. A Great Myth is *a simple
vision of the whole*. It allows us to envision the basic scheme of
existence. Lesser myths are partial, angled visions of reality that
nevertheless reflect something about our relationship to existence. In this way they too help orient us, since they reveal to us
something about our participation in reality. A note of caution is
necessary here: we make a serious error with respect to myth itself
when we take a partial myth as *a vision of the whole*. It is like
taking a leg for a person.

Christianity has wrestled with two different myths, with two
different gospels, we might say. Jesus gave us a Great Myth, his
vision of reality as a whole and our place within it. Jesus' gospel
was an invitation to us to participate directly, just as we are, in the
fullness of reality, what he called "the Kingdom of God." St. Paul
offered us a different vision, not a grand vision of reality as a
whole, but what I feel was only a partial myth, an angle on things.
St. Paul's vision was limited by *his experience* of our human
condition—I speak here of Original Sin. When Paul communicated his understanding of his experience it was taken as a divinely
revealed statement regarding our basic human situation. This
amounted to a kind of counter-gospel. So in the historical context
where St. Paul's writings were accorded the status of orthodoxy,
it is probably better not speak of them as a *gospel* at all, since
Paul's vision appears more like bad news than good news. There
exists a kind of biblical fundamentalism that might be offended at
my suggestion that Paul's religious vision may have been more
limited than that of Jesus. Such a biblical fundamentalism sees
Sacred Scripture as all of one cloth. Everything in Scripture
comes from the hand of God and is of equal truth, according to this
biblicist mentality. However we might understand the divine
inspiration of the bible, both Catholic and Protestant scholars
discountenance a magical mentality as applied to Scripture. St.

Paul's letters were written to the various spiritual communities he had started or influenced by his teaching. The content of the letters was *ad hoc*—they addressed particular problems and circumstances. It is biblical magic to elevate to eternal, irrevocable, dogmatic status what is mentioned, sometimes casually and in any case in a limited context, by a spiritual teacher as he or she is trying to iron out particular difficulties or is simply offering words of encouragement and spiritual *ferverinos*.

Moreover, it has been fully acknowledged even in official Catholic teaching that the limitations of the human authors of the various books of the Bible create a limitation in the Scriptural writings themselves. We are more true to spiritual communication when we abandon mindless magic and accept the written word of any holy scripture as no more and no less than the degree of divine realization of its author. Unless St. Paul is to be made an exception and granted a unique status, it is fair to measure Paul's vision of our human situation against Jesus' understanding, at least as much of Jesus' understanding as can be garnered from the written accounts of the gospel.

To suggest that St. Paul had a limited appreciation of the full gospel of Jesus is by no means to discredit Paul or his spiritual value to us. He was unquestionably committed to a spiritual way of life. He was gifted with exceptional introspective insight. He was a serious, even a profound, person. Most importantly, Paul's spiritual connection to Jesus is, to me, undeniable. My only suggestion is that even a most worthy apprentice is not necessarily as good as the master. To the Philippians St. Paul confessed this about himself: "It is not that I have reached it yet, or have already finished my course; but I am racing to grasp the prize if possible, since I have been grasped by Christ. Brothers, I do not think of myself as having reached the finish line. I give no thought to what lies behind but push on to what is ahead. My entire attention is on the finish line as I run toward the prize to which God calls me."[1] Here, as elsewhere, St. Paul acknowledged his own spiritual limitations. I highlight Paul's limitations only to compare his vision of life to that of Jesus.

St. Paul's lengthy letter to the Romans has gained almost classical status in outlining his vision of our human condition. Paul envisioned a great distance, a gulf, between our human situation and God or Reality. He viewed the basic human condition as one that came to be called *Original Sin*: In Adam we have all sinned.[2] Paul's elaboration of sin, made dogma in the Church, did not focus only on separateness. Paul concluded that we are rotten. We are depraved in our very core. The dogma that elaborated the idea of Original Sin declares that we are actually conceived in the womb as morally corrupt beings.[3] We are turned toward evil and damnation prior to any thought or action on our part. Yet even after being cleansed from Original Sin by baptism, we are still not in a position to do much about our sad plight. For we suffer a weakness in our nature even after Original Sin has been removed. This moral debilitation continues to incline us strongly toward sin. St. Augustine emphasized this idea so far as to describe our born nature as *corrupt*.[4] Following Augustine's thought, the dogma of Trent likens our inclination toward evil [concupiscence] to a tinderbox [Latin *fomes*].[5]

This, Paul suggests, is the cosmic situation into which we have been born. We are born enemies of God and world. The mood of Christian culture, dominated by this sense of Original Sin, was articulated by seventeenth century Saint John Eudes, the "Wonder of the Age" as he was known.[6] John urged the meditation that "...we are only fit to be 'cast into the fire'." Why? "This is our fitting destiny as children of Adam. Hence we are good for nothing but to be cast into eternal fire." Lest this seem unfair, he reminds us of just the sort of thing we are: "By our own corrupt and depraved nature we are children of wrath, because we are children of sin and iniquity...We are children of sin and perdition for we were born in sin and in damnation." To support his view John quotes St. Bernard, who lived half a millennium earlier, "We were damned before we were born." The precise meaning of this prenatal condition is detailed:

> "It is a subject of humiliation of all the mothers of
> the children of Adam to know that while they are
> with child, they carry within them an infant...who
> is the enemy of God, the object of his hatred and
> malediction, and the shrine of the demon."

If St. John Eudes' view seems singular, one might read the discourses of Luther and Calvin, or of Jonathan Edwards and Karl Barth, to get the full impact and pervasiveness of this vision of our nature as corrupt. For Edwards, the first president of Harvard University, even the apparently good life of "the natural man" is perverse and hateful; he deserves eternal damnation.[7] Barth taught that Original Sin means

> "...that we are dealing with the original and radical
> and therefore the comprehensive and total act of
> man, with the imprisonment of his existence in
> that circle of evil being and evil activity."[8]

A more direct statement of human alienation is hard to imagine. We might recall the observation of that old Zen sage, D.T. Suzuki:

"God against man. Man against God. Man against
nature. Nature against man. Nature against God.
God against nature—very funny religion."[9]

As human beings, supposedly the very subjects of this divine malediction, we have every reason to question whether this view of our basic condition is correct. Paul himself would certainly advise us to turn this question over to Jesus. As I read Jesus' communication to us, I do not find the same sense as I get from Paul. Jesus does not see us as rotten, helpless creatures, turned toward sin at every chance. The contrary seems true. Jesus always turns us toward our human responsibility. He even encourages us to meet the highest imaginable moral potential: "Be perfect as your heavenly Father is perfect."[10] Why should we think Jesus said this in order to show us our weakness and shame us? Why should we not accept his instruction at face value? "Do it!"

Certainly Jesus' description of our relationship to the Kingdom of God is in terms of our own growth toward a potential that we already have, that we actually *are*: "Behold! The Kingdom of God is within you."[11] His parables of the Kingdom, as found, for example, in the thirteenth chapter of the Matthew's gospel, were entirely in terms of growth. He likened the Kingdom to a mustard seed, "the smallest of all seeds," but which grows so great that "the birds of the sky come and find a dwelling in its branches." He also likened this Kingdom to a piece of yeast, which over time "ferments [enlarges] the whole."

This Kingdom is our responsibility. As in another parable, "The sower went out to sow his seed,"[12] the seed [Word of God] is already sown. Whether this seed takes root in us or not is up to us. Are we "good ground" for it? Jesus was not playing strange metaphysical games with us. His spiritual instruction to us presumes our capacity to live it: "Blessed are the poor in spirit; blessed are the merciful; blessed are those who hunger and thirst after justice." "If a man forces you to walk one mile with him, walk two." "If someone asks for your shirt, give him your coat as well." "If someone slaps you across the face, turn the other side of your face to him."[13] "I was hungry and you gave me to eat; I was thirsty and you gave me to drink; I had nothing to wear and you clothed me; I had nowhere to go and you brought me to your home."[14] And finally, "Greater love than this no person has than that he lay down his life for his friend."[15] In a word, "Be perfect as your heavenly Father is perfect."[16] Jesus' spiritual advice is

difficult, to be sure. But it is workable. Those for whom the empty
promises of the world have become transparent—death itself
should be evidence enough for the still unconvinced—do have the
capacity to turn to another way.

It is true that we need help in order to meet our spiritual
potential. But by the same token we need help to meet all our
potentials. Who could fulfill her or his potential for music or art
or mathematics or science, for anything at all, without help? St.
Paul was deeply aware of our need for help in meeting our greatest
potential of all, overcoming our egoic self. His epistle to the
Romans, which describes our felt need for help, is insightful and
can be read to one's spiritual advantage. It is not, however, an
expression of our ultimate condition in reality. I think Paul had
something practical in mind, and his letter can serve as useful
spiritual instruction. Paul's feel for life obviously resonated with
that of many others, particularly with Augustine, and then with
Luther. It is not surprising that his experience speaks to others.
The problem is that Paul's sense of his own life, which he
projected as a description of all human experience, is so powerful
that it came to be seen as an ultimate statement of the human
condition.

My criticism here, then, is that Paul's sense of our predicament
was raised in the Church to a metaphysical description of our
ultimate condition, even to the point of eclipsing the gospel of
Jesus. It is this error, I assert, that became a doctrinal misdiagnosis
of our human condition and a tragic error in spiritual teaching.

It can happen that the misdiagnosis of a serious problem is a
fatal flaw in addressing the problem. This, I feel, is precisely the
case with the place of Original Sin within Christianity. A partial
vision was substituted for a vision of the whole. Paul's insight into
our need for personal spiritual help supplanted, within Christendom,
the good-news-gospel of Jesus. The acceptance of this misdiagnosis of our basic human condition by the Church has had
spiritually devastating consequences. Before detailing these
consequences I would like to point out what I see to be the
meaning and validity of the myth of Original Sin.

Like all myths, the myth of Adam and Eve's Fall does have
significance. But the myth of the Fall presents only an angled
vision. Joseph Campbell recognized the myth of the Fall as an
expression of a common mythical theme of the separation of
heaven and earth. It is not, however, the ultimate truth; indeed it
must finally be rejected if we are to be united with our Source:

"Once you reject the idea of the Fall in the Garden, man is not cut off from his source."[17] Nevertheless, we human beings do experience our life and our earth as separated or disconnected from heaven, its source. But both our impulse and our desired goal is unity.

What is to be noted about the myth of Original Sin is that the separation it envisions is essentially a matter of *our experience*. Disconnection is the way *we happen to experience life*. This does not make disconnectedness the essential truth of our existence. That we experience life in some particular way does not demonstrate that that is the way *life is*. There can be a great gulf between how things really are and how we experience them. In other words there is often a great discrepancy between appearance and reality.

The distinction between appearance and reality is a well known theme. Illusion is a common experience. When a stick *appears* bent in water, for instance, this does not mean that the stick *is* bent. Or to take a more personal example, we can easily imagine an adopted child who *feels* unloved, cut off. The child may feel this way even though her or his new parents and family are loving and caring persons. In this case the problem is basically within the child. Being unloved is not this child's truth; it is only the way *s/he experiences* family life.

Original Sin cannot be considered a Great Myth. With its focus on separation, it does not speak our full truth. It offers only a partial vision. In a word, the story of the Fall does not present us with a vision of the whole. Original Sin only highlights our experience of disconnection. It lights up our subjective feeling, the feeling that gives rise to our religious impulse. This is its simple truth: *we do feel* a radical disconnection; we do feel our earth, ourselves, as separated from heaven. For that reason the myth of Original Sin can help us ponder the yearning of our own heart, our felt urgency to make connection. Paul's description of our subjective experience has that much validity. It does not, however, envision for us our ultimate condition in relationship to the whole of existence.

The primary effect of elevating to dogma Paul's emphasis on our condition as sinful has had devastating effects. First is the diversion of attention from Jesus' Gospel, the Kingdom of God. The central gospel of Jesus, that the Kingdom of God is within us, was eclipsed when Paul's reflections became the doctrine that we are a radically sinful humanity in need of salvation. Taking Paul's experience as the central truth led, logically, to a misinterpretation of the life and work of Jesus. It made Jesus a savior rather than a spiritual teacher. Further, our self-image as being radically corrupt proves personally and spiritually demoralizing. It obstructs a right relationship to Christ, and it divests us of a proper sense of our own spiritual responsibility. Finally, the very idea of intrinsic human corruption has created in our culture a false moralistic sense of sin and wrongdoing. Our culture is tainted to the core by a viewpoint about our condition and our problems that is untrue to human nature. It is a viewpoint that prevents us from deeply understanding ourselves and one another. We must examine at some length each of these effects of making Paul's experience and instruction a counter-gospel to the gospel of Jesus.

First we might note again that Jesus' communication presumed our capacity for goodness. Jesus always encouraged. He elicited growth in us. The vision of the whole that Jesus communicated to his hearers did not speak of human depravity. It oriented us in the opposite direction. The myth of Jesus, his Great Vision of *The Kingdom of God*, orients us toward the true nature of reality. "The Kingdom of God is within you," he declared. "God," he told us, "is our Father," whose perfection we are to duplicate. Surely Jesus did not see us as originally corrupt; we are originally pure. It is of central importance that we read and appreciate our innermost nature correctly. Jesus advised us that we are inherently free. But we must realize this freedom through our own effort. Any communication that tells us something radically different from this is not true to the teaching of Jesus. It has the effect of diverting us from our real condition and from our spiritual task. In this way it subverts our life and our destiny.

The second major effect of dogmatizing Paul's vision of our radical corruption is the corresponding interpretation of Jesus' presence and work in the world. Our fallen condition became the basis of Paul's theological explanation of the appearance and of the work of Jesus. Jesus' work was, for St. Paul, a work of salvation.[18] While I do not dispute our need for spiritual help, even in the way of the personal influence of the Spiritual Teacher, I feel Paul's thinking on this matter was so limited as to be misleading. Paul thought Jesus somehow took our purported sinful condition upon himself and then died in order to wash away this sin. His purge of our sin, in Paul's view, effected a redemption or buy-back of the entire human race from this sinful condition. The metaphor of redemption with its idea of ransom is basic to Paul's understanding of the spiritual work of Jesus. Yet these ideas prove quite problematic for theological reflection. Just *who was paid* this redemptive ransom? The Devil? Hardly! God?

Hardly! We must conclude that the metaphor of redemption or ransom clarifies nothing. St. Paul's understanding of the presence and work of Jesus in the world became distorted when he took the myth of Original Sin to be a vision of the whole.

The third negative effect of Paul's gospel flows from the second. The gospel of Jesus allows us to envision both Christ and Christianity without the distortion of Original Sin. Therefore, the understanding of our nature as radically evil undermines both the teachings and other spiritual helps that derived from Jesus. The reason is this: anyone who will enter into a real relationship with Christ must do so on a positive basis. Real relationship is always based on what is common to both. If, for example, we are to be helped by the influence that our relationship to another person makes possible, it is because what is strong in that other person resonates with a real potential that is already our own. Hence we imbibe the musical, or artistic, or literary, or mathematical influence of a great teacher because of our own innate possession of music, or art, or literacy, or mathematics. The influence of our teacher *draws it forth* from us, which is the literal meaning of the Latin root of the word *educate*. Often enough we come to feel and use a potential we have because it was first recognized and encouraged by a teacher. A student who is convinced that s/he has no capacity for some skill will never bring this skill to realization in her or his own life. But it is precisely a wrong self-image that blocks the teacher's influence. Then the student's attempts to study become a struggle. S/he comes to see education itself as boring and demoralizing. Yet this entire syndrome of failure traces back to a would-be student's false sense of him/herself. Experienced teachers recognize this.

The dynamics of personal influence that are felt in all human endeavor hold also for our spiritual development. Our relationship to Christ is able to be there because of our basic purity. This relationship would be impossible if we were radically corrupt. For the kind of influence this relationship energizes is one that has a genuinely transforming effect. Transformation means that what is already in us potentially becomes actualized or realized through this influence, this relationship. But the potential must be there to start with. We would not, for example, try to teach mathematics to a bird, not even to a parrot, because we know the potential is not there. Likewise, without the presence of our own innate goodness (godliness), we could not experience the influence of Christ or any other spiritual teacher in our life.

The image of Jesus as redeemer deforms the right understanding of his influence. As redeemer, Jesus is not thought of as affecting us directly. Rather Jesus' influence as redeemer is principally between himself as godman and God. This makes Jesus a unique lawyer who pleads our sorry case before the highest authority. Such an idea of the influence of Jesus in our life prevents our relating to him as an authentic spiritual master. He is not recognized as one who can help bring our original purity to completion (a more accurate word than "perfection") through spiritual transformation. Rather, our spiritual life is trivialized as if we are to cop a pardon from the Almighty through the work of a remarkable advocate. Yet even in these terms, the ransom aspect of Jesus' work remains enigmatic to our thinking: what does it really mean "to be saved by the blood of Christ?" It is the misunderstanding of our condition as one of corruption that hinders a genuine relationship to Christ. Our self-image as corrupt keeps Christ separate. It makes of him a person who did our spiritual work for us, and who forever stands infinitely above unworthy us as our undeserved savior. Spiritually this makes us like puppies at the pound looking longingly at a divinity who may hopefully, and for no reason at all, choose to liberate some of us, *only some of us*, from our misery.

The truth of the rituals and the sacraments of the Catholic Church is that they symbolize and help vitalize a living relationship to Christ. But the kind of thinking that made Jesus a redeemer has also turned the sacraments of the Church into quasi-magical instruments of our salvation. The sacraments of the Church came to be understood as mechanisms that we activate to ensure that our name is on the list of those pardoned. As a practical consequence, for most Catholics the use of these rituals and sacraments is not a matter of enlivening their spiritual relationship to Christ and thus submitting to spiritual transformation. Moreover, despite the fact that we do experience our disconnectedness, it somehow got lost that our spiritual growth will likewise be something that belongs to experience. When our spiritual life is seen in terms of salvation, then it is not a matter of our experience. The issue turns on whether *God accepts us*. Our spiritual work consists in finding out if we are among the saved. This has nothing to do with our intrinsic state, with how we truly are.

How demoralizing this view about spiritual life has proved within Christianity! If we have no conscious access to our own spiritual state, how can we stay motivated and energetic about it? No one stays vitalized without any recognizable feedback about her or his efforts. No one would persist in a strenuous diet, for example, if no weight loss were observed. None of us persists in anything unless our efforts show results in our experience.

This estrangement from our own spiritual condition has had the debilitating effect of eclipsing a genuine spiritual practice in the lives of Christians. For most Catholics the meager remnant of spiritual practice, if we can call it that, amounts to showing up for Mass on Sundays and "Holy Days of Obligation" as they are tellingly called. We could expect little else from a self-image based on human alienation. We are told to look upon ourselves as perverse children, saved from ourselves and from our deserved destiny by a divine force that remains outside us. What can we do but be obliged against our felt impulses?

This brings us to the fourth negative effect that the gospel of St. Paul has worked into our life. Following the idea of Original Sin as a radical corruption of our nature, the idea of our own sin (personal sin) also came to be seen as a pervasive quality within a person. It makes the person a sinner. He is a corrupt person. This alienated feeling of being steeped in sin is what has anchored most Christians to the life of practical religion. Relatively few Christians—only the saints—have felt the responsibility to cultivate an inner life, actually to become transformed. Only they have taken seriously Jesus' word to "be perfect," to live a transformed life. The rest have known little more than to pattern themselves in an externalized life that they are told is pleasing to God. They feel guilty when they sin. Catholics use the sacrament of penance (confession) to secure still another reprieve from the Almighty. Is it not, after all, the sense of moral life as obedience that maintains most Church members in childish dependency on a human moral authority that over the centuries has often demonstrated itself to be the most ignorant, foolish, and at times the most wicked force on earth.

It is this theological understanding of man against himself and against nature and against God that has instilled in people a morality of obligations, of moral *do's* and *don'ts*, as if human life is essentially about good behavior rather than personal transformation. Joseph Campbell cites a highly respected nineteenth-century Hindu saint who spoke pithily to this matter: "Ramakrishna once said that if all you think of are your sins, then you are a sinner."[19] The generalized formula for this insight is "You become what you ponder." Does this not capture the quintessence of prayer? Who will not vouch for the validity of this saying, based on his or her own experience? Why else, for example, were the Puritans such a grim lot, except that their psyches conformed to their thinking?

It is fair to say that Augustine engineered the notion of Original Sin into its central position in Christian self-understanding, which I maintain is a distortion of Jesus' Gospel. Although no one can deny Augustine's overwhelming influence on medieval culture, it is certainly legitimate to dispute its value. Augustine was a politically powerful and argumentative personality with exceptional erudition and literary skills. These garnered for him an intellectual authority that he did not deserve, as he was simply not a first rate thinker. In the words of my own mentor Bernard Lonergan, Augustine was *parum metaphysicus* ["not much of a philosophical thinker"]. Nowhere is Augustine's intellectual insufficiency more evident than in his views on Original Sin, especially in respect to unbaptized infants. Concerning these he asserted,

> "I affirm that an infant born in a place where it was not possible for him to be admitted to the baptism of Christ...Rightly by virtue of that condemnation which runs throughout the mass [*i.e.* of human-kind] is not admitted into the kingdom of heaven, although he was not only not a Christian, but was unable to become one."[20]

It is this view that prompted the following reasonable comment of a major historian of morals:

> "That a little child who lives but a few moments after birth and dies before it has been sprinkled with the sacred water is in such a sense responsible for its ancestor having 6,000 years before eaten a forbidden fruit, that it may with perfect justice be resuscitated and cast into an abyss of eternal fire in expiation of this ancestral crime, that an all-righteous and all-merciful Creator in the full exercise of those attributes deliberately calls into existence sentient beings whom He has from eternity irrevocably destined to endless, unspeakable, unmitigated torture, are propositions which are at once so extravagantly absurd and so ineffably atrocious that their adoption might well lead men to doubt the universality of moral perceptions. Such teaching is in fact simply daemonism, and daemonism in its most extreme form."[21]

As Lecky notes, this is exactly the teaching of Augustine! Augustine's peculiar reading of scripture meshed with his perverse views on human sexuality to insist that we are a radically corrupt race. While Augustine was not an innovator in either of these views,[22] it was his authority that brought this outlook to dominate western Christendom for nearly a millennium and has indeed proved to be "demonism in its most extreme form."

The common understanding of sin as personal corruption does not even belong to the essential meaning of the Hebrew word for *sin*. The literal meaning of sin is *to miss the mark* or *to wander astray*. This sense of the human condition seems to be on target. It locates our human problem in our own subjectivity rather than in so-called objective reality. *We* are wide of the mark; *we* feel separated. This feeling of disjointedness on our part has the effect that, in living out our lives, we necessarily make mistakes. As "The Lord" in Goethe's *Faust* puts it: "Humans err so long as they are striving." [*Es irrt der Mensch, solang' er strebt.*][23]

However, this kind of "missing the mark" does not imply that corruption is our essential nature nor eternal damnation our due. While we do make mistakes—*es irrt der mensch*—we are not corrupt. And although we inevitably pay for our mistakes—the universe does have its inexorable laws—damnation is not eternal. The idea of moral corruption is a superficial understanding of our nature. It is itself a sin against the true and simple idea of sin. Nor does the view proposed here deny all meaning to the sense of hell. Most of us know hell first-hand. But, like everything else, our hells come to an end. Those who are spiritually astute come to discover that hell is of our own making, and that we can be free of our hell whenever we summon our courage to hit the mark instead of miss it. In the words of John Milton,

> The mind is its own place, and in it self
> Can make a Heav'n of Hell, a Hell of Heav'n.[24]

The stunted spiritual life that resulted from understanding spirituality as a game of salvation to free us from our inbred corruption bred sheer insanity in Church life. No one can study the history of post-Augustine Christendom without standing aghast at the human absurdities that at times seemed to affect every aspect of Church life. The hawking of indulgences became perhaps the most famous bit of foolishness, but it pales before, say, the Inquisition.

Martin Luther was a medieval monk who was spiritually serious. Nurtured by the established vision of humankind's radical corruption, Luther prayed and sought for a *gracious God*. When Luther made his pilgrimage to Rome, however, he discovered the pathetic condition at the center of Church life. He witnessed the absence of anything that even remotely reflected the Jesus of the gospels. He found no semblance of a gracious God anywhere in the Church he experienced.

Luther and other reformers began to see the Church itself as deviant from the gospel taught by Jesus. These reformers then sought to recapture the pure teaching of Jesus. But they seemed to stumble at St. Augustine and come to a halt at St. Paul. The corruption they witnessed in the Church at large tended to support Augustine's view of the radical corruption of human nature. The reformers did not reflect on the possibility which modern knowledge of the psyche suggests: the terrible self-identity induced by the dogma of Original Sin has a self-fulfilling quality. If you diminish or destroy a person's self-image, you will soon discover a diminished or destroyed person. If you convince a person that s/he is worthless and helpless, you will soon discover a helpless person of little worth. In any case the reformers sustained the theological error of Original Sin as the radical corruption of the person. This was a blunder of tragic proportions.

In our twentieth century we can only wonder and speculate what Christianity might look like today if the spiritual understanding of St. John had prevailed in the Church over that of St. Paul, and if Augustine had remained a Manichee. Would St. John's teaching presence have enabled others to come more readily to the wisdom of Jesus? Would, then, the wisdom-teaching of Jesus have been preserved, through a lineage of *realized* spiritual teachers, as a spiritual force more powerful than the cultic distortion of spiritual teaching that became so strong within Christianity? Of course we cannot now say. But it is a thought-provoking question.

The dogmatic proclamation that Original Sin is our basic condition has had to be reckoned with in the modern Church. There were early attempts to hold onto the story of the creation and fall as history. But maintaining that this story is history required considerable accommodation to modern knowledge about the earth and sky, the cosmos. Attempts to reconcile the creation story with modern knowledge included things like "each *day* in the story of creation means a *thousand years*" and similar devices of interpretation. In due time all of this came to be seen as unfounded human speculation. It was finally recognized to make no sense at all and was abandoned by most scholars. Although this may surprise some Christians, there are relatively few scripture scholars or theologians today who think that Adam and Eve really existed, or that the creation story is at all an historical narrative.

Most scholars and theologians acknowledge the mythological character of the story of the creation and fall. The odd thing is that they nevertheless remain in dogmatic bondage and accept Original Sin as the Great Myth of humankind.

The fact is, modern theology's attempt to salvage some dogmatic meaning to an Original Sin after the "original sinner," Adam, has been relegated to the mythological has been nothing short of orwellian. What is this "sin" that is not quite sin, since the sinners, especially babies, did not participate in it? It is nevertheless most certainly sin, according to traditional dogma. Following Vatican Council II theologian Father Alfred Vanneste set forth the present state of the question, taking account of our modern world which has become sophisticated concerning myths of the past. Vanneste makes clear his view that "...this ancient doctrine retains its full actuality and remains a most important aspect of the Christian...religious experience."[25] Yet Vanneste explicitly sets out to "...proceed with the re-interpretation and *demythologization* [emphasis mine] of the dogma...in order to justify it in the face of modern Christian thinking."[26] He briefly outlines the history of the dogma he hopes to update, while he offers his own interpretation and takes account of other modern interpretations which he finds inadequate. Although I do not challenge Vanneste's work as an instance of good scholarship and intelligent, albeit tortured, reasoning, I do challenge its dogmatic premise.

More recently Karl Rahner reflected on current problems in making sense of Original Sin. While noting that on the Protestant side "...there is no general agreement as to the existence of any original sin," he also sees that "...on the Catholic side too the situation is not different."[27] Although Rahner affirms that the Council of Trent's doctrinal definitions regarding Original Sin are binding, he nevertheless allows that "...this still does not clarify the situation." To what purpose, one wonders, a doctrinal definition that "does not clarify the situation?" After discussing unarguable problems that the modern world has raised against this dogma, Rahner offers his own sense of its meaning, which he does affirm. In a different context, however, Rahner asserts that

> "...one could equally say in the nature of things and
> *in abstracto* that man is not a sinner through
> Adam—without necessarily teaching something
> thereby which is objectively contradictory to the
> Church's teaching on original sin..."[28]

Avery Dulles has taken a similar position on the dogma of Original Sin. While unwilling to deny the validity of any proclaimed dogma, Dulles acknowledges that

> "In order to bring out the deeper and divinely
> intended meaning [of any particular dogma]...it
> may be necessary to discard the human concepts as
> well as the words of those who first framed the
> dogma."

In Dulles's view "this process is now going on with respect
to...original sin."[29] It is fair to say that, for Dulles, the very
concept of Original Sin is obsolete, although not the "divinely
intended meaning" or revealed truth that mysteriously underlies
it. Despite Dulles's caution, even today theological attempts are
being made to validate and find meaning in the dogma of Original
Sin. Without entering this dogmatic briarpatch, I simply deny the
underlying premise in regard to dogma itself, namely the presumption that dogma tells us "what is so."

Free from such an unnecessary dogmatic bind, our reflections
have more than suggested that the dogma of Original Sin, together
with the doctrine of salvation/redemption that necessarily followed it, is anything but an innocent mistake. It is a harmful
mistake. For Original Sin misdiagnoses the root cause of our
suffering. It creates a fiction of an illness or corruption under
which we stand helpless. It rests our only hope in the mercy of a
saving divinity who may or may not tender salvation to any
particular individual. Joseph Campbell has described the results
of this kind of misreading:

> "...our story of the Fall in the Garden sees nature as
> corrupt; *and that myth corrupts the whole world
> for us* [emphasis mine]...You get a totally different
> civilization and a totally different way of living
> according to whether your myth presents nature as
> fallen or whether nature is in itself a manifestation
> of divinity..."[30]

We do not remain true to the gospel teaching of Jesus unless we
acknowledge that our life is honorable. We are born intrinsically
pure, even if our potential is not yet fulfilled by us. This is exactly
why human life and destiny presents each of us with a great task
and the responsibility to meet it. There is considerable spiritual
work that each of us is born to undertake. It is our reason for living.
Being born human is a serious business. Without a correct sense
of ourselves, however, we will surely be left with our potential
unfulfilled.

The gospel of St. Paul, despite good intentions, has deprived
many Christians of their inheritance, the gospel of Jesus. These

two gospels, that of Jesus and that of Paul, have become fused within Christendom. Only the spiritually astute, the saints, have aligned with the gospel of Jesus. For most Christians the gospel of Paul has prevailed, although a good number have experienced the conflict of a double-gospel. It is time for every Christian to recognize the conflicting demands, as well as conflicting promise, of these two gospels. Are we inherently corrupt or intrinsically pure? The answer to this straightforward question will orient our life either toward a plea for salvation or toward responsibility for a spiritual practice that will strengthen truth and lessen hypocrisy in our life.

I feel that most of us already enjoy a wholesome native instinct about our real nature. Yet our intuition has been abused and confused by an instruction that would reduce our spiritual life to one of childish obedience. Like mentally abused children who have found healing, we could abandon distorted views about our inmost being that have been inculcated into us. Perhaps we are ready to be restored to a proper sense of ourselves.

To give an example of what I mean: If a grammar school teacher of the early grades, say a kindergarten or first grade teacher, were to instill in a little child that s/he is an unworthy, corrupt person, the child's parents would likely take action against that teacher. To such parents the teacher has demonstrated his or her unfitness to teach their child or any child. They are right. But for some reason these same parents may then attend a church or listen to a purportedly religious broadcast that tells them that their own innermost nature is sinful and corrupt. Although this is nonsense, they listen attentively. We may ask, if what these parents hear in their religious setting is true, why would they not return to the school teacher and congratulate him or her for communicating this truth to their child?

As I see it, the reason is that, at the level of *belief*, these parents actually think that they believe the traditional religious palaver they are hearing. But in real terms they do not adhere to it at all. The common experience is that when we have a newborn baby we do not look upon him as depraved and worthy of eternal hellfire, as St. John Eudes described it following precisely what St. Augustine taught about an unbaptized baby. We know better. We love and cherish the little tyke. We would do well to follow this natural intelligence of ours when we come to reflect on the matter of *our own nature* in respect to Original Sin. We do not have to cheat ourselves. We can dismiss those who see evil and depravity in us while they claim to speak for God. The truth of Original Sin does not refer to our profound and pristine condition, our innermost nature. Still, taken as a partial vision, an angled vision of *our experience of life*, it does reflect our feeling of separation and our need to reconnect.

The spiritual teaching of Jesus was profound. It had its effect. Jesus was not an ordinary man. He was not even an ordinary prophet. His very life was sacrificed to his teaching. The Good Friday of Jesus' death is celebrated in conjunction with his resurrection, celebrated as Easter. The liturgy of the Church rightly emphasizes Easter as its focal point. The liturgical year of the Church rightly veers toward and then leads away from Easter. Easter celebrates the sacrifice of Jesus into Christ. The earthly Jesus, and for him the world (the *cultic* world that falsely promises us happiness), was surrendered. The Christ, the Kingdom of God, arose and has remained. Only a Christian who is spiritually ignorant is unmoved by this reality and by the liturgical representation of this reality at Easter. The spiritual Christian, partly in and through this liturgy, hankers for The Kingdom. He desires the Resurrected Christ.

Yet the surrender of Jesus was not the solitary instance of an absolute surrender of this (cultic) world. Similarly the vision of *The Kingdom of God* is not the only vision that has arisen from a full realization of our pristine religious impulse. Nor is the Christian path the only path that can lead to human completion, to the surrender and transcendence of this world. So while the Christ, the Kingdom of God, remains the basic Christian vision, this vision can serve authentic religion without being the only vision that serves authentic religion. A path can be true without being the only true path. It will be instructive to examine the chauvinism that arbitrarily denies the validity of other human paths which open onto the fullness of reality.

NOTES

1 *Philippians* III, 12-13.

2 This complex teaching is elaborated by Paul in *Romans* V, 12-19. In its dogmatic proclamation on Original Sin the Council of Trent made explicit use of this passage from *Romans*. See *The Sources of Catholic Dogma*, pp. 246-8.

3 See *The Sources of Catholic Dogma*, p. 247, para. 791.

4 Many of Augustine's writings emphasize this. One may consult "On Marriage and Concupiscence" or, for easier accessibility, "On Nature and Grace" [*De Natura et Gratia*], Whitney J. Oates, ed., *Basic Writings of Saint Augustine*, (Random House, Inc., 1948).

5 *The Sources of Catholic Dogma*, p. 248, para. 792. [The awkward English translation reads "concupiscence of an inclination" for the Latin *"concupiscentiam vel fomitem,"* (which really means "strong desire or tinderbox").]

6 These views are found in St. John's treatise on Original Sin and in a more readily available book, *Meditations on Various Subjects*, tr. Charles Lebrun, (P.J. Kenedy & Sons, 1947). See in particular pp. 111, 117, 118, *et al.*

7 *Jonathan Edwards: Selections*, eds. Clarence H. Faust and Thomas H. Johnson, (Hill and Wang, 1962), "Doctrine of Original Sin," pp. 316-39, esp. pp. 319f; "Sinners in the Hands of an Angry God," pp. 155-72. See esp. pp. 159 & 161: "Natural men's prudence and care to preserve their own lives...do not secure them a moment...God has laid himself under *no obligation*, by any promise to keep any natural man out of hell one moment."

8 *Church Dogmatics*, IV, 1, p. 500.

9 Joseph Campbell, *The Power of Myth*, (Doubleday, 1988), p. 66.

10 *Matthew*, V, 48.

11 *Luke* XVII, 21.

12 *Matthew*, XIII, 3ff.

13 *Matthew* V, 39-41.

14 *Matthew* XXV, 35ff.

15 *John* XV, 13.

16 *Matthew* V, 48.

17 *The Power of Myth*, p. 32.

18 The meaning of the Christian dogmatic and theological tradition's central focus on this "redemptive" interpretation of the life of Jesus is presented in the brief and easily readable work of Karl Barth, *The Faith of the Church: A commentary on the Apostles' Creed*, (Meridian Books, Inc., 1958), "Doctrine of Exinanition" [*i.e.* self-emptying of God in Jesus], Questions 55-72. Note that there is little difference between the Catholic and Protestant views at this basic level. Modern theological speculation on the origins of a "mythological" interpretation of the life and death of Jesus can be found in John Hick, ed., *The Myth of God Incarnate*, (The Westminster Press, 1977); for a summary see especially Hick's own chapter and the Epilogue, pp. 167-203. Although Hick's book is a reasonable attempt of the post-modern western world to make sense of the human personality of Jesus, it simply does not account for who Jesus really was.

19 *The Power of Myth*, p. 66.

20 *"De natura et gratia,"* Chapter IX, *Basic Writings*, p. 526.

21 William E. H. Lecky, *History of European Morals: from Augustus to Charlemagne*, (George Braziller, Inc., 1955), p. 96.

22 Regarding Original Sin St. Cyprian had enunciated Augustine's basic views over a century earlier [see Jaroslav Pelikan, *Development of Christian Doctrine*, (Yale University Press, 1969)]. In regard to sexuality, many ancient Fathers of the Church were of a radically sex-negative position, deriving their views in good measure from the earlier pagan philosophers of Rome [see Peter Brown, *The Body and Society: Men, Women, and Sexual Renunciation in Early Christianity*, Columbia University Press, 1988].

23 *Faust*, Part I, "Prologue in Heaven."

24 *Paradise Lost*, Book I, ll. 254-5.

25 *The Dogma of Original Sin*, (Vander, publisher, 1969), p. 31.

26 Ibid., p. 65.

27 *Theological Investigations XI*, "The Sin of Adam," (The Seabury Press, 1974), p. 247.

28 *Theological Investigations V*, p. 56.

29 *The Survival of Dogma*, p. 161.

30 *The Power of Myth*, p. 121

IX

Off and on during the journey, I wrote about Christ because I felt I was beginning to see him in a totally new light, beginning perhaps, to see as he had seen.

Bernadette Roberts

JESUS CHAUVINISM OR CHRIST UNIVERSALISM

A teacher of American history put this question to her class: "Why did the Puritans come to America?" A provocative answer came from a lad whom the teacher had, until then, considered one of her dullest pupils: "They came here to worship God in their own way and to make everybody else do the same."

In his *Treatise On the Gods* H.L. Mencken would have been more accurate, I am convinced, had he cited the Puritans or some other particular religious body he was so abundantly criticizing, rather than religion itself, when he observed that "Religion does not necessarily make better citizens, whether of their neighborhoods or of the world."[1] In this striking sentence Mencken rightly indicts a common experience of religion. But it is the provincial attitude of religious exclusivism and dominance over matters outside its domain, and not authentic religion, that he fittingly indicts.

Exclusivism of any sort seems to show a weakness in our inner sense of self for which we compensate by making outward claims of superiority. This confused superiority status is called *chauvinism*, named after an enthusiastic footsoldier in Napoleon's brigade, Nicolas Chauvin.

Religious chauvinism is the attitude that one's own religious affiliation is alone the carrier of spiritual truth, and that all other religious forms are substandard. To look at this matter of religious chauvinism I will draw on my own experience, when I confronted an instance of religious chauvinism that was even more exaggerated than my own chauvinistic attitude.

I was in either sophomore or junior year of high school the time the lady knocked so assertively on our door. Home alone, I answered her knock with whatever graciousness was available to me at that period of my life. The lady was selling some kind of religious form. She was sure she was right about it, but I knew she was dead wrong. She wasn't even Catholic. There was a particular angle to this lady's vigorous sell that got to me. Her cocksure attitude about being absolutely right was bad enough, especially since I had full evidence that she was wrong. But her particular religious form had this very strange quality: It allowed salvation to only one hundred forty-four thousand people. Not one hundred forty-four thousand three; not one hundred forty-three thousand nine hundred ninety-six. No, exactly one hundred forty-four thousand persons were going to be saved. Now let us say that there are over five billion human beings alive today. Let us admit further that we will all soon be replaced. This will make some ten billion people who will have lived in just two modern generations. So how many billions of human beings will have been born and died from beginning to end? Whatever approximate figure someone might arrive at, we can all agree that there are a lot of us. This lady's aggressive manner in trying to get *me* to be numbered among that very, very elite group of heaven-bound—and, of course, to hell with the rest—intrigued me.

Consider this: If you were on a fully booked passenger ship that was sinking in the middle of the ocean, and if there was just one very small raft that could bring, let us say eight or so, persons to safety, would you knock vehemently on all the cabin doors to get everybody to be one of the eight lucky ones? Even if you were assured that you were going to be one of the saved eight, what difference would it make to you exactly who the other seven were? This lady did not know me. What an odd god she was selling, that his so spare gift of salvation would be tendered to me on the basis that I happened to live on the block where a particular woman rather indiscriminately took up her missionary position. It was ludicrous to me even then. As I was so inexperienced at the time, I disputed with this lady. I feel that today I would be easeful, sensing how her mentality was fixed on a terrible need to have her own saved status confirmed.

Every kind of chauvinism is born of inexperience, of being provincial in the narrowing sense of the word. Provincialism reflects our tendency to recognize the value only of what we are familiar with, only of what exists in our own backyard, our own province so to speak. It is like the person who hears an unfamiliar language and calls it gibberish. Such a person does not even recognize, let alone acknowledge, that the limitation is within him/herself.

Religious chauvinism is the attitude and belief that the essential core and truth of religion is the very thing we happen to have inherited as *our* religion. What luck! Of all the billions of human beings who have existed and who will exist on the face of the earth throughout all time, we alone, together with a relatively few like us, have happened upon *the real thing*. Religious chauvinism finally amounts to this: It is our heart's commitment to the thought that the Infinite One has, out of this Infinitude, focussed on a minute raft (which holds exactly one hundred forty-four thousand, or some equally arbitrary number, of people) on a small clump of dirt (planet earth) that wheels about a mediocre star (the sun), which is an unimportant member of a gathering (galaxy) of one hundred billion or so such stars, which galaxy belongs to a cluster of like unfathomables, which cluster is *just one* among billions of such clusters in the total conglomerate of a universe that obviously exceeds the human imagination. Religious chauvinism goes on to assert that some particular person (the chauvinist) has word from the Infinite One about this raft (Church, or whatever) with explicit directions about how to climb onto it. It is further believed that this raft alone is destined to bring a tiny percentage of human beings to their desired goal—and, of course, to hell with the rest.

The lesson I missed at the time is that this lady was only bringing me a mini-version of an attitude that was essentially also my own. For I was then equally a religious chauvinist. The only difference between this lady and me was that my imagination created a slightly bigger raft. It was nonetheless a pitifully minute raft by the great standard of existence.

It is sometimes necessary to go back to basics. By all means worship as a Puritan if you will, or if you must. Let it even benefit you if it can. But about the great matter of existence, humility is our key. We know our heart's desire, or at least through careful attention we can acquaint ourselves with it. For the real evidence of things is within us. We need not let any person or any system cheat us out of our natural inheritance, the resource of our own heart. Humility, however, marks our respect for others. We can take what seems good for us without condemning or belittling others as they take what seems good for them.

It is easy to understand how early Christians were so influenced by the spiritual presence and power of Jesus that he did appear absolutely unique to them. To them he was unique. They lived in a very limited and scurrilous world. The personal quality required to confront that world from the angle of truth and genuine humanness, without losing one's own personal integrity, was, and remains to this day, a rare phenomenon. Through his life and action in the world, Jesus did cut a superhuman, heavenly figure. As he came to be recognized as the very presence of Truth in human consciousness, Truth-in-person we can say, his whole life easily appeared unique.

By itself Jesus' powerful influence does not make another instance of the personal appearance of Truth in this world unthinkable. In the minds of Christians what clinched Jesus' life as a once-for-all event was the interpretation of his death as a saving or redemptive event for all of humankind. Taking Jesus' personal mission as absolutely universal took on an intriguing character in modern times. Intelligent life beyond our world has become plausible speculation. Yet according to the idea of Original Sin *all* creation is corrupt. Certain theologians, following this logic of Original Sin, have felt forced to ask just how the saving, redemptive work of Jesus applies to possible extra-terrestrial forms of intelligent life. While many theologians would scorn this issue as bizarre, it does highlight certain implications of taking the myth of the fall of humankind, and its consequent salvation myth, as literal truth.

Whatever the case concerning possible extra-terrestrials, Christianity did come to view Jesus as the unique means of salvation for all human beings. It was not a large jump to the dogmatic conclusion that everyone must belong to the Church in order to make connection with Jesus and be saved. The classical formulation of this view is: Outside the Church there is no salvation. We have considered this teaching of the Catholic Church at some length when we discussed dogma.

We have seen that modern theologians, and the Second Vatican Council as well, acknowledge "plentiful salvation outside the Church." However, this more generous attitude is not consistent with certain fundamental beliefs of the Church concerning Jesus Christ. What I have insisted on is that these irreconcilable beliefs are not intrinsic to the gospel teaching of Jesus. They come from an inadequate spiritual understanding concerning Jesus, and concerning Christ, and even concerning the world itself. Limitations in St. Paul's spiritual understanding seem to be the source of these misleading beliefs of Christian orthodoxy.

Paul's vision of Original Sin tells us that the world, including ourselves, is fallen away from God. The idea of a redeemer is appealing and credible to those who feel the painfulness of our separation and who believe that separateness is indeed our cosmic situation. Consequently, being restored to perfect wholeness looks like an impossible task, when it is thought of as a matter of our personal responsibility. It would appear to be as difficult as getting to the moon on our own. Hence, seeing the spiritual work of Jesus as repairing this cosmic breach between heaven and earth ["God in Christ reconciling the world to himself" in Paul's words[2]] does imply a unique and universal event.

But as we came to discover the spread of the world beyond our own provincial western culture, Christians were faced with the question as to just *how* Jesus has affected the whole world. As we now stand some two thousand years after Jesus, we know that most of the world's populace have never heard of him. This has held true throughout the history of Christianity. Given the relative smallness of the Church compared to the whole of humanity, it has become intolerably provincial to restrict salvation just to Christians, and then only to some of them. But by the same token we cannot have it both ways. How can we hold both that Jesus of Nazareth is the unique savior of the world and still allow for "plentiful salvation outside the Church?"

Modern times have seen the efforts of Catholic theologians to explain how people who have never even heard of the Catholic Church are nevertheless saved through it. A famous effort of this kind was made by the Jesuit theologian Karl Rahner. Rahner was convinced of the traditional view that human reconnection to the Source happens only through Jesus and the Church. He explicitly asserts that "In this sense there really is no salvation outside the Church, as the old theological formula has it."[3] Still Rahner was reluctant to deny that good people of every stripe are reconnected to their Source. The conclusion was clear to Father Rahner: The earthly life of good people is being lived through Jesus and the Church, although they have no palpable connection with either Jesus or the Church. He described these persons as "anonymous Christians."[4]

Rahner's speculation about anonymous Christians looked plausible to theologians in those days when pure Catholic/Christian chauvinism ["Outside the Church there is no salvation!"] became untenable. But in the final analysis Rahner's position entails too much magic. It makes people of various non-Christian religions Christians, even though they have never even heard of either Jesus or the Church. A personal anecdote, which I believe is factually based, concerns Father Rahner in ecumenical dialogue with Buddhists. After hearing how Father Rahner considers good Buddhists to be anonymous Christians, a Zen monk, the story goes, spoke of Father Rahner as an "anonymous Buddhist." The word is that Father Rahner did not relish that thought.

Rahner's views did not transcend a provincial outlook. He was too entrenched within the entire Catholic belief-system to view honestly the spiritual content and force of other religious forms. It seems that his native intelligence and generous heart were not sufficient to overcome his Catholic chauvinism, a Jesus chauvinism. Although Rahner acknowledged even supernatural elements in non-Christian religious bodies, he nevertheless felt forced to hold out for an absoluteness that is unique to Christianity: "We must begin with the thesis...that Christianity understands itself as the absolute religion, intended for all men, which cannot recognize any other religion beside itself as of equal right."[5] For whatever reason, Rahner felt compelled to express this superiority in a way that was unnecessarily negative as well as untrue: "...a non-Christian religion can be recognized as a lawful religion...without thereby denying *the error and depravity contained in it* [emphasis mine]."[6] Rahner's assumption is that Christianity, Catholicism in particular, is the perfect expression of religion, although he certainly would not have denied the error and depravity of individual Christians. But the knee-jerk language of *error and depravity in non-Christian religions* is another matter altogether. Rahner did not have a sound understanding of other religious forms. Yet his story reveals the blinding chauvinism to which an inbred provincialism can subject even the talented among us.

Certainly our fast-moving age continues to undermine limitations in particular viewpoints. Rahner should not be faulted for belonging to an earlier moment of this age. The present Pope, John Paul II, for instance, has recently expressed a more respectful appreciation of non-Christian religions, and spoke of them in the language of Vatican Council II rather than in the accustomed disparaging language.[7] Coming as it does from the highest Catholic authority, this Pope's statement is welcome. While his view falls short of what I am saying here—and has not been well received by Buddhists, against whose forms of meditation he "cautions"—we cannot expect a wholesale reversal of a major teaching—in this case, what I have named "Jesus Chauvinism"—to come from this level of authority. Things rarely happen that way. As in every other instance of radical doctrinal change, such as the case of "outside the Church there is no salvation" and what will soon be the case regarding artificial contraception, the rationale for change and the new wording will seep up from below. Yes, one can envision a Pope John XXIII both understanding a needed change like this one and expressing it forthrightly. But human history has not seen many John XXIIIs at that level of power. It is useful for now that Pope John Paul II has spoken less abrasively, if not at all adequately, on this matter.

Theological efforts alone have not and cannot resolve the central issue. We must return to the doctrinal problem that lies behind theology. Is Jesus unique? Does it take anything away from the greatness and the fullness of Jesus, from the Truth of Jesus, if we suggest that his communication of Truth was not necessarily directed to everyone? Is it unreasonable to suggest that Truth can present itself to the world in ways, and perhaps in personalities, that exceed the limited imagination of Christians? Is it possible that Jesus *was* The Christ, absolutely and fully The Christ, yet not the only or unique presence of The Christ to this world?

A personal circumstance forced me to face these questions directly. It may be helpful to share my experience: In my early days as a university professor I was invited by a colleague to attend a guest lecture in his course, Eastern Religions. The lecturer was to be a highly respected Swami from India, Swami Ranganathananda as I recall. Swami's special talent was an ability to bring his heartfelt, experienced Hinduism into the sphere of the experience and mental framework of his listeners. At this lecture most of his audience, including myself, were Christians.

Swami opened his talk with this remark: "Christians believe that Jesus was the Son of God, that Jesus was actually God." This was unexceptionable, so "Yes," I thought. But Swami's next line got my attention. "Hindus too believe that Jesus was the Son of God, that he was actually God." "The only difference," Swami continued, "is that Hindus feel that this same divine presence has been manifest also in other human personalities." Then the Swami asked, "Do any of us have certitude about what God can or cannot do or about what God has or has not done?" When the question is put this way, it makes us reflect on how we tend to filter the great matter of existence through our limited ideas. It is more true to admit that, "No, we do not have certitude about what God can or cannot do or has or has not done."

In effect, Swami's two sentences and then his question, because of their universal implications, broke the bondage of religious provincialism for me. At the time I did not recognize the full impact on me of this Swami's communication. My mind responded with just another thought, "Yes, but of course!" Yet in that moment for me the dam was broken. Barely noticing it, I was catapulted from province to cosmos in my spiritual thinking. The interesting thing is how quickly it all became fully obvious to me. My thinking moved in an instant from the limitations of Jesus Chauvinism to the grandness of Christ Universalism.

Christians' devotion to the personality of Jesus is not what I mean by Jesus Chauvinism. The image of Jesus, from before his birth to his resurrection from the dead, plays an important devotional role in the religious imagination of Christians. True devotion has an authentic spiritual effect. It would be neither true nor useful to deny the past and present influence of Jesus in the lives of Christians. Through his influence true devotees begin to make connection with The Christ.

The issue of Jesus Chauvinism questions the uniqueness of the incarnate personality of Jesus of Nazareth as the presence of The Christ to the human world. The word Christ bespeaks the depth of the divine. What exactly did Jesus have to do with Christ? The confession of the earliest Christians was "Jesus *is* The Christ." "Jesus *is* Lord." It is not necessary to deny this. The question is whether The Christ is in every way simply identical to the human embodiment and personality of Jesus of Nazareth.

This difficult matter might best be approached by looking at our own fleshly [incarnate] lives. There is something paradoxical about being born an embodied human being. We sit where we are today, and each of us can say "I am here." At the same time we can recall some particular place where we were ten years ago and say, "I was there." We mean this very precisely, "The one [myself] who sits here now is exactly the one [myself] who was in that other place then." When we consider our body, however, there is not a single cell, not a single molecule present here today that was present in that other place ten years ago. There has been a total exchange of parts. Nevertheless we are embodied [incarnate] today and this same person was embodied ten years ago. A careful look at the living process of embodiment shows that our loss and rebirth of cells, of our entire bodily constitution, is an ongoing process. It is our bodily *life*. We are not inert. Yet somehow we keep the very same identity throughout all this change. Paradoxically, this identity is what is embodied. Nor is it true to say that we are only inhabiting a body, like we inhabit a house or a coat that still remain outside us. *Paradoxically, we are embodied.*

Jesus of Nazareth was embodied [incarnate]; but unlike ourselves, at some point Jesus awakened fully to his true identity. When he said "I" he *knew* exactly what he was talking about. The "I" that was present at his birth, that lived as a child and adolescent, that grew to manhood, that taught, was threatened, and was finally executed, was the selfsame "I." Nevertheless the incarnate form (Jesus' bodily existence) was continuously changing. *Still he was embodied* for a time. Jesus' true identity and the culmination of his historical life is known as The Christ. But just as there was no particular moment of his everchanging incarnate existence that was perfectly identical to The Christ, so his surrender of bodily existence at the moment of his death did not affect his true identity in any significant way.

Our own embodied being in the world is a profound mystery that goes beyond our ability to understand it; it is a paradox. But paradox belongs to our mind, not to reality. Paradox expresses our mind's inadequacy *vis-a-vis* reality. But the inadequacy of our mind does not hinder our own conscious presence as we are incarnate in this world. The embodiment of those rare people who become fully conscious of their true nature is an even greater paradox to our mind. It is a mystery that far exceeds our rational powers. But this does not stop our ability to discriminate between their true nature and the everchanging forms of their embodiment—from the time they are babies, to when they are youths, to when they are adults. Their life represents the presence of the Divine to the world over and above the ongoing changes in their worldly embodiment.

In the case of Jesus, his incarnate existence became the presence of The Christ to this world. Yet God's revelation [unveiling] in the life of Jesus is basically the same as the awakening of true faith in the hearts of all men and women in whom it actually happens. This is the simple but profound reality that came to be called Christianity. It is unreasonable to deny for Christians the irreplaceable influence of the incarnate Jesus of Nazareth, through his own realization of The Christ, in this great, historical, shared awakening. But by the same token, there is no reason to take the one instance of Jesus' everchanging bodily existence to be the single instance of a human being awakening fully to her or his true nature, to The Christ.

The issue before us is this: Is Jesus of Nazareth the solitary instance of the human presence of The Christ in our world? Is the extraordinary life of Jesus, who surrendered the limitations of his mere humanness, the only human life to surrender all limitations and so realize the presence of God in this world? The tendency of Christians is to say, "Yes!" Yet is this not a tendency toward Jesus-Chauvinism? Is it not arrant chauvinism to take what is true and meaningful and great *to oneself* to be the only instance of its kind that is true and meaningful and great?

The harmful thing in Jesus Chauvinism is this: it sets a boundary to and so limits the complete and straightforward reality of The Christ. Jesus Chauvinism attempts to possess the Divine-Presence-to-consciousness (which is The Christ) as if it were one's uncle. It takes nothing from Jesus or from his realization of God to suggest that the historical personality, Jesus of Nazareth, did not place a limitation on the Divine Presence to the world of human consciousness. Nothing of the power and influence of the Nazarene is diminished when we begin to understand the spiritual truth he communicated. St. Paul spoke of "God emptying himself"[8] in the incarnation of Jesus. But by the same measure Christians might recognize that Jesus emptied himself back into God at the time of his death. This *emptying* is what gave rise to The Spirit of Christ, Jesus' lasting influence in the world. All of this can be true without its being the single, sole, solitary play of the Divine in this world.

Many of the early Christians had deep appreciation of this reality. They told it as good news [gospel] to others. But they did not share their experience of human/divine love in order to threaten or belittle or deny the validity of their hearers. The core good news of Jesus does not condemn anyone at all. His life on earth was full of non-condemnation. Love simply does not express itself in condemnation. Exactly the opposite is the case. Love first acknowledges the truth in every person. This is why love can draw it forth. To condemn another is *not to see* his or her truth. So where there is condemnation, there is surely not love.

The spiritual meaning and force of The Kingdom of God simply abated in western culture, no matter how *Christian* this culture thought itself to be. This was due to the absence of the kind of spiritual instruction and spiritual work that are needed to cultivate the true Kingdom in the life of each individual. For the great mass of Christians only a memory of something better has remained. Having lost the living spiritual understanding, the Church concocted worldly means in order to recapture and control the Kingdom that it felt was its automatic inheritance.

But the Kingdom is never an automatic inheritance. It is always a personal accomplishment. Can a child, for example, inherit the musical virtuosity of her mother? Absolutely not! If the child becomes a virtuoso herself, it is because she applied herself to music. The influence of her mother and the musical environment created by her mother definitely provide a nourishing atmosphere for a child. But the child must make use of it and do the work herself.

The loss of spiritual knowledge and the attempt to recapture it through worldly means is something like the situation of a husband who has not fostered and cultivated his love-relationship with his wife. When he notices that she is truly apart and that love is no longer there, he may try to force it back, to recapture it and control the situation. He may tend to use means that are not love: gifts, money, promises of every sort, even threats of deprivation or lawsuits. Such a man is bewildered by his loss and cannot see the irrelevance of all his tricks for restoring the love he has lost. Only love itself, once again come alive, can reestablish a lost love-relationship.

When spiritual understanding faded in the Church, the rich spiritual atmosphere that sacrament and ritual could provide for spiritual work were debased into a means of mechanically produced grace for the spiritually deprived masses of Christians. This loss of the very meaning of spirituality magnified the *worldly* dimension of the Church, what in these pages I am calling The Cult of This World. The Cult has not, however, totally eclipsed the power of The Spirit of Christ to influence exceptional persons throughout the ages. Rare as they have been, there have always existed genuine saints, those persons who have had the inner genius to recognize and apply the universal spiritual knowledge that was reenlivened in our human sphere through the presence and teaching of Jesus.

But actually living the gospel of Jesus is a tremendous demand. A person has to make a choice between God and World [in the biblical sense of *mammon* or *wealth*, the most essential symbol of the world] in Jesus' own words. A choice for God in the spiritual sense comes only as the awakening of faith, the initial experience of the Kingdom. Even the necessary conversion of heart that Jesus emphasized is but the beginning. The hallowed New Testament word for conversion is *metanoia. Conversion* can be translated accurately as "a turnabout of the heart-mind." But living out the disposition of faith *after* conversion—what is here called *spiritual practice*—requires much more of us for the rest of our life. Spiritual practice cannot occur without correct instruction. Spiritual practice is the application of this instruction after it has been rightly understood. Such instruction is the whole point, and the only point, of Sacred Scripture. It is the single mission of the Church.

The mere conviction that Jesus was right is not conversion. It is not an awakening. Such conviction is nothing more than a mental calculation and assessment that comes from taking a good look at life. That kind of assessment is not ignorant. It is smart. It even suggests wisdom. But the difference between such mere mental assessment and *reality that is felt* is total. It is the difference between knowing *about* something and actually *being* it. *Being it* is true spiritual practice. The practice is fulfilled in the possession of the Kingdom. Only "the violent bear it away," as Jesus has said[9]. These are strong words. But true spiritual practice is a mighty affair. It is the ultimate human challenge.

Why did Jesus' spiritual communication and challenge fade? This question reminds me of the symbolic meaning of an old favorite Protestant hymn, "Were you there when they crucified my Lord?" If we hear the words of this hymn only literally, of course we were not there. After all, it was almost two thousand years ago! But if we allow the symbolics of the hymn to touch us, we might begin to notice our distance, our separation, from The Christ. We are hardly present [there] to the abandonment of Jesus to The Christ—"when they crucified my Lord." Authentic Holy Communion is very difficult for us.

Yet our movement away from the spiritual communication of Jesus has been gradual. Like Peter in the Garden of Gethsemane, there was no particular point at which we decided to go to sleep, to abandon our interest in The Christ. It is a gradual and easy movement from wakefulness to sleep; from clarity to confusion; from sobriety to drunkenness; from seeing to delusion; from Kingdom to Cult. The slide is often imperceptible to us. This is true in our personal mental and emotional life. It is true in our social, historical life. But it is particularly true in respect to the eclipse of our interest in authentic religion, our impulse and need actually to reconnect to our Source.

In the case of our experience of the pain in the heart, our fundamental disconnectedness, well might we expect an immediate reach for a palliative. Those who are too experienced to fall once again for worldly things as a cure for our basic ill are easy prey to the vision of a this-worldly heaven. Once again we are able to see why only a person of genuine spiritual knowledge can guide us on a path beyond every palliative toward the reality. Jesus' spiritual communication, the challenge of The Kingdom, faded because the line of direct influence, the begetting of full spiritual understanding in successors, did not happen with sufficient strength. The magic of ritual and an authority *not based in spiritual understanding* were thought to suffice. The long history of cultic religion within Christianity, especially within the Catholic Church, with its suspicions of heresy, its persecutions, its inquisitions, false accusations, condemnations, its garnering of worldly power, then worldly riches, pomp, glory, and then a final determination that it alone is true—of all things!—this has replaced the humble submission to and communication of the genuine spiritual, world-transcending practice that Jesus taught.

Christianity became provincial and chauvinistic when it was no longer lived. Its good news was turned completely around. Perverted is the exact word. It came to be very bad news to all those who were going to be tortured and murdered because they could not receive a gospel as presented by preachers who had not the least trace of spiritual understanding. The spiritual reality which Jesus was is the same profound and simple thing he taught. It is called love. Spiritual understanding is nothing more than the recognition of and submission to this reality. Love does not require an intellectually deep or complex understanding, because love is not mental. What is important and true about love is that it is very hard to *do*, or more accurately, to *be*. Love requires that we surrender our most basic position, our self-centeredness, as well as the life we have built to defend our centered self. In a word, love demands that we give up our own little world and be fully present to the real one. That total presence to reality *is* love. Love, we remember, was St. John's definition of God.[10]

The word used to express the presence of the Sacred in this world is Sacrament. The human life of Jesus Christ was the sacrament of God, the work of Love in this world. Certainly the memory of Jesus in the minds of Christians (prayer) is sacramental. Also, the concrete words and works of Love were likewise sacraments. The imprint of those works in the world-memory as ritual is also sacrament. In the next chapter we will explore the magnetic field, if we may call it that, which takes shape in the world as the sacramental presence of the Sacred.

But we must also account for the human response to this presence which has marked western history for the past two millennia. After the murder of Love Incarnate, and when the residual sparks of his spiritual instruction were smothered in an unnurturing atmosphere, we witness a long, sad history of the human caricature of the life and teaching and memory of Jesus. This caricature can be seen in boldest relief in the lives and teachings and minds of many of the popes.

Some centuries after the death of Jesus, the bishops of Rome came to see themselves as singularly entrusted with the care and propagation of the Radiant Love of Christ. Somehow they believed they could exercise this responsibility of making Absolute Love, The Christ, present to the world without participating in it themselves. They looked upon their responsibility as a job in the world created and handed on by Jesus to bring salvation to people through mechanical means. They did not shy away from the use of force, including the threat of torture and death and the actual delivery of these, to bring and keep people within the fold of the Church. Oddly, it appears that even the most degraded of popes—and numerous popes can credibly compete for this notorious distinction—even the most degraded of them seems to have felt he was somehow doing God's work. Such is the confusion to which life within a system fraught with hypocrisy can reduce us.

The Church did not easily accept the implications of her minority status in the vast world of humanity. Modern times nevertheless forced her to deal with a human world that far exceeds her own boundaries. We have seen that only a little over a century ago, Pope Pius IX still held to a one true Church outside of which no one could be saved. "It must, of course, be held as a matter of faith," he preached, "that outside the apostolic Roman Church no one can be saved, that the Church is the only ark of salvation, and that whoever does not enter it will perish in the flood."[11] This 1854 speech of Pius IX was given at a time when the inhabited world was known to be large indeed, and when the minority status of Christians, not to mention Roman Catholics, was fully recognized. Unlike his predecessors who proclaimed the same "outside the Church there is no salvation" doctrine, Pius IX felt forced to account for such a large non-Catholic world. He could hardly maintain that absolutely everyone outside the pale of the Catholic Church is truly hell-bound. So Pius acknowledged that *ignorance* relieves a person of guilt for not adhering to this true Church. In fact he became almost magnanimous in pointing out how extensive such ignorance may be: "...taking into consideration the natural differences of peoples, lands, native talents, and so many other factors," to cite his words. Pius IX's interpretation of a longstanding dogma can be put in plaintalk: The vast multitudes of people are so ignorant that they will be excused in the long run. There is some irony in making *ignorance* the entry to eternal salvation for the vast majority of people. His view on this matter alone might well throw into question Pius IX's spiritual understanding.

The world of the twentieth century has so expanded that each of its parts, its power centers, has, relatively speaking, shrunk. Likewise has the worldly power of the Catholic Church, particularly at her center, the papacy, shrunk most noticeably. The Church has not been particularly gracious in suffering the erosion of power.

In the final analysis it came to be a matter of power. The gospel teaching of Jesus centered on the distinction between God and mammon, between the Kingdom of God and the powers and principalities of this world. St. Augustine made the distinction between the City of God and the City of Man. In the words I have chosen in this book, the distinction is between Church and Cult. To give any account of what is necessary for an effective reform of Christianity, we cannot avoid a detailed consideration of the quality of its presence in the world. Following our general discussion of the meaning of sacrament, we must then enter into this most ambiguous of topics, the Church as a spiritual body that is at the same time an institution in a world governed by power.

NOTES

[1] (Alfred A. Knopf, 1965), p. 270.

[2] *II Corinthians*, V, 19.

[3] *Theological Investigations VI*, (Darton, Longman & Todd, 1969), p. 391.

[4] Ibid., pp. 390-398. Rahner later used the expression "implicit Christianity." See *Theological Investigations IX*, (Darton, Longman & Todd, 1972), pp. 145-164.

[5] *Theological Investigations V*, "Christianity and the Non-Christian Religions," (Helicon Press, 1966), p. 118.

[6] Ibid., p. 121.

[7] *Crossing the Threshold of Hope*, (Alfred A. Knopf, 1994). See esp. pp. 80-83.

[8] *Philippians* II, 7.

[9] *Matthew* XI, 12.

[10] *I John* IV, 8.

[11] *The Church Teaches*, p. 80.

X

The most beautiful and deepest experience a man can have is the sense of the mysterious.

Albert Einstein

MAGIC OR MYSTERY

We should be awe-struck by our whole life. "Wonder," said the ancient philosopher Aristotle, "is the beginning of philosophy." We have all experienced wonder, that open disposition of the heart-mind. Wonder is a bright feeling-relationship to everything. Wonder is full awareness and interest in the mystery of life. Things somehow produce themselves. They arise and grow and change and then give birth to new forms. This great and uncanny process is what we call *life*. The processes of life in this grand and total sense happen out of an unseen and inexplicable source. This is true mystery.

If authentic religion will speak to our total condition, it must come to terms with mystery—with the ultimate in which "we live and move and have our being,"[1] in St. Paul's words. The ultimate is anything but obvious. The context of our existence is not an open book to us. Nevertheless, we are undeniably involved in what is ultimate. It is our own proper element. Nor can we reasonably deny in advance any counsel that may come from others who, perhaps, may have seen more than we have. Therefore, on the one hand we may well expect authentic religion to tutor us in a mystery that far exceeds our rational grasp. But, on the other hand, we can ill afford to be duped by religious pretenders. These claim to do commerce in the great mystery and pretend to trickle it down to us second-hand, as if the mystery itself must remain beyond us and come to us in a form that can only be looked upon as magic. A sort of *supply-side* religion.

Indeed there are words and symbols, gestures and rites, that arise out of human experience and associate our experience with the mystery that envelops all things, including all experience. But this sacramental dimension of religion requires our intelligent engagement and response. When we only busy ourselves and

128

manipulate things, we ignore the mystery. If our main concern is to figure the world out and then twist it into shapes that we have created in our mind, we are apt to lose the mystery. There is little mystery in astroturf, on a highway, in a restaurant or even in a hospital operating room. This is not to disparage science or the technology it enables. However, science must be constantly recalled to its rightful place. We do have the ability to identify and name those processes of nature we are able to observe. This is what science is. Obviously we can also work with the processes we identify. This is technology. But such recognition of the processes of nature is not the same as knowing things in themselves. Observing and naming and working-with is not knowing in the sense of overcoming the mystery. Francis Bacon, seeking to engender a new scientific spirit, observed that "Knowledge and human power are synonymous."[2] Exactly so. But the power of our knowledge is possible only when we consciously cooperate with the powers already in existence. It behooves scientists to reflect on their own behavior to discover what the scientific-technological enterprise really amounts to. The human mind with its science and technology does not even approach, let alone comprehend, the mystery that undergirds it.

Before we learn to relate to the world as manipulators, we already live in an enchanted world. Our entire universe, as well as our personal life, is filled with mystery. Children intuit this, at least until they are inducted into the rationalization- knowledge-power scheme which we too often identify with *education*. The great science fiction authors intuit mystery, until they notice scientists lurking behind them, assessing where next to hunt and so reproduce in the artificial world of technology some faint semblance of the wonder that is intrinsic to nature and revealed to the science-fiction seer. The greatest of scientists confess the mystery of nature. Isaac Newton compared his own work to a single grain of sand on the vast seashore. Einstein confessed that his own aim was to discover the mind of God. Artists feel the mystery. They experience the mysterious mirroring back and forth between their subconscious mind and the world of forms. Artists know that their art is not their own doing. They admit to having been touched by a Muse, "a certain dose of inspiration, a ray from on high that is not in ourselves," in the words of van Gogh. Above all, the great realizers of the Self behold the mystery of existence. It belongs to the very substance of their realization. To them the mysterious visible universe is but the transparent body of an all-pervading consciousness or Mind.

In fact we can all free ourselves for a moment from being engrossed in our rational minds and wonder afresh at the mystery made present in our own experience. How even a nuclear explosion pales before a great thunderstorm! How slack a roller coaster ride feels compared to a storm at sea! Who would dare to say that the identifying-naming-classifying work of chemistry and biology captures the unfolding of the small acorn into the mighty oak! Who would even suggest that we rationally understand the substance and structure of a tiny seed whose process of living will *grow* into a flower? What *is* "to *grow*" anyway? Who can still suppose that our scientific laws govern the movement and operation of things? What does our mind have to do with the great living movement of reality?

Even human manufacture and artifacts, when we see them in perspective, clearly belong to the mystery of nature. It is a delusion to think that we control nature by manipulation. Our most ingenious manufacture is deftly canceled by nature when it falls out of alignment. What we think of today as an ecological crisis is but our awareness that our manufacture is presently out of alignment with nature. The somber fact is, *we* are what will be adjusted. And we have no say about it.

Whenever the authentic, the real and the natural, drifts from our life, it is quickly replaced by the inauthentic and artificial. When, for example, we lose contact with the ebb and flow of nature, with sunrise and sunset, with the seasons, we find ourselves prompted by calendars and clocks. These latter, like a virulent virus, soon take over our life. A person's life is first guided, then governed, and finally dominated by his calendar. He cannot do things that are right for him to do because he cannot "fit them in." He cannot tarry a while with a friend he chances upon, for his clockwatch will not permit this.

To take another example, when our sensibilities have been bombarded by the artificial, our own sense of proportion is diminished. We no longer discern between the beautiful and the grotesque. The true aesthetic of our personal environment soon gives place to knickknacks, then to plaster images, and finally to plastic everything.

Authentic religion is part of the living process of reality. It has nothing artificial or contrived about it. In a word, religion meets us in the actual mystery of the existence we already have, the mystery that we *are*. It enters the life that we are already living. It enters our world. We are not strangers in our world. The world is our present home. Religion is not an alien force that tries to snatch us from this world and place us in another one. Rather religion connects us to the truth of *this* world.

Therefore, the idea of *secular* is a false idea. There is nothing outside the mystery of existence itself. Nor are there two existences. There are not two realities, a sacred reality and a profane one. So the word *sacred* in the context of this book does not point to a reality that is distinct from the reality we already experience. *Sacred* does not depict some fake divinity, a *god*. For it is not true that we are down here and he (god) is up there. We are much closer to our happiness than many of us may suspect. "More inward to me than I am to myself [*Intimior mihi meipso*]," St. Augustine said of God. Everything is rightly thought of as sacred. The idea of *profane* or *worldly* does not describe our life in contrast to another, *sacred* life. *Worldly* refers to a wrong relationship to the world. A relationship in which we involve ourselves in the world in a dishonorable way because we ignore the mystery that is its source and context. There is no profane world outside the sacred. Profane is the desecration of the sacred, an abusive attitude toward life itself. Just as the common notion of *profanity* denotes an abuse of language.

Yet, to say that existence, including our entire world and our whole life, is sacred does not deny that there are some words and activities and things and places that have a special sacredness to them. Few Americans, for instance, can walk the Vietnam War Memorial in Washington D.C. and remain untouched by the personal intensity of the place and by the names of the dead inscribed there. Then, something of their own feeling remains when they depart. The part of their soul they leave behind intensifies the experience of those who follow. Thus do places gain personal potency.

To use an analogy, love between a man and a woman holds for their entire relationship. If marriage is more than a "sex-contract," as one spiritual author has chided, then it is a living personal relationship. It persists morning till night, then through the night and the morrow, and thereafter. It is a personal constant. Still, no one would question that in every marriage there are moments and places and words and gestures of intimacy that are special. Yet this specialness does not reduce the intimate nature of the partners' whole life together, the entire love-relationship that is their marriage.

In like manner, a true seeker lives her or his entire life in the spiritual mood. St. Paul captured this fact in his encouraging words, "Whatever you do, in word or deed, do it in the name of our

Lord Jesus Christ."[3] Jews of those days used the word *name* to refer to the very essence of something, especially of persons. Paul's words might be translated more accurately, if less literally, "Whatever you do, do it in the essence of Christ."

A communication of this same teaching, as simple as it is beautiful, is found in the conversations and letters of seventeenth-century Brother Lawrence, a humble cook and bottle-washer in a Carmelite monastery. In the brief collection of his letters and conversations, *The Practice of the Presence of God*, we read of Brother Lawrence's first full experience of the mystery. It worked a radical change in his life. The language and images are appropriately Christian, the only religious form Brother Lawrence knew. But his life in the Spirit had a universal quality: "He was eighteen at the time and still in the world. He told me that it all happened one winter day, as he was looking at a barren tree. Although the tree's leaves were indeed gone, he knew that they would soon reappear, followed by blossoms and then fruit. This gave him a profound impression of God's providence and power which never left him. Brother Lawrence still maintains that this impression detached him entirely from the world and gave him such a great love for God that it hasn't changed in all of the forty years he has been walking with Him."[4]   We should be cautious when we try to understand an awakening like that of Brother Lawrence. The experience that occasioned it is common. Who among us has not seen a barren tree in winter? And did we not know that the tree would come alive again in the spring? More-over, the words that describe his experience are simple. It is not hard to envision that occasion. It was an ordinary event, looked at externally.

But there is an indescribable difference between Brother Lawrence's experience as told and the awakening to mystery that graced it. A distant analogy might be found in the story, probably apocryphal, of Isaac Newton and the falling apple. This scientific genius, the story goes, was lying under an apple tree when an apple fell from it. Unlike most people, Newton's mind was attracted to this simple event: Why does an apple fall? People have witnessed things fall to the ground from time immemorial. But Newton brought a distinctive kind of genius to the experience of a freefall. Its *lawful* implications, in terms of gravity, added something immeasurably superior. The insight this experience occasioned in Newton's mind was of an intellectual order that was wholly different from the experience.

Brother Lawrence not only experienced the processes of

nature and enjoyed correct insight into the lawfulness of the mysterious power behind nature. That experience and insight occasioned in him an awakening to a new and permanent state of being. Mysteriously and uniquely, the sighting of a barren tree became for Brother Lawrence a sacramental occasion.

Despite the sacredness of every moment of our life, there are, I must agree, times and places and things and actions in the world that touch our religious need and impulse in a special way. In Christianity these special moments that recall to us and enliven our spiritual awareness have coalesced into formal occasions that are called sacrament, in the general meaning of this word as I suggested above. The essence of sacrament is its spiritually reconnecting power. All by itself sacrament is nothing in particular—just a barren tree. But when we consciously engage ourselves in it, sacrament becomes spiritual empowerment.

In another place I will speak positively of the sacramental radiance of authentic religion. Here, however, we must meet a prior requirement. There is much hocus pocus, pure fakery, under the banner of Christianity. We need not concern ourselves about the personalities who promote fakery, whatever their status or their intention. High status and good intentions do not, for example, enable us to make a silk purse out of a sow's ear, as an old saw goes. The reality has to be there.

The mystery of which we speak could be said to have magical qualities in one real sense of this word. But in this context I am using the word *magic* in its superstitious sense. It denotes the spurious games of magicians. Magicians show us something. But they pretend a power and an effectiveness that are not there. Such contrived magic is false. We deceive ourselves when we accept superstitious magic as authentic.

We human beings have a strong tendency to be superstitious. I have seen this quality in many others and have experienced it in myself. This tendency needs to be looked into. There seems to be some connection between our sense of the ultimate mystery behind everything and our vulnerability to superstition. We discern an intelligence behind the uncanny powers of nature. We perhaps anticipate that human consciousness, itself highly creative, should be able to associate with that great intelligence which moves all things. To this extent I think we are precisely correct.

But if we will avoid superstition we must ask what is required of us to associate with the power behind things in this profound sense? It is here that the line between superstition and spirituality can be drawn. Superstition rightly senses the mystery of things.

Experience points to an invisible source—the philosopher Schelling called this the "Ground of Being." Our feeling that we can relate to this source is likewise valid. However, serious work on our own conscious life is necessary for us to make this connection. Our failure to account for this work is what gives rise to superstition. Superstition is our tendency and attempt to relate to the spiritual realm through external or mechanical means, without the required inner effort on our part.

In Christianity the spiritual instruction and practice that mark a religious way of life became sparse over time, as I have already more than suggested. Other than in remote pockets, the Church was at times nearly void of spirituality. It has nevertheless carried the sacred word that speaks to every person's deepest aspiration— for we all long for happiness. Likewise it has borne a tradition of sacrament—sacred elements—that had arisen spontaneously when spiritual know-how still prevailed in the Church. No matter how formalized—mere formality—Word and Sacrament have often become, their basic structure remains, like a great cathedral, ready to be reempowered by persons alive in the Spirit.

As spiritual know-how waned, it was only to be expected that the larger populace turned to superstition. Sacrament as empowerment through the work of one's own conscious participation became, for the most part, lost. The majority of people looked upon sacrament as an external ritual that was supposed to produce mechanically a spiritual effect in their soul. The dubiously creative idea of indulgences extended this spiritual effect even to the souls of the dead. Their spiritual estate was thought to be altered independently of their own conscious participation.

This superstitious desecration of sacred symbols and rites was at times positively promoted by the entire ecclesiastical machine down to the lowest cleric. Through the sale of indulgences, sacrament as a kind of pseudo-spiritual mechanism became an important source of revenue. Payment for certain of these sacred mechanisms supported wars and whores, as well as sumptuous palaces and artworks, including cathedrals.

It should be mentioned here that, in reaction against the apparent foolishness of superstition and credulity, some people are liable to an inverse superstition. They become committed unbelievers, naysayers. They back away from the mystery and retreat into their own heads. They take their own paltry minds [and whose mind is not finally paltry in the face of existence itself?] as their single access to Truth.

Inverse superstition can take the form of scientism, which is really a pseudo-scientific stance. Scientism in this sense is the posture that we are to some significant degree knowers of reality. This is a presumption that is not true to the facts. The scientistic stance bypasses the need to inspect exactly what it means to be a knower of reality. This very complex matter concerning the ultimate nature of human knowledge is ignored by the scientism that naively implies that it has privileged access to knowledge. Authentic science, like authentic religion, will take account of its foundation. For like everything else, science cannot be stronger than its foundation. Devotees of *scientism* remain naive in their assumptions about the issue of foundations. They feel free to ignore the very thing that supports and validates the entire scientific enterprise.

In their naivete they do not cut as foolish a figure as did, say, the credulous peasants at the time of Luther. After listening to the Dominican friar Tetzel, these poor folk dropped their hard-earned coin into the coffer, at whose sound a soul of their dead loved one was promised to spring to heaven. Tetzel's meretricious but memorable jingle went:

> Sobald das Geld im Koffer klingt
> Die Seele aus dem Fegfeuer springt.
> (As soon as coin in coffer rings
> The soul out of purgatory springs.)

It is easy to ridicule the superstition of those who knew only this way to relate to the mystery of life, death, and a possible afterlife. But reverse superstition is equally naive about its own foundation. The fact is, there is no substitute for self-reflection on anyone's part. No one can afford to remain uncritical in respect to her or his own basic assumptions. Therefore, the wondrous complexities of theories and mathematical formulations are no more self-validating than the blandishments of fake but charismatic preachers. As mere statements about reality, scientific theories are just speculation. They become valid *to us* only when, in their very root, they become transparent to our consciousness.

Reverse superstition takes on other guises as well. It appears as secularism, a seemingly earth-based, no-nonsense realism. The secularist stance rightly rejects what it sees as superstitious. It does not, however, take full account of one's own place in the mystery of existence. Secularism is a stand that would keep us insulated from the most fundamental desire and impulse of our own heart.

Reverse superstition appears in a less sophisticated form as simply a global dislike and distrust of everything that goes under the banner of religion. It is not hard to understand why people surrender in this way. Yet this attitude, too, readily results in a day-to-day "unreflective life" in Socrates' sense. We do well to recall Socrates' view of it, that "the unreflective life is not worth living."

The spiritual way lies beyond both superstition and the naive reaction to it that I called reverse superstition. The spiritual way begins with the wonder that Aristotle said awakens the love of wisdom [philo-sophia] within us. In fact, there is but a single ultimate desire of the heart, one love of wisdom. Therefore, since they are both rooted in our heart, religion and philosophy are not two distinct things. But as philosophy developed historically in the West, it has retreated into the rational mind. In many schools philosophy has become almost identical to mere logic. For many, rational understanding has replaced wisdom as the intended goal of philosophy. For its part religion, as poorly as it has often performed, has remained in the full element of the total mystery that envelopes us. This mystery supports us even when we turn away from it with all our might. It pursues us like a "hound of heaven." In a word, we just cannot get away from our felt need for happiness.

It is thus that the spiritual way places a heavy demand upon us. It requires that we go beyond the superstitious attitude that would have our own transformation (salvation) happen outside us while we somehow receive the results as grace. The spiritual way will also prevent us from rejecting our necessary destiny just because we are offended at the mismanagement with which religious bodies have often shaped themselves in our cultural setting. The spiritual way imposes upon everyone to become responsible for his or her total existence. We must find our own way. A man stranded on an island, for example, will either find his way to safety or die. He must discover and use whatever means are at his disposal. Imminent death awaits him if he becomes sullen or petulant at the scanty helps he may chance upon. He is forced to inspect everything in his environment to see what might help. Clearly, ingenuity is required. He might well expect to make some mistakes. He may work with materials that finally prove ineffective. But if he is faithful to his need for a way to safety, he will likely find his way.

The person who has become possessed by the Great Question is in a similar circumstance. Unlike the stranded man who would finally die in any case, however, the self-aware know that our total human destiny is at stake. We have to become intelligent about it.

We must test the means to our safety. Childish credulity—the Jimmy experience—will not do. When we look around us at the spiritual means at our disposal, we must not forget the task at hand, our own transformation. We have to become insightful as to how any particular means relates to our real goal. Intelligence and insight can take us beyond superstitious gestures to the essence of those spiritual helps that belong to the Christian heritage.

A critical spirit does not throw anything away because of its mere appearance. In the case of the spiritual elements of Christianity, we cannot afford to let superstitious use and abuse hide the spiritual potential of sacred places, words, symbols, or rituals. It is wise to critique superstition by inspecting the actual condition in which superstition arises. But the mystery of existence, which occasions superstition in some persons, should not be avoided just because others approach it irresponsibly or superstitiously. Hence we are obliged to return with a critical but open mind to the spiritual elements that have evolved within the greater Christian tradition. The point is to understand them right so their spiritual power will be effective for us.

The first spiritual element is the Church itself, a community so bound up in the person and teaching of Jesus that St. Paul called it "The Body of Christ." This title was later expanded to "The Mystical Body of Christ." Rather than "mystical," I suggest the Church be recognized as "The Body of Christ immersed in the mystery of existence."

It is not enough to complain about the Christian Church gone worldly. If we are to make a clean break from a worldly Church, we must become discriminating: What is missing in the worldly Church that separates it from the mystery and makes it go magic?

There is one absolutely necessary condition for a spiritual community—any spiritual community—to maintain its integrity in this world. There must be a living teacher of authentically spiritual understanding who constantly recalls the community to its spiritual life and purpose. Great spiritual teachers of humankind appear from time to time to recall all of us to a sense of our purpose. Such a one was Jesus. They are the voice of the living spiritual reality, what the Christian tradition has always called "Holy Spirit" in general and "Spirit of Christ" in particular. The voice of the Holy Spirit comes into this world through a human voice, it is true. But it is the human voice of men and women of profound spiritual understanding and of an utterly transformed heart. It is never the mechanical voice of a spiritually mediocre person, or group of such persons, just because they have achieved power in a religious organization or Church.

The magical idea of possessing the Holy Spirit is contrary to every prophet or other spiritual authority. The Spirit is not and cannot be institutionalized, dispensed, or withheld by official decisions. In a word, She is not the backup of any worldly institution or form at all. This fact was unmistakably understood and clearly articulated by St. John and St. Paul. John's words can be pondered often and with great value: "The Spirit blows where she will."[5] St. Paul: "Where the Spirit is, there is freedom."[6] Paul goes so far as to say, "When you are under the Spirit you are no longer under the law."[7] The freedom that connects us to the Spirit of Christ presupposes a profound sacrifice on our part. The True Spirit is certainly not a "treasury of the merits of Christ" whose key is held by a pope. Such superstitious trading in forgiveness and indulgences—for money, no less—was indeed a rampant feature of medieval Christendom. But it was a false magic. Protestantism offered some corrective within Christianity for this attempt to control and govern the Holy Spirit.

Genuine spiritual teachers must criticize vigilantly the encroachments of self-centeredness into the politics of a spiritual community. Historically, the thrust of egos into the life of spiritual communities was mostly for power. The late Bishop Fulton Sheen, whose work often put him in the center of Church politics, remarked that "Ambition is the ecclesiastical lust." One among others, I suggest.

More importantly, a genuine teacher is one who is able to give effective spiritual instruction. Such instruction continuously enables and encourages the transformation of the lives of community members. Yet a teacher's words and influence must actually work a change in the lives of people. For without a spiritual way of life actually being lived, there is no spiritual community. If a community without authentic spiritual leadership nevertheless puts on the externals of spirituality, we are well advised to look for the traces of Cult, an encroachment of this world into our spiritual interest.

Jesus had the personal presence and instructive power to maintain a spiritual community. The early Church showed some fidelity to Jesus' teachings, so long as his memory remained strong. The memory and lingering influence of Jesus was able to remain strong because of the continuing teaching of his disciples, those who had been taught and influenced by him personally. However, Jesus' instruction and influence did not seem to flower fully in his disciples, and even less so in those whom the disciples taught. So the living gospel of Jesus became increasingly more a memory than a reality. This made for a severe defect in the Church. It meant that the revelation of the gospel was not in fact being transmitted heart to heart so as to remain a living revelation. As the living gospel weakened and the living memory of Jesus faded, the worldly, egoic brand of politics began to wax within the Church. In the absence of a strong spiritual discipline in the lives of practitioners, it could not have been otherwise.

This loss of the living presence of the gospel has been implicitly recognized. But the problem has not been addressed in these simple terms: The gospel exists only when it is *realized*, when it comes alive in the life of a person. For only a person can continue the process of revelation. Only Spirit-filled men and women, those who actively engage the presence and instruction of the Spirit, have any power to help others spiritually. The rest are pretenders at best, "blind leaders of the blind,"[8] or worse, "wolves in sheep's clothing,"[9] in Jesus' words. Too readily do we excuse the sorry state of the Church gone worldly: "We are only human." "God's power of forgiveness is greater than our ability to sin." "God is powerful despite our weakness," and so on. All of this is spiritually irresponsible. The blind have no right whatsoever to direct others along a path. Wolves have no right whatsoever to wear sheep's clothing. Who would dare to use the teaching of Jesus to defend the spiritually ignorant when they assume positions of spiritual authority?! Such, nevertheless, has been the historical fact.

A magical idea of Church arose because it was presumed that the revelation and influence of Jesus will prevail whether or not it is received personally, whether or not persons engage it in an ego-transcending way of life. It was presumed that Jesus left behind a heritage of grace and faith, of instruction and symbolic ritual, that can be distributed and received mechanically. According to this mechanical view, we simply put ourselves in place, go to church, take a sacrament, or whatever, and the spiritual thing becomes ours. I have argued above, and I will repeat it: This is not so. We grow spiritually only when we are truly transformed. Is this not too obvious to have to mention? Yet a false magical notion of Jesus' presence and instruction has assumed a strong place in the Christian tradition, both Protestant and Catholic.

We have already discussed the reinterpretation of Jesus' influence into a purported salvation that implies he did our work for us. "If we accept Christ as our savior we are saved." I observed this attitude at close quarters when I was a young child. A friend of my mother, a nice person long since dead, insisted that she was saved. She urged my mother to enjoy this condition by accepting Christ as her Savior too. I also remember my father's mock of this woman's preemptive strike on salvation: "Saved?! Hell, she ain't even dead yet!" The large matter of one's very existence resolved so easily? It was highly suspect to me even then.

Yet in less obvious ways many people create a similar ruse for themselves. It amounts to making a one-sided contract with god. The only hitch is, they do not receive back any signed copy from god. They only believe that god stands behind their vision of their salvation. Brooklyn Bridge for sale, anyone? Credulity, however innocent or well-intentioned, does not change reality. If you try to take possession of the Brooklyn Bridge with the title you purchased "in all good faith," you will understand exactly what I mean.

Salvation is nothing short of self-transcendence. "The grain of wheat must fall to the ground and die" before it bears fruit, in Jesus' words.[10] This spiritual matter is profound. It is barely mentionable here. It requires one's total interest and a willingness to learn and accomplish what this entails. To cite again Jesus' words: "The violent shall bear it away." Magical salvation is false. Aside from the indescribable influence, the sheer grace, that we can allow into ourselves from the great ones, who represent the Great One, no one *saves* us.

The Word of God, Revelation, the first and most basic communication and fruit of the Holy Spirit, is said to exist, magically somehow, elsewhere than in the human heart-mind. Superstitiously the Word of Revelation came to be conceived as a bag of truths which could be infallibly determined and then contained in irreformable dogmas of the Church. This deposit of faith is thought to be held in place and authenticated by not less than the Holy Spirit.

We must inspect this magical idea. To take an ordinary example, we know that the mere words of any book are, by themselves, nothing more than ink. Similarly with the voiced sounds that we also call words. Parrots can utter them. Likewise with word formulas, the abstract structure that we think of as language. The ink and the sounds and the formulas are only the garb of the real word. They are but servants or tools of the ideas they hope to mediate. In pondering the deep meaning of the sacred sense of Word as Revelation, as found in St. John's gospel, the Word that "became flesh," Goethe snubbed the conventional translation, "word." He considered translating it "thought," but realized that the real word is beyond thought. Indeed it is even beyond "power." Goethe finally translated it as action or "deed" [*Tat*]. "In the beginning was the Deed."[11] We know that ideas must and will be expressed differently in different human settings if they are to become effective in peoples' lives. The actual function of ordinary human words is so obvious that it is almost pedestrian. At best they are weak carriers of Revelation.

In real life we consider it frivolous to shift attention from the real issue of understanding to word games. We do refine our words and language with great care, just as a good worker in the trades takes proper care of his or her tools. But we deem it a mark of personal immaturity to get caught up in mere talk or language at the expense of meaning.

If even ordinary talk is basically about communication, what about spiritual talk? "The Word" in spiritual communication is called *Revelation*, as we know. But how can there be a *showing* except to our consciousness? Revelation itself can only occur as our understanding. Not merely intellectual understanding, but spiritual understanding or understanding of the heart—the understanding that makes a change in our experience of life [Goethe's *Tat* or deed]. Therefore, revelation is not a word-thing that can be possessed by a Church. It is not a "deposit of faith" as it has often been called in traditional Catholic theology. Revelation is not an event in the past. The only true Revelation is a literal showing, heart to heart, in the present living moment. Revelation taken as a mere assemblage of words is both a contradiction and a superstition. That such "bag of truths" revelation is possessed *infallibly* by any human being just by power of office—aside from spiritual understanding—is superstition that tampers with sound logic.

Sacraments as they have been narrowly defined in the Christian churches are often compromised, not to say trivialized, by a false magic. In the Catholic system, for example, sacraments are often reduced to a kind of mechanics: Perform this ritual, and you will get this effect. The promised effect is a spiritual goodie of some kind. Yet the Catholic theological definition of sacrament is sound: An outward sign (words and gestures and elements such as water and bread and wine) of an inward grace (or gift of the Real). There is surely much to be said about the spiritual influences made possible by the Spirit of Truth at work in the elements of this world. But before we can participate effectively in sacraments, we have to understand something about the connection between our inner and outer life, between consciousness and the world. It is the quality of our conscious attention to the

active influence of the Spirit that makes a sacrament real and
effective within us. Protestantism "protested" vehemently against
the mechanical notion of sacrament. Rightly so. However, with
Protestantism, to recall an old saying, "The baby went out with the
bathwater." Protestant theologian Tillich was firmly committed
to "the Protestant Principle" which insists that nothing less than
God should be accorded the absoluteness that is God's alone.
Nevertheless, with his customary insight Tillich made this important point:

> "The rejection of sacramental
> superstition was one of the
> main points in the Protestant
> protest. But historical
> Protestantism removed through
> its protest not only cultic
> superstition but also the
> *genuine meaning of ritual,*
> *and of the sacramental sym-*
> *bols* [emphasis mine]."[12]

I am in wholehearted agreement with Tillich on this.

Finally we should consider the magical approach to the name
of God. Contrary to nearly all theological presumption I assert
this: All talk about *god* that comes from *our thinking* is idle
speculation. The name of God can rightly be used only in
invocation and celebration. Consider it: What do our minds or our
tongues have to think or say about "god?" Is it not obvious that
every human idea or concept of God is a contradiction in terms?
Both idea and concept refer to products of our mind. Surely, no
idea of ours *is* God. So on what basis do our ideas refer to God?
In fact, when we think and talk about God—modern theology calls
it "god-talk"—we only fall into empty imaginings, delusions of
our own mentality. We remove ourselves from reality. The
figments of our mind become reality to us. This is why one ancient
sage wisely advised us, "Stop talking, stop thinking, and there is
nothing you will not understand."[13] Ironically, it is our mentality
itself that prevents our conscious realization of the mystery-
source of our existence.

The blindness of leaders and the superstitions of followers are
easy to spot from a distance, whether in time or space. When we
look back upon the human carnage of crusades, inquisitions, and
witchhunts that were commanded by popes in God's name, we are
rightly appalled. When we look across at young boys who, at the
directive of ayatollahs, rush headlong toward the slaughter of their

fellow human beings as well as to their own death, all for the supposed glory of Allah, we understandably wince. For it is all tragic nonsense that has pretended to promote, in absurd ways, our impulse toward happiness.

Here is the important issue: Why are we credulous? What is it in us that prompts us to sacrifice our intelligence to superstition? There is no doubt that we have regularly been abused by blind spiritual leaders. But what kind of blindness do we have that prompts us to follow them? It appears to me to be nothing less than our failure to be fully responsible for our existence exactly as it is. We do not attend to the mystery into which we were born nor do we pursue questions exactly as they arise in us. In short, we want an answer without doing the work of the question.

Thus we make ourselves easy prey to Jimmy as I have described this in the opening chapter. We choose to remain children in the face of our own felt condition, the pain in our heart. For what else do we have but the feeling-intelligence of our own heart-mind for our ultimate guide? I understand the Jimmy phenomenon quite well. I experienced it fully and have no regrets about it. For I was only a child, and Jimmy was for some reason a necessary episode in my life. In any case it was a fact. But I am no longer a child, and I have been willing to learn something from my Jimmy.

We have grown up in so many ways. We have learned not to be naive about the ways of the world. Those who remain naive tend to lose what they have. Most people take Jesus' advice to become "sly as a serpent"[14] regarding the ways of the world. But he meant it for our spiritual life where it seems very lacking. Thus "dovelike innocence" in spiritual matters is out of balance without the serpentine, discriminating wisdom that is required to assess and rightly use the sacred persons, words, places, and gestures that can assist us on the path we must tread to our destiny.

The most demanding discrimination must be applied to the political reality of the Church itself, the community that is to carry the Kingdom of God through human history. "Only the violent shall bear it away," we are told. Indeed, violence there must be, as the world has demonstrated great power in infiltrating the political reality of the Church. We might now turn our discriminating intelligence to contrast the politics of a truly spiritual community with the Church we know from history.

NOTES

1 *Acts* XVII, 28.
2 *Novum Organum*, Book I, 3.
3 *Colossians* III, 17.
4 Brother Lawrence, *The Practice of the Presence of God*, (Whitaker House, 1982), p. 7.
5 *John* III, 8.
6 *II Corinthians* III, 17.
7 *Galatians* V, 18.
8 *Luke* VI, 39.
9 *Matthew* VII, 15.
10 *John* XII, 24.
11 *Faust*, Part I, *"Studierzimmer"* [Faust's Study].
12 *Dynamics of Faith*, pp. 120-1.

XI

We must bear in mind that there is nothing more difficult and dangerous, or more doubtful of success, than an attempt to introduce a new order of things.

Niccolo Machiavelli

THE POLITICS OF SPIRITUAL EXISTENCE

I was not politically canny in 1961, the year I began classes in Canon Law at Rome's Gregorian University. Canon Law defines the inner legal structure of the Roman Catholic Church. Its somewhat rigid form traces back almost a thousand years.

I had come to Rome imbued with two great American principles. First was the principle of freedom: freedom of conscience, freedom of self-expression, and freedom of choice respecting religion. Equally ingrained in me was the principle of separation of church and state. Ideas and attitudes opposed to these basic principles seemed outmoded and oppressive. I had nevertheless long viewed Paul Blanshard's POAU [*Protestants and Other Americans United for the Separation of Church and State*] to be a benighted and paranoid anti-Catholic organization. At that time I had felt no need to read this thoughtful lawyer and journalist's well-argued book, *American Freedom and Catholic Power*. The book had already been thoroughly bashed by numerous Catholic writers of note as well as by numerous non-Catholics—who perhaps secretly feared the very power Blanshard documented in his highly researched work. My later reading of Blanshard convinced me that he respected American Catholics as citizens who are loyal to American principles of freedom. Blanshard even respected certain spiritual teachings of historical Catholicism, and acknowledged that, in her long history, the Catholic Church has accomplished considerable good in the world. Blanshard's argument had to do with the current worldly political power of the Catholic Church's hierarchy in America.[1] His concerns might be better appreciated by reading, for example, a critical biography of New York's famous Archbishop, the late Francis Cardinal

Spellman.[2]

A further element in my thinking at that time was this: It seemed to be a strain of unfettered ignorance in American Protestantism that, as late as 1960, this religious body still pondered whether a Catholic would be acceptable as president of the United States. Many Protestants seemed to question whether a Catholic could be other than a puppet for the pope. My own thinking was: What conceivable interest could the pope or any other Catholic Church leader have in garnering political power in America in this day and age! Particularly an interest in influencing American affairs or interfering with our freedoms!

My new study of Canon Law in theology school, therefore, had an unsettling effect on me. In this class I learned what was still, in 1961, the Catholic Church's official position regarding church-state relations. The position was simply this: The Roman Catholic Church, since it alone is the *true Church*, is to be the privileged religious body favored by every government. All other religious organizations, including Protestant Churches, should ideally be suppressed. At best they might be tolerated. The principle behind this practical matter was stated succinctly: "Error has no rights."

This doctrine was taught in Canon Law class in terms of *thesis-hypothesis*. The *thesis* describes the ideal situation: The Roman Catholic Church is the privileged religion supported by every government. The underlying reason is that the state, like everything else in life, is not an end in itself. It is only a means. The state exists to support our ultimate goal, which of course is our spiritual well-being. *Ergo*.

However, our Canon Law class did acknowledge that in pluralistic times such as ours this thesis cannot be made to prevail everywhere. Thus the practical matter, the *hypothesis*. In this context hypothesis means *in case that*. To wit, in case the Catholic Church is not able to prevail in some particular nation, then all religious bodies in that nation are to be treated equally. This was the hypothesis in the language of our Canon Law class. In the America of the fifties Paul Blanshard and his small POAU were not the only Americans suspicious of Catholic designs on American politics. Many Protestant church leaders were equally wary, if slightly less aggressive, about Catholic power in America. Let us now admit that they had their point.

The sheer genius and spiritual import of the American Constitution's clear separation of worldly politics from the spiritual realm was not to the liking of many Protestant churchmen either. In 1863, for example, representatives from eleven Protestant denominations formed the National Reform Association. It proclaimed "the nation's allegiance to Jesus Christ and its acceptance of the moral laws of the Christian religion, and so indicate that this is a Christian nation, and place all the Christian laws, institutions, and usages of our government on an undeniably legal basis in the fundamental law of the land."[3] This movement grew rapidly and its influence extended well into the twentieth century. Forrester Church sees in this movement the prototype of Jerry Falwell's Moral Majority. In our America of the 1990's we can add other self-styled "Christian" political influences as well.

Ironically many Protestant leaders who have been recently concerned about the political power of the Catholic Church do not hesitate to look upon America as a *Christian Nation* founded on Christian principles. How does the gigantic presence of this large Christian majority in America appear to Jews, to Muslims, to Buddhists, to Hindus, to small and powerless religious sects, or even to people with no outward religious affiliation at all? Are they all aliens in this great Christian Church called America? Our American Constitution insists not.

Even aside from that dangerous constitutional angle, the presumption that America is a Christian nation raises more basic questions in regard to Christianity itself: How did Christianity ever get from Jesus' "My kingdom is *not* of this world"[4] to a *Christian nation*? Exactly when and why did the Church reknit the clean break Jesus made between "what belongs to Caesar" and "what belongs to God?"[5] When, why, and how did the community of those committed to Jesus as their spiritual master transform itself from Jesus' spiritual kingdom to a Church that is to be supported by all civil governments to the exclusion, or mere tolerance, of every other religious body? Or to be effectively included as the centerpiece of American politics in spite of our Constitution? Was this a natural growth of what was in seed in Jesus' teaching? Or did the actual succession of events compromise his teaching? When the issue is put this starkly it becomes clear that Jesus' teaching was compromised. Quite beyond America we know of the vast array of worldly political parties that dare take the name "Christian." "Christian Democrat" names a major political force in many nations. This issue is complex. It concerns the history of Jesus' teaching as it was adapted by persons who obviously twisted it to serve purposes that were alien to it. And all in his name! To address this large, complex, and long-standing issue, we must break it down into more manageable elements.

We will begin by returning to the image of Jesus as the exceptional spiritual figure that he was. Jesus did enter the human world, and his spiritual influence here clearly outlived him. We must account for this in a way that pays attention to the kind of human world it is in which Jesus offered his teaching. This raises questions about worldly politics. What sort of thing is worldly politics? Here we once again broach the theme of Cult and Church which I have signalled prominently in this work. We must face the issue of how The Cult of This World may have worked its way into the politics of the spiritual community that gathered around Jesus. Did Jesus' teaching and influence suffer distortion when it became a worldly power—when it was brought into Caesar's realm, to use his own image? How did this happen? No one with the least knowledge of western history will dispute that Church leaders and the institutional Church itself were often worldly, crassly and embarrassingly so. At some point we must put the discriminating question: What would the politics of a spiritual community look like if it were purged of the ways of this world? If it were exorcised of the Cult?

JESUS AND THE SPIRIT OF CHRIST

While it is nigh impossible to trace a personal biography of Jesus' day-to-day life, it is equally impossible to deny the force of his personality in history as well as in his own time. In our day we are faced with the difficult task of extracting Jesus' spiritual teaching and of discerning his spirit out of a religious system that has been less than faithful to these.

After the death of Jesus his abiding influence was called "Holy Spirit" along with other descriptive terms. The title *Holy Spirit* effectively expresses the spirit-presence of God to the human world. Holy Spirit is also called "Spirit of Christ" to designate the continuing influence of Jesus. Spirit of Christ is the quintessence of the Christian heritage.

The language of the earliest Church, already seen in St. John's gospel, describes a great struggle between Spirit and world. It was symbolized as a battle between light and darkness. It was seen as a choice between freedom and bondage. This struggle became the pivotal issue of Christianity. It was the point where authentic religion struggled with the Trojan Horse, *the world*, as worldliness crept into the precincts of authentic Christianity. That is why I have identified it as the struggle between *The Church* and *The Cult of This World*. Perhaps this ambiguity will remain as long as there are both world and Church. An image created in Jesus' own words acknowledged that the "wheat and the tares"[6] will grow together until they are separated at the end. This is the situation Pope John confronted by adopting the traditional Protestant phrase, *Ecclesia Semper Reformanda*—the Church *always* to be reformed.

This phrase means that Church reform is always in order. The *radical* reform I propose recommends only that we quit our half-measures and go to the *root* problem. In order to probe the root problem in the context of the social nature of the Christian community, I pose this question: When and how did worldly politics infiltrate the spiritual community of Jesus' devotees? To begin to answer this question we must have a brief look at the nature of human politics.

POLITICS

Every situation that involves more than one person is political. A spiritual community is no exception. Politics in this broad sense embraces all interactions among human beings. It includes all social relations. We can define politics in this broad sense as "the art of structuring our communal life in a way that enables and enhances human life on earth." We must get beyond the notion that politics is always associated with government. Although government leadership is an important facet of human politics, it is by no means the whole of it. Every single time we associate with one another some kind of politics is in formation. This is not a criticism; this is our nature. Politics is not a bad word. It simply points out the play of personal power in all human interrelationships.

When we make laws to regulate our socio-political ways, we should not mislead ourselves about what is cause and what is effect. Our politics—how we in fact relate to one another—comes first; laws and other norms only reflect, with more or less accuracy, the ways by which we already interact with one another. Laws may reflect our political ways somewhat adequately. More often the reflection is rough or vague. Sometimes certain laws of a society do not reflect the real interactions at all. In America, for example, many state laws regarding sexual activity could, if prosecuted, land a majority of adult citizens in jail. A society can get crazy when fools try to execute laws that are out of sync with the established ways. One might well consider prohibition in this context. For social systems never work backwards: laws never establish our ways. Personal politics, not laws, prevail in our interrelationships. This is just the way it is. It could not be otherwise because we are alive and laws are inert. An important reality follows from this fact: Laws and related social structures can never be better or more effective than the human character of the people who formulate and try to live by them.

Politics pertains only to our association with and responsibility toward others. Turned to ourselves, to our inner, spiritual life, we are apolitical. Jesus spoke directly to our spiritual, apolitical nature. Although his fundamental myth spoke of "the Kingdom of God," Jesus always separated this kingdom from worldly politics: "My kingdom is not of this world." In a word, spiritual reality is like a kingdom in some sense—for it is not an aggrandizement of the individual. But this realm is not a humanly political one. It is not "of this world."

Nevertheless, the community of Jesus' disciples had to take shape in this world. This community *incarnated* and took on a worldly body, the Church. This necessarily presumes a human political cast. However, just to take shape in the world does not of itself entail a compromise of the spiritual purpose of the Church. For there is nothing intrinsically bad about the world. Neither is there anything intrinsically bad about the politics of human life. And there is nothing intrinsically bad or compromising about the social interactions, the politics, among a community of persons when their purpose remains spiritual. St. Paul captured in an apt metaphor the political dimension of the early Christian community when their central purpose remained spiritual. He spoke of this Church as the "Body of Christ."[7] Yet the worldly dimension of the Church places upon her the same spiritual struggle that faces each person: Will you *serve* God or world [Mammon]? Addressed to today's Christian community it might read: Will you be Church or Cult? This struggle is central to spiritual life, both of each person and of a community.

We still must consider the essential difference between worldly politics and the politics of a spiritual community. Worldly politics has no choice but to take us as we are and to do what is necessary to structure social life among people who remain radically self-centered or egoic. It has to mediate conflicting (egoic) interests. Our self-centered condition is known. It prompted Freud's harsh observation that "...every individual is virtually an enemy of civilization."[8] That is, society tends to suppress the natural instinctual life of the individual. In short, our self-centered life in the world involves estrangement. So when a person of spiritual maturity, one who has passed to a notable extent beyond the egoic struggle, graces worldly politics, yes, both individual and social life is made better for many. People witness a form of life that goes beyond the estrangement of communal self-centeredness. To cite a modest example, in the nineteen-fifties the civilized world felt briefly the political presence of Dag Hammarskjoeld. This kind of person tends to relieve us, however slightly and temporarily, of our self-centered conflicts. But with the death of that personality, things pull back quickly to the egoic power struggle. For the nobility of mature human character cannot be institutionalized.

A genuine spiritual community, however, is not built on our self-centeredness. On the contrary, according to its very purpose a spiritual community continuously undermines the force of our egos, our self-centeredness. The essence of a spiritual community is that it relates its members to one another non-egoically. Nothing says that we *cannot* relate to one another in a way that goes beyond our self-centeredness. The notion of love implies as much. So there is nothing that necessarily prevents a spiritual community from flourishing as an institution in this world. For no matter how we are or feel, we definitely appreciate love.

When we look to the original Christian community, it seems that it was governed by the spiritual principle. Jesus' final instructions were directed at the community life of his followers: "This is my commandment: love one another as I have loved you."[9] He obviously assumed that there is no intrinsic conflict between living as a genuine person [love] and living in society. If his disciples would live by his teaching, then a spiritual community would flourish in the larger world without losing its integrity. It is only in such a community that Jesus' promise makes sense: "Where two or three come together in my name, I am among them."[10]

The Acts of the Apostles suggests that it actually happened this way in the earliest days of the Church: "They devoted themselves to the apostles' instruction and the communal life, to the breaking of bread and the prayers...Those who believed shared all things in common; they would sell their property and goods, dividing everything on the basis of each one's need."[11] *A Letter to Diognetus* [possibly the tutor of Marcus Aurelius], found in the body of early Christian writings, describes the life of the Christian community in words that remind us of the vision expressed in *Acts*. The writer poses the question, "What is the character of the love that links them [Christians] one with another?" He answers his question: "They share in all duties like citizens and suffer all hardships like strangers...In the flesh as they are, they do not live according to the flesh. They dwell on earth, but they are citizens of heaven. They obey the laws that men make, but their lives are better than the laws. They love all men, but are persecuted by all."

If these are the visible qualities of the politics of spiritual existence, then we must acknowledge that another form of politics has overtaken Christianity at large, although not necessarily every single community within it. How Jesus' teaching presence became so distorted is not easy to understand. Yet I feel we can find the key to this distorting process and examine it in its broad contours.

THE WANING OF SPIRITUAL PRACTICE

To put the issue in personal terms, do you feel that you have access to a spiritually profound way of life? A life that leads to deep inner peace and happiness? The evidence suggests not. I think we have a right to ask if our spiritual leaders are giving us the spiritual substance we need. What is the quality of instruction that the ordinary run of spiritual leaders gives us? Of course there have always existed spiritually outstanding persons at every level, from the local minister or nun or priest or deacon to bishops and higher church officials. Even a pope, in the case of John XXIII. But my experience tells me that these tend to be more the exception than the norm.

We have already discussed the necessary condition for a community that is founded in wisdom to maintain its integrity in this world. To review the argument briefly in the present context, wisdom cannot persist as mere words. Words are easily twisted by the unwise to suit their own purposes. How often I have heard the words of Jesus uttered by ignorant preachers to support preposterous views. To remain alive wisdom must incarnate in the flesh and blood and mind and heart of a teacher of authentically spiritual understanding. Only such a teacher can recall a community to its spiritual life and purpose. She or he must stay vigilant over the encroachments of self-centeredness into community politics. Even more importantly, this teacher must be able to give spiritual instruction that continuously fosters the transformation of the lives of the members. And his or her teaching and influence must actually work a change in the lives of others. Without this personal accomplishment of a spiritual way of life, a way that is actually lived by community members, there is no genuine spiritual community.

In the place of effective spiritual instruction we too often hear Christian leaders preach in the mood of condemnation. Their occasional pious platitudes are almost a relief. On Sunday mornings spiritually bereft and hungry multitudes tune into their TV evangelists to be fed an insipid christ-crispies. Recently this TV brand of lazy-man's religion has begun to wane as the disparity between word and deed among so many of these preachers, especially in monetary and sexual matters, has caught the public's attention.

I do not say this to disparage religious leaders and preachers. Sheer charlatanry is not universal among them. It could be that even a good number of them believe what they are saying, at least mentally. But too often they themselves have not been nurtured in a truly spiritual environment. It is likely that many of them have not realized just how shortchanged they are in the matter of spiritual instruction. I think spiritual leaders are often unaware of a spirituality that goes much beyond good behavior. Not even to know that such spirituality exists, much less understand the demands of an effective spiritual discipline. The majority of today's spiritual leaders, from Protestant or Catholic TV Evangelist to pope, seem limited to a mediocre belief-system and an attempt to lead a decent life. Even if they feel their particular system is true, it is still not spiritually challenging to a public that, as I see it, is becoming increasingly needful of spiritual depth. By this I mean that increasing numbers of people are beginning to question whether chronic dissatisfaction is the necessary truth of our life.

Referring to this sad condition, I have spoken of the absence of a commonly accessible spiritual practice, which is, ironically, a discipline of happiness. I say this because only actual practice counts spiritually. Only through spiritual practice can growth toward our desired happiness occur. Nothing less than actually living a spiritual way of life validates spiritual ideas (beliefs) or talk or writings or Church structures, including even the physical buildings. Apart from a transforming practice, it is all Cult.

I am convinced that the key to understanding the deformation of Christianity is its failure to maintain the teaching-presence of Christ as the way by which to live life. Dogma became the *rigor mortis* of Jesus' life-giving and life-transforming teachings. Jesus himself was misinterpreted as one who undertook and fulfilled our spiritual responsibility. Our simple task, in this view, is to find out how to coattail Jesus through the pearly gates and get saved.

How contrary this chimera is to Jesus' own instruction!

Yet, it is not that at some point Christians chose to abandon a spiritual way of life. No one would be so foolish. It seems that the heart of a spiritual tradition becomes deadened another way. A valid spiritual tradition wanes when it is not made real in the lives of enough people through the engagement of practice. What would become of our scientific heritage if only a very few persons mastered the various sciences? Surely science as we know it would be lost. The books might remain. But who could read them and know what they are saying? Oh, occasionally a genius might pick up a book, say of higher mathematics or physics, and it might make sense to her or to him. But unless that genius had the ability to turn the tide, to attract and teach students who could understand, and thus return society itself back to its scientific heritage, the tradition of science would remain essentially lost.

It seems that something like this has happened within Christianity. The teaching-presence of Jesus was not put into practice by enough people to keep the authentic tradition fully alive. Without blaming, we must acknowledge that the heart-to-heart transmission of revelation, with a continuing transformation of persons, began to decline early in Church life. Mere words and ideas increasingly replaced deeds and a transformed heart as the Christian ideal. Words and ideas became *the faith*, as has already been discussed at some length. We have further considered how the dogmatic attitude was a distortion of spiritual doctrine. However, dogma not only marked the failure of spiritual instruction. It also came to serve an insidious function within the Church.

So at this point we must explore the corruption of the politics of the Christian spiritual community on two fronts. First we will inspect the political role that dogma came to assume in the Church. Then we can examine briefly the process of deformation as the interpersonal structure of the Church took on first the garb, and then the very essence, of worldly politics.

THE POLITICAL DISTORTION
OF JESUS' TEACHING

Corruption has its own laws. Corruption is not only the loss of something. It is also the creation of something else. To use an ordinary example, little bugs and vermin and bacteria get busy and create a whole new enterprise out of larger living bodies when they die. The general laws of corruption apply also to the corruption of Jesus' living instruction when it succumbed to the *rigor mortis* of dogma. There was a pivotal moment between the message and power of the Gospel and the mentalized abstractions of Christian philosophy. This moment lies sometime between the Gospel of St. John and early Church Fathers.

By the fourth century even sanctity came to be identified more in terms of a person's thoughts rather than of her or his personal transformation. A single example of this can help show what I mean. John Chrysostom is considered a *saint* of the early Church. The name Chrysostom means "golden mouth." It was a title bestowed upon John because of his preaching eloquence. John was indeed learned in Scripture and theological issues. But just what did this man have to say? Among other things, this: "I hate the Jews! I hate the Jews! God hates the Jews!"[12] In a public sermon, no less. Is sanctity compatible with hatred, hatred of an entire people? Can sound theological understanding ascribe hatred of Jews to God? Especially since God is a Jew, literally, according to the traditional Christian dogma of the Incarnation which no competent dogmatic theologian will contest.

Discounting John's theological mistake, can genuine spiritual understanding assign hatred to God in any sense? John Chrysostom was, perhaps, a knowledgeable theologian. But he was also a spiritual ancestor of Adolf Hitler. A saint he was not! Nor was he a man of even mediocre spiritual understanding, if we think of this in terms of the heart-mind and not only of the rational mind. For only an absence of spiritual vision could ascribe to God hatred of an entire people. Nevertheless, mesmerized by his Golden Mouth, people proclaimed John a saint. For our part, we might separate true sanctity from mere intellectual accomplishment and ponder the dogmatic attitude itself, especially when witnessed in people who are blind to the state of their own heart. What does dogmatizing really amount to?

Dogma, in fact, came to serve a worldly political function in the Church, whether this was consciously intended or not. There certainly were times when it was consciously intended, we will see. The political nature of dogma can be observed by looking carefully at four ways in which dogma has functioned. I will first state these four ways; then we can examine them one by one.

The political use of dogma is first noted in this: the Christian dogmatic belief-system was described in terms of *unity* rather than truth. We will see how the ideal of unity describes a political function. The second aspect to consider is how the *intrinsic* content of dogmas became relatively unimportant as the demand for members to commit themselves to dogma was increasingly emphasized. Thirdly we will look at the role of *civil authority* in the creation of dogmas. Emperors called and approved Church councils to clarify doctrinal issues and implemented the dogmatic decisions of these councils. This civil interference began with the Emperor Constantine, despite the fact that Constantine had no interest at all in dogma as such. Fourthly and finally, we must review the blatant *abuse of dogma* by popes. This will entail some discussion of papal power and Church life in general. We will finally come to review the naked aggression of Pope Pius IX, who in the nineteenth century clearly used dogma to secure his own political position and power. The spirit of Pius's disastrous reign reaches into our own time.

DOGMA AS THE PRINCIPLE OF
POLITICAL UNITY

Careful inspection reveals that unity rather than truth became the central purpose for defining something as a dogma. *Una fides* ["one faith," *i.e.* belief-system], even became the hallmark of the Church as an institution. The criterion of dogmatic truth was given a classical definition in the fifth century by St. Vincent of Lerins: "Moreover, in the Catholic Church itself all possible care should be taken that we hold that faith which has been believed everywhere, always, and by everyone." St. Vincent's phraseology for identifying the true faith [belief-system] became this classical formula: *quod ubique, quod semper, quod ab omnibus* ["which everywhere, which always, which by everyone"].[13] Looked at logically, this formula talks about unity rather than truth.[14] A condition of the truth of dogma was its power to create unity.

What does unity in thinking imply? What does it do in our life? Whatever else, unity of mind unquestionably serves a political function. It is the first rule of social order. That is why creating unity of thought is the ordinary politician's first order of business. Rightly so. For without the social order that comes from shared views, human communal life could barely exist in the world. Social systems (whether economic, educational, medical, *etc.*) are primarily accountable for their political significance, how they can be reconciled with the common vision. This means they must fit into the social order that is created and governed by politics.

Great leaders have always implicitly recognized the fact that unity of mind underlies social and political order. This political use of ideas even has its own name, ideology. Our tendency is to disrespect the notion of ideology, because the very word suggests that truth is subservient to political goals. But we would do well to note that ideology has replaced brute physical strength in bringing order to society. In democratic societies, it is true, voters are pandered with appealing ideas only to get their votes. Today even ordinary people increasingly feel manipulated when they realize that truth has almost nothing to do with political campaign strategies and speeches. But they might console themselves by reflecting on this question: Is it preferable to be manipulated or shot? Strangely, somehow, democracy seems to work. Ideology is what creates the group identity. Anyone who does not yet see how ideology promotes social order ought to observe a leader galvanize a crowd and watch how an idea fuses the energies of the crowd into a single force. Although it does not have to do with truth, I have no quarrel with political ideology. While it is just another game with winners and losers, it is less murderous than the politics of brute physical strength. This is perhaps the best that worldly politics has to offer. The question I pose is this: Is this kind of unity the same as the communion Jesus envisioned in his disciples? "Where two or three come together in my name I am there in their midst."[15] "This is my commandment, that you should love one another as I have loved you."[16]

To put it another way, is belief equal to love as the binding force of Christians? Hardly. Do today's Christian communities evince a unity based on love as described by Jesus? Or are they held together by a common commitment to a system of beliefs? The latter, so it seems. Yet is this not more a worldly politics than a politics that is based on Jesus' instruction?

The power of religious ideas and beliefs have been employed in many cultures for worldly political purposes. They were made society's underlying cohesive force, its ideology. For a religious vision offers a bigger-than-life meaning to our life and therefore to society's ways. It was not incidental to their political function, for example, that kings and emperors have been held to be divine. This is true in modern as well as ancient times. It was lately the case with the Japanese emperor Hirohito. It has held recently also in China, where the emperor was "The Son of Heaven." It was because of the connection of religious vision to political cohesiveness that Socrates was executed. His teaching was thought to run counter to the religious ideology that held the state together. Many early Christians were persecuted at various times and places because their views seemed to be a political threat. The role of a religious vision as the cohesive political force in the life of nations is a fact currently evident in Islamic countries. Here we are asking whether this use of spiritual doctrine is a function of the True Church or whether it is an instance of Cult.

A second characteristic of ideology must be noted: It is not the *content* of an idea that makes it a politically binding force. The *political* force of ideology is that it is *held* in unison. When spiritual doctrine becomes dogma or ideology, this means that the doctrine itself is not intrinsically important. The important matter is that the idea be *held* firmly and in common. Regarding dogma, the main emphasis has been, historically, on consent rather than understanding. This becomes obvious by a careful look at the phenomenon called heresy.

HERESY

The word *heresy* refers to an idea of underlings that deviates from the established ideology enforced by persons in authority. To reflect on the history of heresy in the Church is to turn to an ancient and frightful matter. Saints were jailed and killed at the behest of Church authorities because heresy [supposedly erroneous ideas] was imputed to them. Scientists were arrested and effectively stifled by these same authorities due to their imputed heresy. In our own day, we will see, decent men and women are deprived of their work and livelihood—they are silenced by Church authorities—because they appear to deviate from the party line. The irony is, heresy has nothing at all to do with *spiritual* digression or wantonness. In fact the spiritual state of those who have been murdered, jailed, or otherwise stifled for their views has almost invariably been morally superior to that of their church-authority tormentors. The same arguably holds today as well.

In respect to the early Church Justo L. Gonzales has argued, "Soon the impact of the heresies led Christians to join the ideas of apostolic succession and of monarchical episcopacy, and thus began the emphasis on the uninterrupted chain of bishops who unite the present Church with apostolic times."[17] This practical weaving together of dogma and Church structure was a political development aimed at Church unity that was not present in the primitive Church, in which "little emphasis was placed on hierarchy, authority and orthodoxy. There was no papacy and no central bureaucracy."18

The full flowering of ideology that arose in the Christian Church came to be called *orthodoxy* [straight-thinking]. Its contrary, wrong ideology, was known as *heterodoxy* [divergent-thinking]. Interestingly, heterodox or wrong thinking by itself is not yet formal heresy. Heterodoxy in the church becomes heresy only when the idea is held willfully after its presumed error has been pointed out.

Neither the spiritual quality of heretics' lives nor their sincerity belongs to the issue of heresy. Persons were condemned and cut off from the community—excommunicated or jailed or killed— simply because of the ideas they harbored in their minds. More precisely, because they *held* to their ideas when they were commanded to think otherwise. This is how Christian life itself was put in service of ideas. Imagine people being executed, not for evil deeds, but because of ideas they considered true. The fact is, the popes and other Church authorities who condemned these people were often among the most debauched human beings ever to have walked the earth. The condemned, on the other hand, are now often reckoned our saints and profound spiritual teachers. In the Catholic Church itself think of Meister Eckhart and of St. John of the Cross. Or at least men and women whose insights have been validated by history. Consider Galileo.

A look into heresy shows how doctrine becomes political when it is taken as dogma rather than as spiritual instruction: If you presumably hold to a wrong (heterodox) understanding of a doctrine, but you do not recognize your supposed error, your faith and good-standing remain intact. In theological language, your wrong-thinking (heterodoxy) is only *material* heresy, not full-fledged or *formal* heresy. It becomes formal heresy only if you realize that you are in conflict with official Church teaching and still insist on holding to your views. On the face of it, this might look fair enough. Why should you be held accountable for a mistake you do not even realize, much less insist upon? In daily life we indeed excuse one another for our unintended mistakes, especially when we are not adamant about them.

But I propose that our existence runs much deeper than this. We do not exist in life like children, whom we do tend to excuse for mistakes that come from their inexperience. The great laws of existence do not excuse even children. If children fall off a cliff, for example, they will be hurt or even die. Nor do the great laws of existence excuse us because of our ignorance or good intentions. On the contrary, the lawfulness of existence puts the demand of reality upon us. Even if we are only factually wrong, we still pay the consequences. If, for example, you are mistakenly convinced that the ice on the lake is thick and solid, you drown anyway. Or again, if you do not know you are allergic to a particular medicine, you react anyway, maybe even die. If you had not noticed the defect in your tire, you crash anyway. If you misread a map, you miss your destination. The laws of existence simply do not indulge our carelessness or even our simple ignorance. Not even our good intentions. Maintaining our life and well-being requires a lot from us, and we are given no choice about it.

Spiritual doctrine belongs among the great laws of existence. In fact, spiritual teaching outlines for us the Great Law as it pertains to our purpose and destiny. This Great Law is the literal meaning of the Jewish *Torah* and of the Hindu and Buddhist *Dharma*. I argue that it is the essential, if not literal, meaning of the Christian *Gospel*. This means, genuine spiritual teaching counts *intrinsically*. If you do not get it right, you get it wrong. And if you are wrong in your spiritual understanding, you will not accomplish the spiritual work. It might seem burdensome to us that we have to have some correct understanding of our life if we are to fulfill its purpose. We might be tempted to swing back to the old thinking: "As long as my heart's in the right place..." But in spiritual terms this is wrong thinking. If your heart were already "in the right place," you would neither need nor be involved in spiritual instruction. You would already have fulfilled everything that spiritual instruction promotes.

It demeans the teaching work of such a one as Jesus to think that it does not have *intrinsic significance*—that if you somehow commit yourself to the teaching, even if you do not understand it or if you understand it wrong, you will nevertheless be spiritually secure. This amounts to consummate ignorance concerning spiritual teaching itself. Spiritual instruction is not arbitrary, as if a correct understanding of it is not particularly important. Spiritual instruction is to make a difference in the orientation and conduct of our life. Merely joining the right church and committing ourselves to its doctrine does not save us or bring us to spiritual wholeness any more than getting into a good college makes us knowledgeable. We are not automatic. We ourselves must engage the process. This is the spiritual way of life, and spiritual instruction shows us how. A spiritual way of life cannot mature without proper instruction rightly understood. Getting the instruction straight—this is genuine orthodoxy, which brooks no excuses—is a serious matter that each of us must finally achieve for herself or himself. It is, after all, our own movement toward our own destiny that is at stake. Real heresy—and it can be a useful word—is a practical rather than intellectual error. When doctrine is understood as instruction rather than merely an intellectual view, then the distortion of doctrinal instruction is serious indeed. It misdirects us and leads us down a faulty path—or, worse yet, it excuses us from the demands of the Gospel. This is a heresy that I hear regularly expounded by many so-called TV Evangelists.

DOGMA AND WORLDLY POLIICS

Lest this analysis of the political function of dogma seems overdrawn we will turn to the third matter, civil interest in dogmatic orthodoxy. Civil interests became heavily involved in Church dogma already with the Roman Emperor Constantine. H. G. Wells identified Constantine as "That very great political genius" who "...was the first to apprehend and to attempt to use this possibility [*i.e.* Christianity's "systematic instruction of great masses of people"] for the preservation and moral knitting-together of the world community over which he ruled."[19]

The reign of Constantine the Great (306-337 a.d.) was a pivotal moment for the Christian Church. While Constantine's leadership naturally involved the total complex of the western history of his time, our interest concerns his impact on the Christian Church. Its dogma in particular. The ordinary theology student who studies history perhaps views Constantine as some kind of savior and promoter of Christianity. Spiritual discrimination may recommend otherwise.

In late 312 a.d. Constantine became the Roman Emperor of the West after defeating Maxentius, being guided by a vision of the Christian sign of the cross, so he insisted. Constantine is credited with the Empire's full tolerance of Christianity through his famous *Edict of Milan*. Constantine himself became only very tenuously a Christian, however. He refused to get baptized until the end of his life because killing fellow human beings was so integral to his life's work. And in those days the Church still considered killing others to be contrary to the teaching of Jesus. Moreover, Constantine was far from nice. He fit easily into the brutish style of worldly politics that prevailed in those days and since. We can perhaps allow that soldiers kill people they are told are enemies. But Constantine murdered also his wife, his son, his nephew, his brother-in-law, and many others. Most of these murders happened long after he won the crucial battle against Maxentius at Milvian Bridge.

It is pointless to try to judge the relative sincerity of historical personalities like Constantine. I do not know what Constantine really thought of Christian teaching. But it is clear that, while he did enable the Church to emerge from the underground, at the same time he used the Church to his own political advantage. Whether true love played any part in this marriage of Empire and Church, it was surely one of considerable convenience for Constantine. And of course it brought the Church right into the politics of this world. Through Constantine the Church was born as a powerful worldly force and, for many Protestants, the time of "the fall of the Church."[20]

The Church in fact proved to be a uniting factor in Constantine's Empire. For when Constantine for all practical purposes abandoned the West by transferring the seat of his empire to Byzantium [now Istanbul] in 330, the bishop of Rome [now pope] became the political leader in the West by default. The Roman bishop, however, remained a kind of vassal of the emperor for many centuries, until strong popes were able to shift the balance of power toward the papacy in the later Middle Ages. Detailing this sad story is the work of historians of western civilization. The enormous consequence for Christianity was that this marriage of caesar to god turned Jesus' community into an established Christendom. When the same merger occurred a short time later in Constantine's new seat of power, the state of course maintained political ascendancy. Historians came to call this untoward submergence of the Church into the state *caesaro-papism*. The political intrigue begotten of this union of church and state is the source of the special, labyrinthine connotation of the word *byzantine*.

Out of the complex entanglement of Church with worldly life, the point to be made here concerns the political role of religious dogma in this story. The issue concerns the emperor's dominating influence in doctrinal controversies. The first notable controversy concerned a North African bishop who had been ordained by a sinner. Is a sacramental rite effective, does it really happen, if it is performed by a sinner? Disunity among Christians about this matter resulted in civic unrest. Constantine responded with an imperial policy. He called a small council or synod to decide the issue. Ultimately Constantine closed the Churches of those who dissented from the synod's decision.

A short time later, after Constantine had achieved full dominion also of the East, a far greater doctrinal issue arose concerning the nature of Christ. It came to be known as the *Arian Heresy*, named for its principal exponent Arius. Constantine first sent his ecclesiastical advisor to counsel peace and to "drop this unprofitable question." When it became clear that the parties were too involved to drop the issue, Constantine called a council of the entire Church, the First Ecumenical Council of Nicea. Constantine himself, although not even baptized and presumably without intrinsic interest in an "unprofitable question," nevertheless attended the council. It is true that religiously interested personalities haggled about dogma in these council sessions. This made dogma take on the appearance of being more religious than political. But we must look behind those scenes where bishops punched one another on the Council floor as each proclaimed some truth—or its opposite—to be Jesus' teaching and God's revelation. Why were such struggles happening in the first place? What was really going on? Looking behind the fray to the source, we find Constantine's interest, not in the "unprofitable question" itself, but in establishing a unity of mind that would restore harmony to his empire. It was Constantine who finally effected the adoption of the Nicene statement of faith. The two bishops who refused to sign this "united expression of the faith," together with the presbyter Arius, were banished—by Constantine.

The statement of belief formulated by this Council is the *Nicene Creed*, which is recited regularly in Christian Churches. Its chief engineer was Constantine who did not have the least understanding of the Creed's philosophical subtlety. But the content of the Creed, not to speak of its subtlety, did not interest him. After all, the whole issue concerned an "unprofitable question." What was important to Constantine was to have a universally accepted ideology that would return unity to the Church and, through it, to the Empire. Calling together and approving church councils, thus indirectly influencing even dogmas and beliefs, became a political role of the Emperor that lasted for many centuries. Over a thousand years later this kind of relationship manifested again when the princedoms of Germany became either Protestant or Catholic dependent upon the whim of the local ruler. *Cuius regio, eius religio* was the coined expression: "Whoever rules the region determines the religion." Is it possible to reconcile spiritual teaching as *truth* with these political whimsies? Ah, Orthodoxy!

RAW PAPAL ABUSE

The emperor, then, used the Church and religious ideology to undergird the political unity of his realm. But the popes raised the political potential of dogma to a higher level. They established their immense power base by controlling the minds, and through this the hearts and the very actions, of the Christian people. A summary review of any accepted manual of western history confirms this. In these pages I can cite only some of the more outrageous presumptions and actions that established and enhanced the tremendous power of the central headquarters that today resides, albeit attenuated, in the Vatican.

It began early, quite before Constantine. The earliest Christians came mainly from the poorer class. However, their Church-centered way of life, together with contributions of certain wealthier members, began to create communal wealth. While money is necessary just to stay alive in this world, it is also a very powerful worldly force. It is the basic meaning of the word *mammon*. We should remember Jesus' warning: You cannot serve both God and mammon. The power of money cannot be kept in tow in a spiritual community unless the community stays strongly centered on its spiritual purpose.

Other than in particular religious groups such as the Desert Fathers, the spiritual interest in early Christianity did not remain at the center of Church life. Increasing wealth drew attention to the many possibilities of wealth: Land and churches and other buildings, all for the kingdom of god, of course. There naturally arose the need to administer all this property, no small task. The growth of bureaucracy absorbed more and more of the attention of the overseer, the meaning of the word *bishop*. Human nature being what it is, overseeing worldly affairs brought an additional human factor into the picture. In sheer worldly terms, those with the position to oversee wealth necessarily enjoy power and prestige. Although worldly power and prestige have no spiritual value, people are drawn to them. Joined to wealth, power and prestige entice the spiritually immature away from every spiritual interest. Which is basically what happened.

No one decided at some point to twist the inner spiritual interest to outer worldly concerns. Such a thing happens more subtly, like the fading of consciousness. Before you know it you are asleep in a world of dreams. To remain a true revelation, I have insisted, the gospel must be realized. It must come alive in the life of persons, for only persons can continue the process of revelation. Yet the strength of Jesus' character and the fact of his gospel gave rise to the presumption that, since he cannot fail, Jesus must have set up a system that would carry on his rich spiritual heritage. Through this system Jesus' legacy of grace and faith, and instruction and ritual, are supposedly distributed and received mechanically, independently of the actual spiritual realization of persons. Thus when the belief in the reality of Christ and his Church met with a decline in applying his teaching to the living of life, undue emphasis was placed on the mechanical and worldly character of the Church to the detriment of its spiritual substance.

After some five centuries the presumption explicitly arose that Jesus had put an entire spiritual system under the charge of the bishop of Rome. This became the papacy. Untutored Catholics are thus disposed to accept the totalitarian papal claim of spiritual authority as if it comes from God. But this aggrandized vision of the papacy is alien to Scripture and it is not true to the history of the Roman Church. Fidelity to history requires us to face the fact that the bishop of Rome was not recognized in the early centuries of the Christian Church as having any power or jurisdiction over all other bishops. Even Catholic scholars who accept the Pope's totalitarian claim of spiritual authority do so on theological rather than scriptural or historical grounds. Beginning with Constantine the emperor enjoyed far greater ecclesiastical power than did the bishop of Rome, as I have already indicated. Constantine considered himself Bishop of Bishops. Historian Jacob Burckhardt described the political conditions:

> "...the imperial power...and its administrative system was far too well established to have to give way to a purely priestly government...Constantine was clever or lucky enough to make himself head and center of the Church and to leave this position...well established for his successors. We have already noticed his claim to comport himself 'as a common bishop' [*Ecumenical* or *World Bishop, author*]. This was not merely a manner of speaking; actually the Church had no other central point."[21]

To the Roman emperor belonged the title Supreme Pontiff [*Pontifex Maximus*]. Only centuries later was this title taken over by the pope. The very word *diocese* designated a geographical division of the empire before it was assigned to the various churches as a geographical dividing tool.

The theological argument for papal primacy runs like this: Since Christians came to believe in the primacy of the pope, it must be true. Otherwise the Church would have fallen into error, which could not happen. Another argument insists that if Jesus wanted a unified Church, for all practical purposes he must have intended a single human leader; this leader must be the bishop of Rome, since there is no other contender. A third line of argument rests on the special place Peter seems to have been given by Jesus. In Matthew's gospel we read, "You are Peter and upon this rock I will build my Church...I will give to you the keys of the Kingdom of Heaven. Whatever you bind on earth shall be bound in heaven and whatever you shall loose on earth shall be loosed in heaven."[22] Jesus' special words to Peter were interpreted by the early Fathers of the Church in terms of *faith*, not of *jurisdiction*, a notion that simply did not belong to the self-understanding of the early Christian community.[23]

Aside from the issue of a special "jurisdiction" of Peter, there is a serious historical problem in associating Peter so closely with the city of Rome. Historical evidence recommends, but does not prove that Peter was ever in Rome, not to mention that he was bishop there. The early Church Father Irenaeus considered Peter the *founder* of the Church at Rome, but not its first bishop, whom he lists as Linus. Irenaeus acknowledges the Church at Antioch also to have been founded by Peter, although that Church too had another man, Evodius, as its first bishop. Even the foremost of ancient Church historians, Eusebius (d. 340), places Linus, not Peter, as the first bishop of Rome. It was not until the fourth century that the claim "successor to Peter" was made with any explicitness, and then only tenuously. Concerning this claim the respected Church historian, Father Francis Dvornik, speculates that "It is quite possible that the transfer of the imperial residence to the East at the beginning of the fourth century contributed to speeding the development of the Petrine idea in Rome."[24] This is centuries after the establishment of the Roman bishopric. We should not today let our distance from antiquity blur the large gaps in time that obtained then. What if someone in America today were to base a jurisdictional claim on something that he asserts was established by Columbus—a claim separated from Columbus by some five centuries. No one would recognize such a claim. So, what was the thinking of the Church in the hundreds of years that separated St. Peter from the first man to suggest that his own personal power derives directly from Peter "by succession?" What was happening in the interim was a Church forming its own polity and basing it on the structure of the Empire. Well known to historians of the period is the struggle for power and preeminence that went on among the bishops of Constantinople, Alexandria, and Antioch. Father Dvornik points out, and this is just one example, that Alexandrian Bishop Theophilus "used every means at his disposal and all his riches to frustrate the Bishop of Constantinople, St. John Chrysostom."[25] He actually succeeded in getting the emperor to depose Chrysostom. A generation later, Dioscorus of Alexandria put together a second council at Ephesus, establishing Alexandria first, Rome second, Jerusalem third, Antioch fourth, and Constantinople fifth in order of preeminence. This Council was repudiated and nicknamed "the robber Synod," as Rome came to be increasingly recognized to have primacy over the other churches.

The issue, however, is whether Rome's preeminent place among the churches of the various cities was by an act of God. Theological speculation, which in time became Church doctrine, that Rome was established by God to be the center of the Church is not supported by the historical facts. Rather, this idea suggests an anthropocentric sense of the divine and a less than fully responsible sense of our own part in our spiritual life. An alternate line of thinking about Church authority is at least equally plausible and less silly about a divinity who arranges human affairs in detail. To wit, given the fact of Jesus' profound revelation to us, must we expect him to have detailed blueprints on what we are to do with it? That Jesus was not attuned to this-worldly politics detracts nothing from his spiritual force and communication. After all, he was the spokesman for a "kingdom not of this world." A community of spiritually minded persons did gather about him. If Jesus' spiritual community found that it could function better with a center, then it was able to create one. In fact it did. The papacy is a human historical creation with well-known historical causes. While Father Dvornik is presumably a supporter of papal supremacy, he has still pointed out,

> "...not all of the bishoprics located in the provincial capitals were of apostolic origin...This shows us that it was not apostolic origin which was the determining factor in the organization of the primitive Church. It was rather the principle of *accommodation* to the political organization of the Em-

pire that was paramount."[26]
Dvornik goes on to assert:

> "...thus it became quite natural for the bishops of
> the capitals to assume the right of surveillance
> over the other bishops of their political districts, in
> accordance with the practice of the magistrates of
> the capital, whose jurisdiction extended through-
> out the whole of the province."[27]

It does not push Dvornik's argument to see how the Church of
the very capital of the Empire, Rome, over time assumed the
capital position *quite naturally*. Personally, I consider the development of a central spiritual authority to have been a potential
asset for keeping Jesus' revelation alive in the world. Many
Protestant theologians and thinkers agree with this assessment. In
other words Christianity could do well with a pope.[28]

But we do not want a pope who mistakes this human determination to be something of divine origin. In particular we eschew
popes who propose their vile application of the worst sort of
human politics—which have indeed prevailed over long periods
in the Church's life—to be the vicarious work of God in this
world. All such popes should be seen for the blasphemy they
represent.

Genuine popes should be measured by Jesus' description of
authority in a spiritual community: "You know how among the
Gentiles their seeming rulers dominate them; their great ones
wield authority over them. It is not to be like that with you.
Anyone among you who aspires to greatness should be your
servant; whoever wants to rank first among you is to be the slave
of all."[29] Once again, Jesus' instruction reverses both the spirit
and the action of worldliness. Jesus depicted spiritual authority
with uncanny accuracy. He explicitly ruled out the worldly,
dominating kind of authority. A genuine spiritual leader does not
possess this kind of authority. Jesus demonstrated in his own life
his unwillingness to blend spiritual with worldly power. When the
political authorities began their assault on him, Jesus clearly
showed that he was not about to respond to them at their level of
worldly power. "My kingdom is not of this world" was his
outright refusal to play their brand of politics. It cost him his life.

But when spiritual understanding began to dim in the Church,
and with it genuine spiritual authority, the Church had recourse to
a worldly understanding of authority. Once again it *accommodated*, to employ Dvornik's word, itself to the nature of state
polity. The Church based its form of authority on Roman Law. It

is true that Roman Law of old had achieved a measure of greatness. Yet it was necessarily founded within the limitations of human jurisprudence. It was immersed in human politics. Yet when the Church's legal structure, Canon Law, was finally established as a binding system, its paradigm was Roman Law. We see here again a clear encroachment of The Cult of This World into the spiritual life of the Church. A papal court modelled on the kingdoms of this world emerged, not surprisingly, out of the worldly politics that waxed as authentic spiritual authority waned.

THE CHURCH AS A WORLDLY POWER

We have noted briefly how the bishop of Rome came into political power in the West. History also narrates the worldly growth and spiritual decline of Christianity as it became a bureaucratic institution modelled after the kingdoms of this world. Together with religious tolerance Constantine granted land and many privileges to the Christian community. In later times fraud on the part of the papacy further enhanced Constantine's original generosity. One of the grander frauds is known historically as *The Donation of Constantine*. This elaborate document, claiming Constantine as its author, derives most likely from the eighth century, when the Pope tried to legalize the power he was busy consolidating. According to this document Constantine had transferred to the Pope "the city of Rome and all the provinces, districts, and cities of Italy or of the Western regions."[30] Only a few astute persons recognized the fraudulence of this bequest until the mid-fifteenth century when the brilliant Cardinal Nicholas of Cusa noted that the language of the document did not jibe with the language of that era, and Lorenzo Valla demonstrated the document's fakery beyond dispute. Even the Poet Dante had believed that the donation was from Constantine and bemoaned its consequences:

> "*Ahi, Costantin, di quanto mal fu matre, Non la tua conversion, ma quella dote Che da te prese il primo ricco patre!*" [Alas, Constantine, how great an evil did you mother, not by your conversion, but through that wealth accepted from you by the first rich father (pope)!][31]

Dante's criticism of Constantine remains valid, notwithstanding the fraudulence of the so-called donation. For Constantine's engineering of the marriage of church and state, together with the wealth he did bestow on the Church, spawned untold evil indeed.

From a society mostly of slaves and the dispossessed, the worldly Christianity consolidated by Constantine began to attract another sort, those interested more in mammon than in God. They came forward as candidates for the priesthood and eventually for the Roman bishopric. Already in the fourth century there were bloody rivalries for the position of bishop. To put it bluntly, the blatant worldly corruption of Church leadership followed almost immediately upon Constantine's edict of tolerance and his generous allotment of worldly possessions with its accompanying power to the Church. It was a corruption that grew boundlessly over the centuries.

The papal court reached such a nadir of debauchery by the tenth and eleventh centuries that Catholic historian Peter De Rosa remarks:

> "Without question, these pontiffs constitute the most despicable body of leaders, clerical or lay, in history...Ancient Rome had nothing to rival them in rottenness...Very many were libertines, murderers, adulterers, warmongers, tyrants, simoniacs who were prepared to sell everything holy. They were nearly all more wrapped up in money and intrigue than in religion."

Many of them were murdered, a few in bed when jealous husbands surprised them in the act of adultery.

De Rosa's observation describes the popes of the tenth and eleventh centuries. There was more than an element of absurdity in their lives. For example, Benedict IX, who became pope at the tender age of eleven, was a brat at the time of his election and was only debauched further over the few dissolute years of his remaining life and reign. St. Peter Damian spoke of him: "That wretch, from the beginning of his pontificate to the end of his life, feasted on immorality."[32] In the same context De Rosa cites another observer: "A demon from hell in the disguise of a priest has occupied the Chair of Peter." A sense of the ugly condition of the entire Church is easily discerned in St. Bernard's strongly worded "advice" to Pope Eugenius III. After helping this Pope ponder ["consider"] the many levels of abuse in the Church at large, Bernard finally turned to Eugene's personal circumstance:

> "You will not deny...you are the heir of him whose throne you hold. This is Peter, who is known never to have gone in procession adorned with jewels or

silks...In this finery you are the successor not of
Peter, but of Constantine."[33]

Although Rome was at the heart of this debauchery, the higher
officials of the entire Church were similarly corrupt. Peter Cantor
(d. 1495) tells a story that gives some flavor of earlier times.
About 1100 the Archbishop of the prestigious Tours prevailed
upon King Philip I, for whom he had done an important favor, to
give the diocese of Orleans to his young lover. Although this
young man was notorious for his sexual exploits (the preceding
Archbishop of Tours had also been his lover) and was called
"Flora" after a noted prostitute of the day, he did become Bishop
of Orleans on the Feast of the Holy Innocents. Peter Cantor cites
a Latin rhyme composed for the occasion by derisive lower clergy
and populace:

> Celebrating the Feast of Boys (the Innocents)
> we have elected a boy,
> Following not our own ways
> but the command of the king.

Reform-minded clergy were faced with false accusations and then
exiled. Truly ardent reformers like Arnold of Brescia (d. 1155)
suffered vague accusations of heresy and were put to death.
Despite the extent and intensity of corruption among lower as well
as the higher clergy, there was an even worse aspect to medieval
Church life: Lust for money led to a merciless exploitation of the
common people.

Over the centuries the accumulation of property made the
Church extremely rich in landholdings. The higher ecclesiastics
had the power to exploit ordinary people. The social impact was
disastrous. It worked this way: Men acquired through some favor
or another, often through literal purchase, a *benefice*. A benefice
consisted in control over an abbey or vast Church property of one
sort or another. It amounted to a kind of ownership for purposes
of profit. Benefices would go at times even to children. When
Pope Alexander III discovered that one bishop was habitually
awarding benefices to boys under ten, he established a minimum
age of fourteen to receive a benefice. Other popes reduced the age
to seven.

Holders of a benefice received all the proceeds from this
property. They were entitled to tax recklessly the poor people
living on or working the land. This they did not hesitate to do. The
higher ranking clerics were thus able to live wantonly luxurious

lives with their wives, concubines, bastard children, boyfriends, or other family members. Most often they hired out the overseeing as well as any work connected with their benefice to lesser clerics at poverty wages. Often enough the holders of benefices never even laid eyes on their property, not to say resided there. The massive evil worked upon ordinary people by higher ecclesiastics led to a belief common among pious Christians that a bishop could not go to heaven. Thirteenth century Peter of Blois narrates the story of a pious monk who was elected bishop of Tournay and was exhorted by both Pope Eugenius III and St. Bernard to accept the office. The monk, Geoffroi de Peronne, is reported to have said: "If you turn me out, I may become a vagrant monk, but a bishop never!" The story continues that on his deathbed Geoffroi promised a friend to report to him on his condition in the afterlife. He did so, the story goes, and told his friend that he was in heaven, but that he had been told by God that had he accepted the bishopric he would have been condemned to hell. Interestingly, the source of this story, Peter Blois, repeatedly refused the office of bishop.

We must not assume that things got appreciably better over time. The fourteenth century Italian poet Petrarch called the papal court

> "...the shame of mankind, a sink of vice, a sewer where is gathered all the filth of the world. There God is held in contempt, money alone is worshipped and the laws of God and men are trampled under foot. Everything there breathes a lie: the air, the earth, the houses and above all the bedrooms."[34]

Over a century later the young Augustinian monk Martin Luther identified Rome as the "whore of Babylon," an epithet deriving from the New Testament Book of Revelation. This epithet had been applied to Rome some three centuries earlier by St. Bonaventure, the General of the Franciscan Order. But even the Reformation Luther supported was unable to root out the lust for money and the subservice of doctrine to money in the lives of the clergy. I have read somewhere Samuel Butler's satirization of early British Protestant clergymen who adjusted and readjusted their beliefs in the changing reigns of Charles I, Cromwell, and Charles II:

> What makes all doctrines plain and clear?
> About two hundred pounds a year.
> [*i.e.*, a cleric's yearly stipend]
> And that which was prov'd true before

Prove false again? Two hundred more.

The Middle Ages saw scarcely a pope who was minimally decent, not to mention a man of spiritual substance. An exception was Pope Celestine V, who was enticed by a Cardinal in 1294 to come forth from his reclusive monastic life to become a compromise pope. For the great Colonna and Orsini families were at a stalemate in selecting one of their respective candidates for the papal office. A few months after Celestine's coronation Cardinal Benedict Gaetani, who had consented to the compromise for his self-promotion, arranged that the voice of the Holy Spirit be piped into the new Pope's cell [Celestine had refused the regal splendor of his palace at Naples]. In response one night to this Holy Spirit's advice, the unworldly Celestine abdicated the papacy after only four months, during which he opposed the licentiousness, regal splendor, and struggle for power of the cadre of reprobates who surrounded him. The tough Gaetani, who had prepared this resignation by piping the Holy Spirit's voice into the Pope's cell, stepped in as Pope Boniface VIII. This monster made sure Celestine would not return with a mind for reform by imprisoning him. Celestine died shortly of neglect and starvation, but was later named a saint of the Church.

The effective murder of his unworldly, perhaps even saintly, predecessor was among Boniface's lesser crimes. This very strong personality went on to attack those who threatened his power, particularly the Cardinals of the Colonna family. After humiliating and stripping the Colonna Cardinals, he took revenge on people who had supported them. He deemed that the magnificent city of Palestrina, which had given refuge to the Colonnas, should be destroyed with all its inhabitants. At the lifting of his arm from a distant hillside, Boniface's armies invaded Palestrina and levelled it, together with its irreplaceable artworks and monuments. Far worse, this invasion murdered thousands of innocent men, women, and children—all to satisfy the thirst for revenge of this monster-pope. Yet even these crimes of passion were superseded by morally more heinous deeds, at least in the view of Dante's Inferno. Dante placed Boniface in the Eighth Circle of hell for his simoniacal mismanagement of Church affairs, a crime of cool mental calculation and therefore worse than his impassioned crimes of revenge.

Even more central to our interest, however, was this Pope's consolidation of the political position of the papacy. Boniface asserted the sovereignty of the pope over all worldly kingdoms. This shift of balance of power from emperor to pope was already implicit in the eighth century coronation of Pepin by the Pope. It lay stealthily behind Pope Leo III's tricky coronation of Charlemagne in 800, although Charlemagne maintained his controlling position. But strong popes, such as Gregory VII, coincident with weaker princes, had prepared the papacy for its assertion of absolute power under Boniface VIII.

It happened this way: When Boniface fell into dispute with the intransigent Philip IV of France, he issued a famous Bull or proclamation titled *Unam Sanctam* from its opening words. In it Boniface laid out God's real design for the papacy. Boniface described the relationship of the Kingdom of God to worldly kingdoms in the image of *two swords*, signifying worldly and spiritual authority. He wrote:

> In his [Peter's] power are two swords. Both swords, namely the spiritual and the material, are in the power of the Church. The latter is exercised for the Church; the former by the Church. The one by the hand of the priest; the other by the hand of kings and knights at the bid and sufferance of the priest. One sword has to be under the other and temporal authority subjected to the spiritual power..."[35]

Totalitarian regimes are frightening, especially to Americans. But what about a totalitarianism that puts the political rule of the entire earth at the service of one man who claims it as an adjunct to his total spiritual authority. We should look again at Boniface's claim: We declare, announce and define that it is altogether necessary for salvation for every creature to be subject to the Roman Pontiff. Join this view concerning our spiritual state with the *two swords* view that the entire political system of the world is subject to the Roman Pontiff's purpose, and you have a vision that exceeds by far any totalitarian design of any worldly ruler in human history. And from the likes of Boniface VIII!

Nevertheless, *Unam Sanctam* became a kind of charter for conducting papal authority. Although over time it was rendered weak as governments of the world freed themselves from papal power, the spirit of *Unam Sanctam* long remained the effective basis of the Catholic Church's theory of Church-State relations even into modern times. Without exaggeration the erudite nineteenth century historian, Henry Charles Lea, could begin his History of Sacerdotal Celibacy with these imposing words:

> "The Latin Church is the great fact which dominates the history of modern civilization...Nowhere

do we see combined effort, nowhere can we detect a pervading impulse, irrespective of locality or of circumstance, save in the imposing machinery of the Church establishment....Far above all, the successor of St. Peter from his pontifical throne claims the whole of Europe as his empire, and dictates terms to kings."[36]

Lea was not attacking the Catholic Church; he was expressing the Church's own view of herself.

This vision of Boniface VIII was not finally put to rest by the Church until the Second Vatican Council of the 1960's. Interestingly, the principal architect of the Church's new view was an American Jesuit, John Courtney Murray. This Council Expert [*peritus*], it should be remembered, had spent many of his scholarly years as a man warned, condemned, and silenced by the Vatican's Holy [*sic*] Office of the Inquisition. For Murray's views, coming from his American experience, did conflict with established Church teaching and policy.[37] Father Murray was, of course, exonerated and welcomed to the Second Vatican Council as a *peritus* by Pope John XXIII.

Without reproducing an historical narrative, it is safe to say that the corruption of high church officials only increased with the increasing power and wealth accumulated in the centuries following Boniface VIII. The Church's most powerful cohesive force during that time remained the dogmatic belief-system that bound the minds of Christians. Until, of course, the questions and the attack of the young monk, Martin Luther. Luther's grand protest [whence *Protestantism*] meant a return to sources, particularly to bible reading. It protested first the personalities and lifestyles, then the very teachings, of the current Church leadership. In addition to the Word of scripture this protest looked for intrinsic meaning also in the other sacred elements, the sacraments. Over time the developing Protestantism eschewed the mechanicalness that seemed to color the ordinary person's understanding of the sacraments. As we have already seen, the issue of indulgences symbolizes most starkly this mechanical understanding. Thus the attack on indulgences ranked prominent in the total protest that spawned Protestantism.

The immediate Roman reaction to this protest was to close ranks and condemn. Yet the protest did prompt the Roman Church to look to its own pathetic condition. Some measure of reform was enacted through the lengthy Council of Trent. Although reformist, this Council was principally defensive, and its strategy was attack. However, its condemnations could hardly be fought on moral grounds. The moral highground lay with the reformers. So the protesters were simply declared wrong on the many matters of the Christian tradition whose intrinsic meaning they were exploring and whose practical import they were trying to apply to real life.

As time passed it became clear that the protestant movement could not be contained. The single Roman defense against this continuing threat lay in its belief-system, a dogmatic complex that would brook no tampering. It was, I am convinced, this protective defense against the living force of Protestant communities that made the Roman Catholic system so unavailable to the vast cultural changes that mark the modern world. This defensive posture, and the intellectual backwardness that resulted, lasted well into the twentieth century. It continues today in an attenuated form, witness the Holy Office's voluminous files on numerous theologians, who are watched, reported on, warned, and kept subtly in tow. Or not so subtly.

For every new phase of cultural change in the modern world had met with resistance and condemnation from the Church. Perhaps the starkest symbol of this ignorance is found in the harsh story of Galileo. This scientific genius was imprisoned for life at the command of Church authorities for suggesting that the earth travels around the sun. Although Galileo died in 1642 while under this cloud, he has recently been exonerated by Church authorities—some three and one-half centuries too late to avail him of any consolation. In fact, from the rise of modern scientific method, the Church has found fault with many major movements that came from scientific discoveries. Perhaps the most famous is the creationism-evolutionism debate. As if the bible's spiritual value lies in describing worldly events! But to take spiritual teaching as dogma rather than instruction promotes just such confusion.

Yet it was not only modern science that posed a threat to the traditional Church structure. The entire cultural transformation that we call modernity was viewed as a threat and came under attack. Even the newly developing political philosophy that undergirds personal freedom and democratic society was bitterly condemned right into the nineteenth century. Political works of Thomas Hobbes, John Milton, John Locke, David Hume, Jean Jacques Rousseau, Jeremy Bentham, and John Stuart Mill number among the many noble titles found on the infamous *Index of Forbidden Books*, a vast list of literature Catholics were forbidden to read so that their faith [belief-system] might be protected.

For a specific instance, in 1832 Pope Gregory XVI called liberty of conscience "an absurd and erroneous position" [*absurda...ac erronea sententia*]. Then, as if to correct any weakness in this description, he went on to call it "madness" [*deliramentum*] to think that our conscience is free.

Gregory was followed by the aforementioned strongman of the nineteenth century, Pope Pius IX. Pius's lengthy reign (1846-1878) was further enhanced by his exceptional strength of will. Pius aimed to fulfill the political vision of absolute papal supremacy articulated so long before by Boniface VIII. But Pius's determination was challenged by the vast movement of modernity, a force Pius, like his predecessor Gregory, came to fear and condemn.

Pius's strategy seemed at first to be benign—he was looked upon as liberal. But over time Pius recognized that his liberal policies tended to undermine the absolute authority he supposedly inherited. Pius turned absolutist, and his absolutism marked the Church during those socially turbulent times. His views about modern movements and developments, expressed in various documents, were collected in a list or *syllabus* that became famous as the *Syllabus of Errors*.[38] This list reckoned just about every mode of modern thought a mistake. Nearly all the principles that undergird our modern sense of democracy and freedom, you might say the American Constitution with its Bill of Rights, were condemned as errors that are contrary to the Catholic Faith.

The cultural upheaval toward modernity was powerful indeed. If a pope were to oppose it, he would certainly need equivalent power. How could Pius IX achieve this kind of power? By then papal military troops had been diminished. Effective power would have to be of another kind. It would have to be power over the minds and hearts of people. This could be effected only through the pope's position as the spiritual leader of the many millions who considered themselves Catholics. Pope Pius IX's bizarre manipulation of Christian doctrine and abuse of dogma in preparation for his final political coup merit special scrutiny.

A blatantly political use of belief is Pius IX's dogmatic proclamation that Jesus' mother was exempt from original sin from the time she was conceived, a dogma known as "The Immaculate Conception."[39] In the first place, that Mary was *conceived immaculately* was either ignored or explicitly denied by nearly all popes and by every recognized theologian for the first thirteen centuries of Christianity. Its new status as dogma is certainly contrary to St. Vincent of Lerin's established rule for true beliefs, namely those "which everywhere, which always, which by everyone" are held to be true. Secondly, this supposed gift to Mary was enabled by the saving or *redemptive* death of her son, although Jesus was years away from being born, not to mention crucified.

Was the condition of this Jewish woman's soul at the time of her conception, some two millennia previous, a burning issue in the nineteenth century, when the Church was embroiled in social unrest of the first magnitude? Was this matter truly weighing heavy on the heart of Pius IX or any other Catholic? No, it was not; no, it was not.

But a show of spiritual authority this proclamation was, and its content could not be argued one way or the other because of its abstractness from all earthly conditions as well as from anyone's genuine interest. Have you ever figured out how the condition of Mary's soul at the time of her conception plays into your spiritual needs and growth? Especially if, like Mary, we are all intrinsically pure.

However, Pius IX had designs on absolutizing the power of the papacy once and for all. The doctrinal issue concerning Mary's conception lay conveniently at hand, even if Pius's declaration was contrary to the Church's position on the matter during its first thirteen centuries, and thus once again failing the established test of doctrine, that which has been held "always, everywhere, by everyone." Making a show of power over peoples' very minds and consciences would certainly enhance Pius' authority. Thus in 1854 Pius made the solemn proclamation that Mary's Immaculate Conception is a dogma of the faith that binds every Catholic to accept without reservation. This proclamation was the first instance in the history of the Church that a pope arrogated a dogmatic issue to himself alone for resolution.

Politically, Pius knew what he was doing. He was creating and solidifying a position for himself, a position that would become more explicit—not to mention outrageous—in the later proclamation he would push through the First Vatican Council in 1870, namely that the pope is infallible all by himself, *i.e.* independently of fellow bishops, of Church councils, and of the people at large. This position, fought bitterly on the Council floor and deemed untimely even by Cardinals and bishops who thought it might be true, was nevertheless railroaded through the Council by Pius. An unsparing account of the behind-the-scenes political machinations that issued in the dogma of Infallibility is recounted by the

Catholic theologian and historian—and Vatican insider—August Bernhard Hasler.[40] Infallibility has remained a strange anomaly in the Church since then. If the pope did enjoy such a privilege, difficult to conceive, it would be mighty helpful to use it in important practical matters such as the contemporary issue regarding artificial contraception. But popes are too smart to put the dogma of infallibility to the kind of test where it might count. Thus Pope Paul VI explicitly indicated he was *not speaking infallibly* when he nonetheless burdened people, particularly women, with his stricture against artificial birth control in 1968. Pope Pius XII, on the other hand, had used his supposed full power of infallibility in declaring that the dead body of Jesus' mother was reenlivened two millennia ago and taken up to someplace in the sky, a dogma named *The Assumption.* Pius XII's declaration was another *Maria ex machina*, ever at hand for political enhancement. Pope John XXIII, to note the contrary, is reported to have said that if he was indeed infallible, he would never use it in his governance of the Church. This John was an historian. In his wisdom he relegated the notion of infallibility to the practical non-existence it had enjoyed for well over half the time of the Church's existence.

The ideological stranglehold of the papacy over the minds and consciences of Catholics, thus sealed by Pope Pius IX, was effective. So even though people would no longer be executed at Church insistence, papal power remained strong through the influence of the hierarchy over the consciences of those called "the people." It is important in this context to review the papal ideological assault on freedom and intelligence after the papacy lost its raw political power.

One assault should be particularly interesting to Americans. It was directed at us. The quality of American Catholicism was partly determined by the lively Protestantism of the first settlers. The sentiment these Protestants carried with them from Europe was distrustful of everything *Roman*. Protestants felt seriously threatened by the large Catholic immigration of the nineteenth century. Anti-Catholic sentiment became a force to be reckoned with. American Catholicism can boast of some intelligent and broad-minded leaders of that time. Cardinal Gibbons of Baltimore (1834-1921) tried to accommodate American Catholics toward their religiously pluralistic home. He was a staunch supporter of the separation of Church and State. This fondness of American Catholicism for democratic principles threatened the ever-jealous Vatican. A vague heresy dubbed *Americanism* was condemned by the Vatican. In 1899 a papal letter was sent to the American hierarchy warning of these "dangers." The real dangers, as the history of this curiosity makes clear, were American democracy, pluralism, and the separation of Church and State.[41] This was the European hierarchy's last-ditch political assault on the American way, a practical application of the thinking of Popes Gregory XVI and Pius IX, which we have seen.

An even more virulent attack on fresh thinking and openness to new ideas was launched when Pope Pius X condemned Modernism. This large movement called *The Modernist Heresy* included the most perceptive Catholic theological thinkers of England and the Continent at the turn of the century. Pius X's reputed personal kindliness did not extend to the most creative of those theological thinkers. Purporting to speak for the Holy Spirit, this intellectually dull-witted Pope excommunicated them. Just because they did not and could not think the particular thoughts that his watchdogs of orthodoxy, The Holy Office of the Inquisition, wanted them to think.

History has vindicated these thinkers. But their vindication cannot be made retroactive to their personal lives. They were made to suffer. The human factor involved in excommunicating someone is easily glossed over by those who have never been cut off from the human association that she or he feels is supremely important. Pius X's protection of his version of dogmatic truth at the expense of condemning the best and the brightest should have weighed stronger in the moral judgment of his character when he was being considered for sainthood. Pius X's ignorance can be excused, as his intellectual talents were admittedly limited. But I find it difficult to acknowledge as saintly the personality behind the insensitive, uncompassionate, and, through history's judgment, erroneous action of this pontiff.

It is a fact that nearly all the finer thinking of Pius X's era was condemned as the heresy of *Modernism*. Much of it has become today's Catholic theology. Still worse, Pius's fear of new thinking set the Catholic Church nearly a century behind her Protestant counterparts. It also reinvigorated the longstanding and sad process of suspicion, interrogation, intimidation, suppression, and often condemnation, of the Church's finest thinkers, a mood that continues into the present. The seriousness of the intellectual stagnation in Catholicism brought about by Rome's heavy-handed treatment of so-called modernism is not sufficiently appreciated, because the muted do not cry out. One must ponder the implications, for example, of the words of Catholic historian Thomas

McAvoy:

> "The effects of the Modernistic controversy within
> the United States have not been estimated—and
> the history of that episode *will be difficult to write*
> [emphasis mine]—because most of the discus-
> sions were oral and were mostly in the formative
> stage when the encyclical *Pascendi Gregis* cast a
> *paralyzing spell* [emphasis mine] on American
> Catholic theological discussion."

More recent victims of this inquisition-intimidation include
Teilhard de Chardin, Henri de Lubac, Yves Congar, John Courtney
Murray, Karl Rahner, and Edward Schillebeeckx, to name only a
few of the more prominent. In time many of these men were
rehabilitated, some of them to become experts [*periti*] and crafters
of the documents of the Second Vatican Council.

This history ought to concern us lest we fail to learn its lessons
and repeat past mistakes. However, the Vatican's inquisitorial
mood remains at work today. Church authorities, with the leave
when not at the directive of the Pope, continue to harass contemporary theologians and bishops who attempt to deal with poignant
human situations within their communities. The most famous
contemporary personality under constant surveillance and condemnation by the Vatican is Father Hans Kueng. However, Father
Kueng now enjoys a professorial post removed from the perni-
cious reach of Vatican control.

Father Kueng's German colleagues have shown themselves
slightly more solicitous of academic integrity than have their
American counterparts. Father Charles Curran, for example, has
become a famous American Catholic moral theologian and professor. No one questions his competence or scholarship. Yet
Father Curran's moderate evaluation of certain sexual matters—
such as contraception, homosexuality, and masturbation—separates him from the hard and unrealistic position taken by Vatican
authorities.

This is not the place to discuss issues of sexuality. But we must
consider some implications of the political suppression of Father
Curran by the Vatican. When the Vatican insisted that Curran be
ousted from his professorship at Catholic University, the American academic community was aroused—a little. Father Curran
was willing to compromise by teaching only courses that would
exclude his views on the issues in question. This seemed fair since
the rest of his theological views are unquestionably orthodox. The
Vatican, however, would have none of this. Its interest was not

only to stop the propagation of Father Curran's controversial views—he was willing to meet this requirement. The Vatican, in its mean-spirited tradition, wanted and continues to want him suppressed and, minimally, out of a job.

There was a time when the Vatican had the power to execute the likes of Father Curran, a power it used all too often. Happily, it no longer enjoys this kind of power. Sadly, however, Vatican power still plays a strong hand in American affairs. In the case in point, the Vatican still influences American academic life, including public higher education, by keeping Father Curran from achieving a secure teaching position. As of November, 1990 we learn that Auburn University, an institution supported in part by public tax funds, suddenly withdrew its offer of a tenure-track position to Father Curran. We are to believe that the President of Auburn University suddenly discovered that his University did not need the position it had opened up and offered to Father Curran after an academic search? How remiss of this President to discover his University's real situation so long after creating a search for someone to fill a position he suddenly discovered to be superfluous.

The Vatican is indeed dead set to teach, namely Father Curran. But how unlike the teaching of Jesus and of all those who have genuine spiritual understanding! The lessons taught by the Vatican are much more like the lessons of the Mafia and similar organizations with which the Vatican has been in intimate association in recent years—a topic that will receive further attention. Looked at only outwardly, this disgrace of our era does not equal the hangings and burnings of the past. But if we consider the human factor, the confusion and suffering currently imposed on theologians who are only trying to think, then our era appears only too close to the disgrace of the past.

Vatican City State is its own country, one of the smallest in the world. Countries do influence one another politically; the world works this way. However, neither American academicians nor even those Americans who appreciate our constitutional separation of Church and State are sufficiently alarmed by Vatican interference in the professional life of Father Curran. Is it acceptable that an American institution of higher learning must have its personnel and its discussion of ideas subject to Vatican censorship? The full background of the President of Auburn's decision to withdraw a tenure-track teaching position from Father Curran still merits public disclosure and discussion. Where is the POAU, since the AAUP [American Association of University

Professors] remains remiss in its vigilance?

Yet abuse of dogma has not been the sole instance of recent distortions of spiritual realities to serve this-worldly politics, *i.e.*, Cultic interests. Pope John Paul II, admired by many for his sensitivity to social justice, also combines worldly politics with church life.

A case in point relative to inner Church life concerns an instance of *canonization*. Canonization is the process by which the Church determines that the moral character of a deceased person was such that she or he may rightly be declared a saint.

Before detailing the particular episode, it is important to emphasize the spiritual importance of sainthood in Christianity and in other religions as well. To do so we must again apply the spiritual meaning of sacrament, the empowering of a physical reality—for example, the *water* of baptism—to draw us beyond merely physical life. The earthly lives of genuine saints are not less than sacramental to those who are able to relate to them properly. This means that the influence of saints is spiritually intrinsic: Saints are able to touch us and influence us at the heart. There is nothing surprising in this. Even secular role models, from sports figures to military heroes past and present, attract people into alignment through the example of their lives. And their lives are usually without sacramental power because these personalities have ordinarily not broken within themselves the bonds of *ego* that separate person from person. So what might be said of the truly *spiritual* influence of those who have broken their inner bonds of separateness and entered the stream of unlimited love? Centuries ago St. Thomas Aquinas spoke of this influence. His Latin verity, *Bonum est diffusivum sui*, can be translated accurately, if somewhat freely, "Love ["the good"] spreads by itself!" A saint is thus a source of love, a sacred reality, a sacrament *par excellence*. Hence the prominence of saints in Christianity and in other spiritual communities from all times.

The *canonization* process was established by the Church precisely to preserve care and authenticity in recognizing the outstanding spiritual character of spiritually renowned human beings who have preceded us. This process includes a sincere effort to discover everything relevant to the person's character. The process brings in witnesses for the sake of obtaining the facts. While the traditional role of *Devil's Advocate* [a kind of prosecutor-role] no longer belongs to this process, the canonization process is still designed to get at the truth. It is not unlike the ideal of our judicial process which uses prosecution and defense to follow up every relevant line of inquiry. Except, we know that both prosecutors and defenders can subvert our judicial system by seeking something other than the truth, for example a conviction for political purposes rather than because of actual guilt. But the canonization process would ideally be free of such political motives. In short, the Church has dedicated itself to determine the *actual* character of those to whose teaching, example, and influence we are advised to submit.

Now to the particulars of the case of Josemaria Escriva [d. 1975]. Despite his own misgivings about the canonization process, Pope John Paul II seems determined to declare this man a saint. The late Msgr. Escriva was the founder of a Catholic organization called *Opus Dei* [Work of God]. *Opus Dei* is a unique, large, traditionalistic, and highly secret organization within the Catholic Church. While *Opus Dei* includes Catholic clergy, it is comprised mostly of laypersons who are dedicated to celibacy and to strict obedience to the pope, while they work at regular jobs in the world. Its secretiveness in particular causes numerous Catholics, as well as non-Catholics, to find *Opus Dei* a scary organization.[42] It is well-known that Pope John Paul II has long been an admirer of *Opus Dei*. This is understandable. *Opus Dei* meshes well with his theology, his need to be obeyed, his views on sexuality, and, as we shall see, his own CIA-connected type of political operation.

To the case in point, the process of canonization is being applied in a unique way to Escriva. Having described Escriva as "heroically virtuous" only a year earlier, Pope John Paul II nevertheless cautioned in 1991 against "undue haste" in the push for his canonization.[43] Greater credibility for *Opus Dei* through the canonization of its founder seems to be the motive for subverting the ordinary process. The usual process of canonization, for example, seeks out the experience of every creditworthy person who has knowledge of someone proposed for sainthood. Something contrary holds in the case of Escriva, a fact implicitly acknowledged by the Pope who spoke of "procedural errors" in the process as applied to Escriva.[44]

Whatever particulars the Pope had in mind, a subversion of ordinary procedures has certainly obtained in Escriva's case. Usually, for example, the nine-member board of examiners are fellow-countrymen who are in the best position to know the person. But in the case of the Spanish Escriva, the board of examiners were almost all Italians. Further, the medical professional who judges on the issue of a possible miraculous cure is, in Escriva's case, himself a member of *Opus Dei*.

More scandalously, serious and credible persons who knew Escriva well, including long-standing members of *Opus Dei*, have been refused a formal hearing in his canonization process. Their knowledge and experience of Escriva is intentionally excluded from consideration. Some of these persons have nevertheless gone public with their knowledge and views of Escriva. *Newsweek* cites a respected architect, the elderly Miguel Fisac: "He [Escriva] is not the figure they presented to the public...[he was a man who] spoke badly about everyone." Father Vladimir Felzmann, a longtime member of *Opus Dei* and now an aid to England's Cardinal Hume, described Escriva's "filthy temper" and, more importantly, Escriva's defense of Adolf Hitler, whose Nazi organization is not wholly unlike *Opus Dei* in structure and procedural ways, if not in objectives and activities. Felzmann is quoted: "He [Escriva] told me that Hitler had been unjustly accused of killing six million Jews. In fact he had killed only four million."[45] A considerable element of the membership of Opus Dei joined Hitler's Nazi forces in its attack on the Soviet Union. Escriva's critics offered additional information that does not square with the image of a person who has gone beyond egoic self-centeredness.

Moreover, contrary to *Opus Dei's* description of this examination process, it has been leaked that the examining board was not unanimous in recommending even the *beatification* (first step toward canonization) of Escriva. At least two members of the board did not consent even to the probability of sainthood of this proposed candidate.

Anyone who still doubts concerning the politics of Escriva's canonization process ought to ponder this: when Father Felzmann, with the knowledge of England's Cardinal Hume, complained to Rome's Congregation for the Causes of Saints about excluding his intimate knowledge of Escriva, the reply to him, which continued to deny any interest in his views, came from the Rome office of *Opus Dei* rather than from the Vatican Congregation to which it was addressed.

The intrinsic nature of sainthood in Catholic devotion is too important ever to create a fictionalized saint for purposes of empowering a political organization within the Church, no matter how valuable a potential that organization may offer to a current administrator, even if he is pope. To tamper with the sacrament of sainthood is, in traditional Catholic parlance, a sacrilege sin.

While sacrilegious politicizing of inner-Church life is terrible, to be sure, it is not the worst of political corruptions that have infected the Church even during this century. Only recently has it come to light how extensively the Vatican colluded with the Nazis before, during, and after World War II.

To touch upon this complexity we might begin with Pope Pius XII [Eugenio Pacelli] prior to his ascendancy to the papal throne. Archbishop Pacelli was the papal emissary (*nuncio*) to Hitler's Germany. It is known that Pacelli, as Pope, retained a strong affection for Germany, a factor that may have played into his ready accords with Nazis and finally into his saving of numerous Nazi war criminals from facing the court of justice after the war.

As Papal Nuncio to Germany, Pacelli had signed the Vatican's treaty or *Concordat* with Hitler's Germany in 1933. The German Catholic hierarchy, it is true, spoke out against Hitler at first. Their opposition softened, however, when Hitler offered money to support Catholic schools. This was not unlike the French. A private archive lately come into public awareness reveals that in 1944 the renowned Jesuit theologian, Henri de Lubac, condemned the behavior of most of France's Catholic hierarchy under the Nazis.

Recently released documentation, moreover, demonstrates an official collusion of the Vatican with Nazi organizations during and after the war. The Vatican's double motive for these intricate cooperative efforts was the defeat of communism and the enhancement of Roman Catholicism. Ironically, the Soviet Union maintained the superior spying advantage by having a mole at the highest level of the Vatican bureaucracy, it is now known.

With the advantage of hindsight we might well question certain political judgments of Pius XII and criticize his distorted anti-communist zeal which led to direct and indirect support of certain Nazi efforts. But It would be far from the truth of the complexities of this history to think of an unambiguous alignment of the Vatican with the Nazis. Pius XII did seek to maintain a position of neutrality between the great warring factions, and he never mentioned "Jews" in his public utterances related to the war. To look upon this *silence* in regard to the Nazi genocide of Jews as merely "church-protective" or, worse yet, a quiet anti-Semitism does not account for Pius's dilemma, even though his silence was questioned at that time and since. Given Hitler's mania, outspoken denunciation might have worked more harm than good to Jews and to others as well, in Pius's judgment. Given Nazi policy, there is obvious truth to this.[46] For my own part, I incline toward the view of major Jewish leaders who lived through those difficult circumstances. For his work to save Jews Pius received high accolades from the likes of Golda Meir, Jerusalem's Grand Rabbi Isaac Herzog, Rome's Chief Rabbi Israel Zolli, and an untold number of Jews whose lives were saved by his assiduous activity on their behalf. Grand Rabbi Herzog visited Pius personally after the war to "officially thank the Holy Father and the Holy See for manifold acts of charity on behalf of the Jews."[47] These Jewish leaders can hardly be faulted as naive.

Notwithstanding Pius's probable innocence on the Jewish question, what has surprised even the historically knowledgeable, except for insiders, is the extent of Vatican collaboration with western governments, especially Britain and the United States, in saving Nazi war criminals toward the end of the war. The Nazis were seen as a highly effective force against world communism. For this reason Nazi war criminals were cultivated by the Church and by Britain and America precisely to become a cadre of "Freedom Fighters" to forestall and hopefully conquer the perceived communist menace.

Mark Aarons and John Loftus have documented this intrigue in their book, *Unholy Trinity*.[48] Catholic novelist Morris West has described their book as "A bill of indictment, meticulously researched, carefully documented, soberly reasoned..." U.S. Intelligence did not discover the extent of the Vatican intrigue, nor the route to safety it created for war criminals, until 1947. It named the carefully crafted Vatican escape route "Operation Ratlines," named after the rope ladder that leads to the top of a ship's mast. This operation provided false identification papers for numerous Nazi war criminals and then smuggled them to the West. Famous criminals like Adolf Eichmann and Klaus Barbie were beneficiaries of this Vatican escape route. Eichmann, a principal architect of the Holocaust who was later found and executed by Israel, was housed by Cardinal Siri in a monastery in Genoa until he could be spirited to Argentina. Eichmann's traveling expenses were paid by the Catholic relief organization, *Caritas*. Similarly, Klaus Barbie was funneled by priests to his penultimate safety. Some war criminals were even housed and protected *within Vatican City State itself.*

Less well-known Nazi fugitives were often equally or even more inhumane than better-known ones. The Vatican gave needed support to the Croatian Nazi leader Ante Pavelic, a Roman Catholic who had once chided Hitler for his *leniency* toward the Jews. This support enabled Pavelic's murder of hundreds of thousands of Serbs who were, after all, *Orthodox* [*i.e.* unaffiliated with Rome] Catholics. This background may help bewildered Americans to understand something of the contemporary situation in Bosnia. Because of Pavelic's publicly known character as a murderer, Pope Pius XII would not grant him an official audience. This Pope did meet with him in the Vatican twice on an informal but friendly basis, however.[49] Deniability intact. This man was, we are advised, a Catholic, after all, and thus belonged to Pius's flock. And he did strengthen Roman Catholicism vis-a-vis Orthodox Christianity. Pavelic's attitudes were shared by many priests and bishops. The Nazi collaborator, Bishop Ivan Saric of Sarajevo, for example, was known to U.S. Intelligence as "the hangman." He was by all common standards a Nazi murderer.[50] Pavelic and his large cohort of criminals were nearly all guided to safety through the Vatican Ratlines. What is significant is that this entire Vatican operation was known and approved by Pope Pius XII and his operative, Cardinal Giovanni Montini, who later became Pope Paul VI.

I do not maintain that in worldly terms the Vatican was more immoral than other governments of the world. The Vatican was no worse than Britain, France, Italy, or the United States. It certainly was not worse than Stalinist Russia. My argument in this book does not concern comparative worldly politics. I am asking: Was the Vatican's role in the situation of World War II that of a spiritual community? The answer to this question is clearly No. Admittedly, those were extremely difficult times whose depth can hardly be fathomed. As a worldly power in those turbulent times, the Vatican fared as it fared, no better nor worse than other powers. I question its performance in terms of "the politics of spiritual existence."

Eugenio Pacelli, Pope Pius XII, was an ordinary human being, possessed, perhaps, of exceptional political position and acumen, but hardly bereft of faults. Pius's personal confusion bared when old age began to strip him of his wonted *savoir faire.* His longstanding housekeeper-confidant, Madre Pasquelina, has offered significant information about the aging Pope. Among other peculiarities, this aged Pontiff required visitors, including aging cardinals, to discuss their issues with him on their knees—and then to walk backwards out of his office.[51]

Therefore, only the historically untutored were appalled to learn from the American weekly *Time* [2-24-92] that Pope John Paul II has more recently aligned Vatican and Polish Catholic Church operatives with a former American President and the

American CIA to subvert and finally overturn Poland's communist government. The historically knowledgeable are only saddened at this revelation, to the degree they are spiritually sensitive. For a new version of Caesaro-papism has arisen fresh from what a Vatican II perspective may have hoped to be a permanent grave. But Pope John XXIII knew that the Cult of This World will never die: *Ecclesia semper reformanda.* Jesus knew this too. The wheat and the weeds must grow together until the end, this Master of Truth had already warned us.

The Polish-born Pope did not like the communist government of his homeland. But this is, I submit, a worldly rather than a spiritual concern. Of course spiritual instruction can be at odds with the objectives and ways of the world, including its political systems. Prophets emerge from time to time as absolute critics of worldly ways, including political and economic ways. But the spiritual community itself is neither a worldly political system nor an operative of any such system.

Although he denied a *formal* alliance, Pope John Paul II defended his association with President Reagan and the American CIA in subverting the communist government of Poland. He argued, "The fact that the Holy See, the Church, defended the victims of a totalitarian system is nothing negative...it is an act that merits appreciation." Yet when Mikhail Gorbachev wrote laudatory comments about Pope John Paul II's *political* [Gorbachev's word] role in the collapse of communism, the Pope quickly pointed out that he did not have "a political role in the strict sense." This splitting of hairs in determining a *strict sense* is unnecessary. Regular collaboration with the United States government and the CIA is worldly politics, *Realpolitik* it is called, no matter the stated goal of "defending human rights and religious freedom." Long before John Paul, St. Peter drew his sword in defense of Jesus himself. But Jesus advised against it: "Put your sword back."[52]

The extent of Pope John Paul II's political intentions was clear very early to the Soviet Union. According to the American *Catholic News Service*, Italy's KGB director from 1976 to 1982, Boris Solomiatin, spoke to the Italian weekly *Panorama* about the KGB's top-level spy in the Vatican. "We couldn't have coped without this—the Vatican had to be watched almost as intently as a superpower," Solomiatin said.

A perverse irony that verges on cynicism attends the particulars of this situation. At the very time Pope John Paul II was in direct collaboration with the American CIA, he was also moving against theologians, *Liberation Theologians* they are called, who were attempting to bring gospel principles of justice into action for oppressed and impoverished people of third world countries. "Too much worldly politics," this Pope admonished. Then, one envisions, back to a telephone conference with President Reagan and William Casey, head of the CIA.

The sheer irony does not end there. The essential difference between rightful action in the world and succumbing to worldly politics can be seen in the practical consequences of this recent unholy alliance. It is known that the Pope had to make political payoffs, which he did by helping the American government's purported *interests* in Latin American operations. This despite the fact that these supposed interests involved activities that are incompatible with what modern Catholicism has stood for publicly regarding wealth and social justice. Can we read the Pope's suppression of *Liberation Theologians* in terms other than his carrying out his part of the Washington-Rome Axis agreement? Likewise on the American home front: the relatively enlightened body of American bishops—relative, that is, to the Church's stance in other times and places—addressed major concerns regarding American economic policy, a policy it criticized as insufficiently addressing the plight of the impoverished and the homeless, while it encourages the Ivan Boesky/Michael Milkin-type economic rape of American society. At least until juries sent many of these principals to jail. This newly refined system of economic chaos took the name *Reaganomics* from its principal unarchitect, the American President. At the other end of the Axis, however, this President had a collaborator high on the Throne of Peter, as it is called. So the American bishops were called by Rome to modify and mollify their document to blunt its prophetic edge and thus meet minimal reaganesque standards. Not to wonder at all of this, however, for to engage worldly politics means to abide by its rules. It can work no other way, as those who are party to effective worldly politics tacitly understand and accept.

The Vatican can correctly argue that it, too, has required and received payoffs from the Washington side of the Axis. As *Time* also reported, "In response to concerns of the Vatican, the Reagan Administration agreed to alter its foreign-aid program to comply with the church's teachings on birth control." In fact, funds were cut off from countries and organizations that did not adhere to Catholic teachings on family planning. In this way the promotion of artificial contraception in overpopulated, underfed countries fell victim as the American Government's payoff to Vatican demands regarding family planning in the world. Major organizations such as the World Health Organization were faced with a significant increase in world poverty and starvation due to American acquiescence to this benighted Roman insistence alone.

I have not even briefly summarized the political intrigue narrated by the Aarons-Loftus book. But the formation of worldly politics that their book narrates is not the main concern here. In these pages I wish only to articulate the salient difference between a purely worldly politics and "the politics of spiritual existence." The point is simple: the politics that modern Catholicism has embraced is not the politics of a genuinely spiritual community. Radical reform is indeed in order.

Closely associated with politics is, of course, money. Here again modern Catholicism has not demonstrated spiritual discernment. By itself money is nothing more than the token by which we exchange goods and services. It is not intrinsically evil. Money becomes untrue when it is treated as other than the ticket of exchange that it is. When money is sought in its own right, therefore, it becomes *mammon* in the sense Jesus condemned.

We must not expect a community of any sort to exist in the world without sharing in the goods and services that contribute to our physical life and well-being. But we have already seen something of how money became mammon very early in the Church. We have also discussed some of the grave consequences of this mistake. Following the Council of Trent the papacy did draw back somewhat from unseemly splendor. And it has often used the wealth that accrued to it to promote worthy causes, at least as it assessed such causes.

Nevertheless, there has not yet arisen the degree of spiritual understanding that is required to restore the Church at her highest level, the Vatican, to a truly spiritual relationship to money. A Vatican department, deceptively named *Istituto per le Opere di Religione* [Institute for the Works of Religion] or *IOR* as it is more commonly referred to, manages the Church's hefty portfolio: some eleven billion dollars in stocks and over three billion dollars in gold reserves. In the words of Luigi DiFonzo "...the Vatican is the largest stockholder in the world."[53] Parenthetically, it is interesting to note that the Vatican divested itself of its ownership in a firm that produced contraceptive devices—but only after the obvious discrepancy became public knowledge.

Important to the Vatican's portfolio have been major blocks of stock in numerous large banks. In 1969 Pope Paul VI met clandestinely, after midnight, with a well-known financier, Michele Sindona, to make Sindona the overseer of Vatican finances. The perplexing thing about this appointment was that Sindona was known to be Mafia-connected[54] as well as a member of an equally surreptitious and in some ways more powerful right-wing group, *Propaganda Due*, better known as P2.

Without detailing what is amply documented elsewhere, the extremely private and careful Sindona moved the enormous Vatican wealth throughout the world in fraudulent enterprises that skirted and even broke the laws of Italy and other countries, that evaded reasonable taxation, that laundered ill-gotten gains, and that promoted subversive political activities. Need we wonder at the starkness of the choice Jesus offered between God and *mammon*? Or of his careful distinction between what belongs to God and what belongs to Caesar? The Vatican invested its own mammon heavily in Caesar. And lost. This exceedingly complex story, starting with Pope Paul VI's clandestine appointment of Sindona, reached its *denouement* in the fraudulent performance and ultimate failure of Milan's *Banco Ambrosiano* under Roberto Calvi.[55] Rupert Cornwell has documented much of the Church's participation in untold mischief by the vast and complex association its bank, *The Bank of the Holy Spirit* as it is unashamedly called, cultivated with dishonest men, indeed with organized crime.

The Bank of the Holy Spirit found itself at the losing end of a monetary entanglement with organized crime in a world-wide felonious enterprise that involved billions of dollars. How much might be ascribed to chicanery and connivance, and how much to the naivete of the Bank's director, Archbishop Marcinkus, is left to others to judge. The Italian government has sought to extradite this Archbishop for criminal trial. Pope John Paul II has protected him. In an ironic twist, the Archbishop, large man that he is, has often served this Pope as a personal bodyguard.

The sordid story of Vatican finances and the loss of much of its treasury need not be detailed here. A spiritually minded teacher may have interpreted the fiasco as a divine sign, the right time [*kairos*] to step away from mammon altogether. It has been rare for the Church to have this kind of teacher, one who draws the Christian community to a world-transcending spiritual discipline. Yet in such a teacher's absence the long-standing community structure of Catholicism will bear more the marks of Cult than of Church.

To put the matter straightforwardly, if we understand the papacy as spiritual rather than merely political, then we must accept that only a person of profound spiritual realization can factually exercise teaching authority as a pope. The rest are frauds, blind leaders of the blind. In the absence of a person of spiritual depth, the real papacy is simply vacant. No one denies that the papacy *can* be vacant. Unquestionably a vacancy occurs with the death of each pope. At those difficult periods in the Middle Ages when there were several claimants to the papacy, it was often uncertain just who was pope. That matter, however, was a problem only from a worldly or juridical point of view. It had no spiritual significance, for all the claimants were scoundrels. None of them was a true pope in the sense of a genuine spiritual teacher. The papacy was simply vacant for a long time. It has been spiritually vacant for great periods of time over and over again.

I am not saying something new here. Sixteenth century Church historian and disciple of St. Philip Neri, the brilliant Cardinal Baronius, expressed the same view. He called ninth and tenth century popes "invaders of the Holy See, not apostles but apostates." I concur fully with this eminent Churchman's conclusion:

> "The chief lesson of these times is that the Church
> can get along very well without popes. What is
> vital to the Church's survival is not the pope but
> Jesus Christ. He is the head of the Church, not the
> pope."[56]

At the same time, a genuine pope, a person of profound spiritual realization as well as the will and the ability to instruct, would be an invaluable service to persons everywhere. Such a person would be a powerful unifying force in the Christian Church at large.

Structural change within the Church is certainly possible. But we must recognize what is required for the kind of change that could make a difference spiritually. Much can be learned from Vatican Council II. This hopeful Council was born of the spirit and wisdom of Pope John XXIII. He called back to the center of Church life many intellectually and spiritually minded women and men who had been to one or another degree stifled by the machinery of his predecessors. Together it appeared that this Council would make a real difference. In fact it did not. We might be prompted to ask, What went wrong?

Nothing *went wrong*, particularly. The Council is not to be faulted. It proceeded wisely on many fronts. It effected sensible institutional changes. But institutional changes, though potentially useful, are always secondary. The main ingredient was insufficient against the cultic force that had been entrenched within Catholicism for a very long time. The necessary leavening ingredient is nothing less than spiritual understanding, which is the only foundation of spiritual leadership. The only reality that could possibly have sustained the spiritual momentum of Vatican Council II was a worthy successor to Pope John XXIII. This was not to be. No amount of good intentions supplies for a deficit in spiritual understanding. While John XXIII was blessed with a good measure of spiritual understanding, his hand-wringing successor, Paul VI, was not. To turn to our own day, Paul VI's neck-wringing successor, John Paul II, does not appear to be either. Thus the Church structure that this occupier embodies is not presently poised to change. On the contrary, through John Paul II this Church structure has designed its own survival. John Paul's technique for maintaining the *status quo* in the contemporary Church is his application of a litmus test, mostly on select sexual issues, before he names bishops. Profound spiritual understanding is not to be found among the trivialities this Pope considers important for selecting bishops. For his main aim is to bring the world-wide Church into alignment with Rome—a Rome as presently constituted, however, rather than an open Rome as a potential center of a renewed Christianity.

In his recent novel *Lazarus*, Morris West offers an eloquent description of this circumstance through his novel's fictional but thinly disguised Pope:

> "In defiance of biblical injunction, of historic custom, of discontent among clergy and faithful, he had appointed as senior archbishops, in Europe and the Americas, men of his own choosing, hardline conservators, stubborn defenders of bastions long overpassed, deaf and blind to every plea for change. They were called the Pope's men, the praetorian guard in the Army of the Elect. They were the echoes of his own voice, drowning out the murmurs of discontented clerics, of the faceless crowd outside the sanctuaries."

In early 1990 Notre Dame University's theologian and department Chair, Father Richard McBrien, publicly scorned Pope John Paul II's continuing selection and promotion of mediocre yea-sayers to major posts in the American Church's hierarchy. It is becoming a hierarchy of sycophants. I call them "litmus bishops," easily identifiable in how they turn yellow upon touching base with Rome. The most unfortunate aspect of this particular abuse of power, of course, is that ill-fated appointments to quasi-permanent positions of authority continue their malevolent influence in any society long after the death of the one who appoints.

The radical reform of which I speak will not arise, therefore, as an institutional decree of Catholicism or of any other Christian body. We should not look to the very thing that has stifled the Spirit to bring it back to life in the lives of people. Lest this seem like hopeless news, the opposite is true. While a politics of spiritual existence is a desirable reality in this world, it cannot be less than a spontaneous manifestation of spiritual life that is already being lived. "Where two or three come together in my name, I am in their midst." We can take heart in the reality of the Spirit, which is ever-present and "blows wheresoever she will." It would perhaps be good to have community leaders, especially popes, of great spiritual understanding. Meanwhile, however, we are not bereft of all resources. We have our own understanding. We can demand of ourselves what is humanly true. We can stop waiting for others to tell us how to live. We can ask questions about our real purpose in life, about the heart of life itself. We can begin to *examine* our lives in the sense that the great philosopher and man of Spirit, Socrates, recommended.

If Christians ready themselves and do what is already possible to them, then persons of spiritual understanding will definitely emerge. They will arise out of our own ranks. Another long-standing spiritual principle reads: *God does not deny grace to the one doing what lies within herself or himself to do [Facienti quod in se est Deus non denegat gratiam].* When enough Christians seek the Christian truth a politics of spiritual existence, which relates us to each other as a spiritual community, will take a clear and identifiable shape in the world quite naturally. How could this not happen? Thus it is the truly important matter, our preparation, our own spiritual development, that we need to consider. It would seem that this belongs to the mission of theology. Now about theology.

NOTES

[1] (Beacon Press, 1958). After my own experience I came to agree with Albert Einstein's reply, on p. 10, to a critic of Blanshard: "Reading your letter, I cannot help to doubt whether you have really studied Mr. Blanshard's publications."

2 John Cooney, *The American Pope: The Life and Times of Francis Cardinal Spellman*, (Times Books, 1984).

3 F. Forrester Church, *God and Other Famous Liberals: Reclaiming the Politics of America*, (Simon & Schuster, 1991), pp. 96-7.

4 *John* XVIII, 36.

5 *Mark* XII, 17.

6 *Matthew* XIII, 25-30.

7 *Ephesians*, V, 23 and numerous other places.

8 James Strachey, ed., *The Future of an Illusion*, (Doubleday & Company, Inc., 1961), p. 3.

9 *John*, XV, 12.

10 *Matthew*, XVHI, 20.

11 *Acts* II, 42-45.

12 *The Fathers of the Church, Volume I*, (The Catholic University of America Press, 1947), p. 361.

13 *Commonitorium primum iii, Patrologia Latina*, ed. J. P. Migne, 50, 640. For a brief but useful discussion of this formula see Jaroslav Pelikan, *Development of Christian Doctrine*, pp. 39f.

14 For a concise discussion of the connection of unity to dogma among prominent early Church Fathers, see *Development of Christian Doctrine*, pp. 64ff.

15 *Matthew* XVIII, 20.

16 *John*, XV, 12.

17 *A History of Christian Thought, Vol. I, From the Beginnings to the Council of Chalcedon*, (Abingdon Press, 1970), p. 150.

18 Donald Warwick, "The Centralization of Ecclesiastical Authority: An Organizational Perspective," in *The Church as Institution*, eds. Gregory Baum and Andrew Greeley, (Herder and Herder, 1974), p. 111. See also *Dogma and Pluralism*, ed. E. Schillebeeckx, "The Creed in the Melting Pot," esp. pp. 135-6: "At least until the conversion of Constantine, when Christianity became the general law of the Roman Empire, the recitation of identical creedal formulas was not considered essential to Christian fellowship."

19 See H. G. Wells, *The Outline of History*, (Garden City Publishing Co., Inc., 1931), p. 451.

20 *Development of Christian Doctrine*, p. 14.

21 *The Age of Constantine the Great*, (Dorset Press, 1989), p. 311.

22 *Matthew* XVI, 19.

23 Karl-Heinz Ohlig, *Why We Need the Pope: the necessity and limitations of papal primacy*, (Abbey Press, 1975), pp 33-35.

24 *Byzantium and the Roman Primacy*, (Fordham University Press, 1966), p. 42.

25 Ibid., p. 49.

26 Ibid., p. 31.

27 Ibid.

28 *Why We Need the Pope: the necessity and limitations of papal primacy.*

29 *Matthew* XXV, 27.

30 Williston Walker, *A History of the Christian Church,* (Charles Scribner's Sons, 1959), pp. 186f.

31 *Inferno,* canto xix, 115.

32 Peter De Rosa, *Vicars of Christ: The Dark Side of the Papacy,* (Crown Publishers, Inc., 1988), p. 54.

33 St. Bernard of Clairvaux, *Five Books On Consideration: Advice to a Pope* [*De consideratione ad Eugenium papam tertiam libri quinque*], Book IV, 6, (Cistercian Publications, 1976), p. 117.

34 Quoted in *Vicars of Christ,* p. 85.

35 *The Sources of Catholic Dogma,* p. 187 (with the author's minor modification of the translation).

36 *The History of Sacerdotal Celibacy in the Christian Church,* (Russell & Russell, Inc., 1957), pp. 1f.

37 See John Courtney Murray, S.J., *We Hold These Truths: Catholic Reflections on the American Proposition,* (Sheed and Ward, Inc., 1960).

38 *The Sources of Catholic Dogma,* pp. 433-42.

39 Ibid., pp. 413f.

40 *How the Pope Became Infallible: Pius IX and the Politics of Persuasion,* (Doubleday & Company, Inc., 1981).

41 See Thomas T. McAvoy, *The Americanist Heresy in Roman Catholicism 1895-1900,* (University of Notre Dame Press, 1963).

42 See Michael Walsh, *Opus Dei: An Investigation into the Secret Society Struggling for Power within the Roman Catholic Church,* (Grafton Books, 1989).

43 *Newsweek,* April 15, 1991, p. 67. The further information on *Opus Dei* recalled here can be found in more recent *Newsweek* reports [January 13 and May 18, 1992] as well as in Walsh's book and numerous other books and periodicals.

44 *Newsweek,* April 15, 1991.

45 *Newsweek,* January 13, 1992, p. 59.

46 A personal, sympathetic account of this period of Pius XII's pontificate is found in Paul I. Murphy, *La Popessa,* (Warner Books, Inc., 1983), pp. 192-229.

47 Ibid., p. 208.

48 *Unholy Trinity: The Vatican, The Nazis, and Soviet Intelligence,* (St. Martin's Press, 1991). Information in the present section comes principally from this source.

49 Ibid., p. 72.

50 Ibid., p. 126.

51 *La Popessa,* p. 294.

52 *John,* XVIII, 11.

[53] Luigi DiFonzo, *St. Peter's Banker: Michele Sindona,* (Franklin Watts, 1983), p. 5.

[54] Ibid. A glimpse of some of the connections of the Italian Church with the Mafia, particularly in Sicily, are mentioned in *La Popessa,* pp. 230-43.

[55] See Rupert Cornwell, *God's Banker,* (Dodd, Mead & Company, 1983).

[56] See *Vicars of Christ,* p. 53, for this quotation from Baronius' voluminous *Ecclesiastical Annals.*

XII

Everywhere there is an overabundance of writing and prattling.
God cannot be seen by writing and prattling.

Rang Avadhut

DEMYSTIFYING THEOLOGY

The theology I studied at the Gregorian University for four years was a grand intellectual scheme. It was a game for which I felt some aptitude. I found it fascinating. The great questions of existence were raised, and we had a longstanding Catholic intellectual tradition that answered them. That the answers changed over the ages did not bother me. In fact, that the present state of the question was unfinished made the game even more exciting to me. It added a creative element to it. I found myself caught up in theology.

Yet even in theology school I remember the occasional experience of this nagging suspicion in the back of my mind: What if all theological questions were fully answered and I knew it all? What difference would that make? I did not allow this strange question much space in my own thinking. It tended to happen on its own, and I did not offer it a warm welcome. It was more fun to return to the great issues of existence and to speculate theologically about them.

The ineffectiveness of the theology I presumed to know was brought home to me in a forceful inner experience. After completing my degree in theology I returned to the United States to take up parish work in a suburban church. One evening a classmate of mine, more enterprising than myself in the activity of parish life, had formed a large group meeting about a current social issue, the economic impact of racism. There were twenty-five or so participants. My classmate brought in experts, including myself, to discuss various facets of this issue. After several of these experts had expounded their informed views, my classmate turned to me and said: "Ed, now what does theology have to contribute to this?" My answer was short: "Nothing." Everything had been said.

Understandably, opinions were arguable about the earthly side of the issue. But it was an earthly issue. At a stroke I realized that there is no divine viewpoint, accessible through a specialized discipline called theology, that had anything whatsoever to add to the substance. Does anyone really need specialized theological thinking to ponder racism? It seems to me that a "heart of flesh" combined with correct information suffices. Ironically, my later study of slave religion in America showed me that theological arguments were often used by Christian preachers to defend racism, supporting the view that peoples of color are inferior. As I have indicated earlier, theology was made to defend the very institution of slavery, can you believe it!

When I became aware of this deficit in theology, I was surprised at discovering how abstract and irrelevant theology is, at least what I had been considering theology. Up to that time I had presumed that not only is there a sacred science about things that is called theology, but that I actually possessed some scientific expertise in this science. However, my illusion was penetrated in that moment. More importantly, this penetrating insight was not delivered to me from a source outside myself—it came from within. *I* saw it for myself.

Interestingly, although I had considerable investment in theology this new insight gave me a sense of freedom. As I look back, I feel I must have been prepared for this insight and the freedom it brought me. I now realize that many ponderous theological problems that had occupied my attention for a long time were not firmly established in my thinking. Already I had quietly wrestled with the question, "What does my limited mind have to do with the truly great matter of existence?" An unraveling of my own mental game had already been happening on its own. Yet until that moment this unraveling of my mental game remained at the *mental* level. It was just another mind-game. But what had been just a vague suspicion in my student days reawakened in me as a living experience in that evening: the theology I presumed to know just did not have any bearing on life. This came as a realization with very practical consequences. It was a subconscious awareness that a philosophy which remains merely in the mind, even when it is about apparently religious or spiritual matters, is not connected with truth or reality. Such speculation does not offer real help. Unrelated to spiritual growth, it remains extraneous to spiritual life itself.

My work requires that I continue to read theological books. But my new angle of vision has made me increasingly perplexed, almost bemused, over many texts: "Who do these writers think they are talking to? Exactly why do they talk the way they do? What do they intend to come from their theology? Do they know something that is truly valuable to communicate? Are they communicating it effectively? Does what they say aid and abet peoples' spiritual growth and transformation?" It is appropriate to bring these questions to a theological text. There are texts that are spiritually useful; many, I feel, are not.

I am not implying that every theologically useful work should be easily understood by every serious reader. This is not the case. Our own inner spiritual development must already be in place at a certain level of growth before we can understand spiritual instruction that is appropriate to that level and can guide us further. If we are befuddled with problems at one level, we are not prepared to understand the simplicity and clarity of spiritual instruction at a deeper level. This does not invalidate the deeper instruction. It means that we are not ready for it, yet. Such *befuddlement* is a *condition more of the heart* than of the mind.

Therefore, yes, St. Theresa of Avila and St. John of the Cross, to cite two highly respected Christian guides, have very useful things to tell us, even if what they say is not yet accessible to everyone. These teachers knew what they were talking about. We realize this even before we can fully grasp what they are saying. Through their own spiritual discipline they came to experience directly what they advise others. This is obvious in their very telling. It makes us realize that we too have to prepare ourselves if we are to understand such teachers and be able to use their guidance in our own life.

Not everything that may appear theologically complex is spiritually profound, however. Much of it does not relate to spiritual life at all, if we understand spirituality as the actual humanization and transformation of our life. A telling incident that involved me concerned a man who, in gospel terms, was asking for bread but was given a stone. Or to put it more literally, he wanted spiritual substance but was given theological mystification.

This man was a university colleague of mine in the humanities. He approached me one day at early-morning coffee in the university cafeteria. He is an intelligent and urbane man of broad experience. He was excited this particular morning. He had read in the public media a feature story of a theologian who, apparently, had important things to say about our spiritual life. I told him:

"Yes, I have heard of this theologian; and, yes, I am familiar with the book referred to. In fact, I have it. I will get it to you promptly." Which I did. As I handed the book to my friend, I knew that it was not going to be of any use to him. Yet this is something he would have to discover for himself. Which he did. Several days later my colleague again approached me at early-morning coffee. This time, however, with uncharacteristic haste. He spirited my book down in front of me with a hurried "Thank you, thank you very much," and quickly walked away. He clearly did not want to discuss the book with me. It was obvious to me that he found it to be a gobbledybook. Which, sad to say, I think it is. I was reminded of the words of Protestant theologian Gerhard Ebeling, writing nearly a generation ago, who spoke critically to the issue of the relevance of theology:

> "Compared with preaching is the danger of
> being out of touch with reality not many
> times greater in theology, which, as a science,
> floats with its abstract jargon in regions whose
> connexion with concrete reality is unintel-
> ligible at all events to the non-theologian and
> —as we may suspect—is often not clear even
> to the theologian himself?"[1]

The point I would make here might best be clarified through contrast. The spiritual leader of the Tibetan people, the well-known Dalai Lama, once finished a discourse of spiritual instruction with these words: "If what I have said seems good to you, put it into practice. If it does not help your practice, then throw it away. It is of no use." This is a simple and straightforward communication. In my view it is also a profound and valid spiritual communication. One who heeds this advice, "If it does not help your practice, throw it away," will keep his or her mind free of thoughts that are not useful. This advice might well challenge theological works: "How does this work help? What potential spiritual effect does it hold for me? Exactly how will the words of this text contribute to the spiritual transformation of my life?"

Such sensitivity to the real nature of spiritual communication has been present within Christianity. The fifteenth century monk Thomas a Kempis offered this famed spiritual advice, "It is better to feel repentance than to know how to define it." Thomas is sometimes viewed askance, as if he belonged to a subtle strain of anti-intellectualism within Christianity. Being anti-intellectual is an indefensible posture from a merely intellectual point of view.

It is easily cast into the same bag as irrationality, philistinism, and even stupidity. However, this issue of intellect and human understanding in spiritual matters runs much deeper than the superficial accusation of being anti-intellectual. I do not see how anyone could contest the validity of Thomas' assertion. How or why would a definition of repentance even come about, if not in order to feel it? So if a person already feels repentant, defining it would serve no purpose except, perhaps, to show others how they too may feel it. Repentance, like all spiritual experience, is more a matter of feeling than of defining.

Long before the time of Thomas a Kempis revelation had lost its spiritual essence as a showing-how of spiritual life and practice. Historically, as the vitality of spiritual discipline waned within Christianity, spiritual knowledge as instruction turned increasingly into dogmas about how things are, as we have already discussed at some length. Displaced from the life of authentic religion, theology was then set to follow both the spirit and the agenda set by academic philosophy. Sadly, even the word *academic*, when it is not referring directly to school matters, has come into everyday speech with a degraded connotation. When we refer to a question or issue as "merely academic," we mean that it has no bearing on reality, that it is inconsequential. Indeed, academic philosophy in our day is too often just such an exercise in irrelevance. It does not always shine forth as love, a real *love*, of *wisdom*, which the Greek words, *philos* [lover] and *sophia* [wisdom], import. Interestingly, the original academy in ancient Greece was a place where lovers of wisdom came together in their search for truth. We recall with some irony that the most ardent of those lovers of wisdom, Socrates, confessed that his very wisdom is the realization that *he knows nothing at all*. A wisdom that consists in the absence of knowing was Socrates' initiation into spiritual understanding.

Apparently our luxuriant world can afford academic philosophy in the sense of intellectual speculation. Idle speculation is the daydreaming of minds that are unhinged from the desire and concern of their own heart. But religion, which arises from the most basic concern of our heart, cannot afford such mental musings. Religion suffers when it is separated from its rightful work. Mere mentalizing remains outside the scope of authentic religion. Yet the fact is that ideas about *what is so* have long distracted us from our felt need for spiritual instruction, how to reconnect. This is the context in which theology has arisen as "the science of the Divine." John Courtney Murray has described "theological reason" as "philosophical reason functioning under the illumination of the Christian faith."[2]

What is theology thought to be? The word itself can tell us something. The word *Theos* is the Greek word for *God*. Theology has to do with God, of course. But more specifically, the word *theology* refers to the God of our *thinking*, which is expressed by the Greek word *logos*. *Theo-logy*, in short, is *our, reflections concerning God*. Yet what do we know, or what do we have to think, about God?

When the early Church fathers adopted the word *theology* from their pagan forebears, they associated it with the knowledge that they presumed was revealed to us by God, which also had very much to do with us. Originally Christian theology was about God-and-us. But alas, the practical matter, what to *do* about God-and-us, *i.e.* how to reconnect, gradually lost its status as the principal task of theology.

So finally, the classic definition of *theology* was articulated by the eleventh century thinker, St. Anselm. Anselm defined theology as "faith seeking understanding." For Anselm the beliefs of faith impel us toward an intellectual understanding of them. Anselm's definition of theology reflects, and probably derives from, an earlier remark of St. Augustine, "Unless you believe, you will not understand." But in the final analysis, even Augustine saw the core doctrines of Christianity, the "symbols of the faith," to be information rather than instruction, "what is so" rather than "how to." Throughout his life Augustine fought hard for dogma, which for him was more an intellectual than a practical matter. At the same time Augustine recognized that a religious life is a spiritually disciplined one.

It is because the teachings of Christianity were pondered more than practiced that they aligned so well with intellectual conceptualization. Theology came to assume that our spiritual task is first to intellectualize information revealed to us by God, and then to live according to the implications of this information.[3] Unfolding an understanding of God's information to us became *dogmatic theology*. Identifying the proper ethical life (right behavior), based on this information, became *moral theology*. Spiritual discipline for the masses was thus reduced, at best, to a decent life of good behavior. The few who are inspired to go beyond the basic requirements of human decency and do what is *supererogatory* ["above the call of duty"]—well, these become our saints, whose cache in heaven will correspond to their extraordinary performance on earth. Dogmatic theology and moral theology tended to remain distinct disciplines. Dogmatic theology held supremacy in theological thinking, since it concerns God's revealed truth, spiritual information. The lesser, merely practical interest was relegated to moral theology. Father Murray was correct in interpreting the dogmatic theology he knew to be "philosophical reason."

This distortion of Christian scriptures and doctrine into intellectualized dogmas was able to persist unchallenged for a very long, and spiritually vapid, period within Christendom. But modern times have introduced vast new humanistic knowledge, even to the point of a knowledge explosion. The modern scientific outlook has simply undermined traditional religious views of a merely intellectual sort. It has created severe instability in the very thing theology considers its domain: The Faith, *i.e.* belief-system. It is true that Protestantism has never been as politically cohesive as Catholicism. Accordingly, dogma as ideology has not been necessary to the identity of Protestantism. It is not a surprise, therefore, that Protestantism responded much earlier and much more favorably to the intellectual spirit of our modern age. Protestant scholars were not forbidden to look at Scripture with new questions. They were more open to a new understanding of the symbols, even the central symbols, of Christianity. It was not until well into the twentieth century that Catholic theologians were permitted some semblance of freedom to reflect critically on the sources and teachings of the Church.[4] Only recently have they become somewhat free to take account of the mindset that we call modernity as well as the "post-modern" mind.

Despite this seeming openness, however, there is no question but that modern scientific knowledge has created endless shifting in our sense of the validity of religious scriptures, beliefs, doctrines, and even morals. Persons who take the Bible seriously, but appreciate it as telling *what is so* rather than as instruction, are unsettled because modern understanding has questioned many matters that were once taken as biblical facts. In respect to doctrines, our contemporary age has worked havoc on the traditional understanding of dogmatic theology. Nearly all contemporary theologians will admit that the traditional explanations of many, if not most (or all?), dogmas are falling apart, if they have not collapsed already.

Much of what today is called theology is little more than mental reflections on increasingly remote issues that are thought somehow to belong to the Christian belief-system. But most of the issues discussed are, in fact, far removed from any spiritual need we feel. Nevertheless, today's theology feels it must salvage some kind of information about God and salvation, despite the fact that the dogmatic posture of Christendom has become obsolete in the face of modernity. What has really happened is that theology finds itself in competition with philosophy and science in the human knowledge game. Alister McGrath offers this general view of modern theologians:

"A theologian is now one who is generally seen to be marginalized as an irrelevance by church and academy alike, whose public is limited to a severely restricted circle of fellow theologians, and whose ideas and methods are generally derived from other intellectual disciplines."[5]

However, neither academic philosophy nor science affect spiritual understanding one way or the other. Merely human philosophy, as well as science, grow and accumulate and change over the years. Authentic spiritual realization [Christ-nature, in Christian terms] does not change, nor does the instruction that guides us toward it. A Jesus or Socrates alive today would not differ in spiritual terms from the Jesus or Socrates of two thousand years ago. Thus instruction relative to our authentic humanization [Christian conversion, transformation, and, ultimately, self-transcendence in Christian terms] does not become obsolete. It applies today the way it did long ago. In a word, our essential human nature has remained the same. Our concerns, our neuroses, our purification, and our freedom are today what they have always been.

Many laypersons, as well as clergy, have gotten some hint of the real condition of theology. They have witnessed the precious symbols of their faith worn thin by being drawn through endless mazes of thought. Some have responded to this situation by taking recourse to a fundamentalist disposition. Although I cannot agree with it, I do sympathize with this disposition. For faith cannot both be a secure link to our Source and at the same time be as vulnerable and whimsical, so "up for grabs," as modern theology has made it. Nevertheless, the fundamentalist disposition also suffers a failure of authentic spiritual communication. Fundamentalism still preserves its faith in intellectual wrappings, *i.e.* belief-systems. Traditional belief-systems are only the product of an old theology. The fundamentalist error is the failure to see that the mere fact of old age does not validate a belief, since the very texture of beliefs is intellectual rather than real, if this can bear repeating. Pouring the old wine of rancid beliefs back into their old wineskins does not make them spiritually potent. Christian life needs new skins filled with the nectar of genuine spiritual instruction.

Authentic spiritual interest sometimes needs to criticize intellectualism. This does not amount to an attack on our intelligence. Rather it is a spiritual critique of the wrong use of our intelligence. We abuse our mind when we abandon our real, felt problem and seek refuge in the pleasures of idle speculation. The spiritual assault on this misuse of our intelligence is well-founded. A modern sage has spoken prophetically to this matter:

> "Everywhere there is an overabundance of writing and prattling. God cannot be seen by writing and prattling. He is not a subject of speech...How can limited speech describe Him who is unlimited. How can the child know of the gladness and joy of the parents' marriage? Oh scholars and learned men, tell me the truth, what have you gained by your learning?...Priests describe Him; scholars describe Him. They know not what He is in fact. They sold away all sugar with a cold heart and did not taste of it even a little...It is just like an ass who bears the burden of sandalwood on his back. The inner treasure fell to the lot of someone else. He is not the subject of books. Logic cannot reach there."[6]

Mere speculation, playing with ideas, is an enjoyable pastime. But it is a diversion. Spiritual ideas are, like medicine, indifferent to our enjoyment. They are not there to entertain us; they employ us. They are created to serve a practical spiritual function in our lives. Ideas that do not engender spiritual growth are a burden at best. More likely they delude us, since they purport to have spiritual significance for our lives, but in fact do not.

It is quite beyond the scope and the interest of this book to detail the intellectual chaos that modernity has worked on traditional Christian doctrine and theology. A symbol that perhaps best represent this chaos is the so-called *death-of-God theology* that arose in the 1960's. Death-of-God theology was mental speculation run amok. Despite this uncritical sellout to post-modernity, god somehow continued to do as well as could be expected. Today this particular oxymoron might more accurately be seen as a harbinger of the death of theology, at least what theology came to be.

From the spiritual point of view, I submit, the knowledge explosion and the melting of fixed ideas that stamp our own era are a blessing for our religious need. They have made it clear that knowledge of what is so, even were it possible, is not our salvation. Mere knowledge of things in any sense is not even spiritually useful, except secondarily inasmuch as it may help our earthly life to support our spiritual engagement. Moreover, as all human knowledge continues both to grow, to fragment, and to bifurcate into paradox, it becomes increasingly evident even at street-level that we are not knowers of reality at all. In fact, this evidence again confirms that knowledge is only functional and is not a knowledge of *what is so*. For by now we are long accustomed to look for the payoff of scientific knowledge. This expectation should lead us to demand of spiritual knowledge that it too offer a benefit beyond itself. Still, to divest theology of its accustomed purpose (identifying, understanding, and expounding "God" and "his" "revelation" of "what is so") is not to say that theology has no purpose at all. Rather, it requires theology to reclaim its true purpose, indeed its very identity. Its authenticity.

Authentic theology has maintained a presence, although often a tenuous one, throughout the history of Christianity. For just as there was the earthly presence of Jesus and his continuing influence as The Spirit of Christ, and just as there was Jesus' teaching about who we really are and about a way of life that corresponds to this truth, so there has always been, and still is, a theology that would help make this teaching effective in the life of Christians. It is a theology that emanates from spiritual practitioners. Unfortunately, this authentic theology is not usually appreciated as instruction that is meant for every human being. Often it is not even called theology but is known rather as mystical literature. It is treated as something reserved for and taken seriously by only rare human beings who are called to be saints. But Christianity itself is shortchanged by leaving sainthood to others. A saint is no more (and no less) than a genuine person. It is a great calling, but it is everybody's vocation. Everybody has the same basic gift, the same ultimate desire, and the same final destiny. But just as people can be cajoled into the idea of a [scientific] "physics for poets," so we can deceive ourselves and others if we accept a "Christianity for the mediocre." There is no such thing. As Jesus has advised, "the lukewarm are vomited out."[7]

To review briefly our argument: as the real practice of the gospel of Truth became rare, and was replaced for most persons by supposedly "intellectual" truths, real theology retreated and succumbed to an intellectualistic identity. Saint Anselm captured this false identity in his definition of theology as "faith seeking understanding." Theologians who have been orphaned of a spiritual practice have maintained, until modern times, this Anselmian ideal. Modern intellectual ferment, therefore, carries a benefit for true theology. It unmasks intellectualistic pretense. When we are stripped of any validity in *knowing what is*, we are left with our naked religious impulse. Theology must then be opened to a more direct association with the practical place of religion and religious instruction in our life.

Therefore, Father Murray misidentified theology when he defined it as "philosophical reason illumined by faith." It is true that faith is luminous. In fact faith is the very luminosity of the heart when the heart stands free in its own place. But real faith does not need philosophical reason; it does not need to be justified. It is a state of being that is its own justification. Faith is not the result of any kind of intellectual speculation, no matter how clever. St. Paul correctly stated that "Faith awakens through hearing" [*Fides ex auditu*[8]]. Authentic theology comes *after* faith. Theology follows *hearing*. It has to do with bringing the faith that follows hearing to fruition, to *realization*.

Jesus addressed our felt disconnectedness in order to instruct us about reconnecting. The foundation of Jesus' instruction, its validating principle, is the same and only validating principle of any genuine spiritual instruction. This foundation was Jesus' own *realization*, his actual possession of spiritual knowledge as his own inner experience. We can call this God-realization or Self-realization; we can call Jesus Son of God, Christ, or any other name. But it is the realization or full-partnership in *reality* that qualified Jesus as a genuine spiritual teacher. There is plenty of authentic mystery in this. The abstract, philosophically induced mystification *about* Jesus—which has solidified into intellectual dogmas—can be dropped without a loss. A human being will come to a real understanding of Christ only by experiencing the Christ-nature herself or himself. Spiritual knowledge of Christ is *Being-That*. Real theology instructs us into a spiritually disciplined way of life that opens toward this real, experiential knowledge and being. It tells us what is required of us, and it tells us *how*. Theology primarily affects our real life, not merely our intellectual life. It communicates to us about actually reconnecting to our Source. St. Anselm's definition of theology must be modified. Theology is not "faith seeking understanding." I suggest that theology is "spiritual instruction, born of mature faith, which nurtures the life of faith in others." It is a practical, not merely an intellectual, discipline.

If faith awakens spontaneously, as if through a leap, then let theology too leap into its proper work. Many persons who have truly understood—*realization* has become their actual condition—have turned to tell us how. And they continue to do so. For our part, let us listen so that we may *hear*. Facilitating the teaching work of spiritual masters is the right activity of theology within living religion. There is plenty to do, since spiritual teaching, as one teacher put it, must "respond to every detail of our life." Theology is the work only of those whose heart-mind is first and foremost engaged in spiritual practice. Their practice is what enables them to help a spiritual way of life in others. For only their own spiritual practice lets them know what they are talking about. Paul spoke concisely to this matter, "Lest having preached to others, I myself become a castaway."[9] Much of what today is called *theology* is also in need of radical reform.

NOTES

[1] *Word and Faith*, (SCM Press Ltd, 1963), p. 198.

[2] *We Hold These Truths*, p. xx.

[3] A theologically explicit instance of this attitude can be found in the work on *theological method* of Bernard Lonergan. The ingenious methodology disclosed in his work, *On Method in Theology*, clearly categorizes the intellectual component as independent of, although intimately related to, the total spiritual dynamic of faith. Despite his intellectual prowess, Father Lonergan, my own most important mentor in theology, was fully committed to the kind of intellectualism I am criticizing here.

[4] Certain of Pope Pius XII's major encyclicals—*Divino afflante spiritu, Mediator Dei*, and *Humani generis* have already been mentioned in these pages—began to create a more open disposition toward theological discourse which has continued to develop in that vein.

[5] *A Life of John Calvin*, (Basil Blackwell, Inc.), 1990, p. xi.

[6] This is found in the modern Hindu classic *Songs of the Avadhut*, Rang Avadhut Maharaj, (Avadhut Parivar, 1972), p. 1.

[7] *Revelations* III, 16.

[8] *Romans* X, 17.

[9] *I Corinthians* IX, 27.

XIII

Without edifices or rules or trustees or any arguement,
The institution of the dear love of comrades.

Walt Whitman

EPILOGUE

Twice in the recent past I have had occasion to spend time in Rome. The subconscious tugs that brought me to St. Peter's Square almost daily, and inside the Basilica itself nearly as frequently, surprised me. I could easily say it was the majestic beauty that drew me there. Or it was the long history which this basilica represents—despite the ups and downs of that history. Beyond these appeals, though, it was the Catholic Christian *culture*, a culture that so profoundly affected my own formation, that I needed to visit and revisit at this physical center of Christianity. Somehow St. Peter's became to me a hazy mirror of myself.

It is almost unthinkable that either Christianity or the Catholic Church will become obsolete in this world. Such is the profound, the complex and, indeed, the all-pervading nature of culture. For culture, to speak generally, is the mother and sustainer of the human soul. We can no more divorce ourselves from our cultural heritage than we could separate ourselves from our nationality, the mother of our physical embodiment. It is for this reason that we must account for our spiritual heritage, the religious culture that has served to represent our link to the very meaning of life.

The daring words in the title of this book, *Radical Reform*, may have suggested an ambition that the book did not show. In ordinary culture the notion of radical reform suggests revolution and points to drastic institutional change. If such were possible in the case of Christianity, it would be useless anyway. The unregenerate would take control over new structures before the smoke cleared. What I learned recently from St. Peter's is that institutional change is far from the main point. Merely changing its cultural form is not the business of religion. Enabling and supporting the transformation of human life and consciousness is the business of religion.

211

The canny but difficult age in which we live has relativized many aspects of the world, indeed of our own lives and culture, which we had previously taken as absolute. Most notably our age has confronted us with issues regarding our mind. It has challenged the validity of conceptual thinking as our access to truth. In this regard the latter half of this century looks upon itself as a "postmodern" era. Ironically, this "newest of the new" of our postmodern world is but a confused and still incoherent discovery about qualities of our inner nature and mind that have been well known and discussed in the Great Spiritual Tradition for well over three millennia, as I pointed out while speaking of the meaning and function of spiritual doctrine.

Christian culture, as a form within the world, has undergone the same "deabsolutization" as every other dimension of the world and of human culture generally. Many persons feel bewildered at the instability of their newly relativized world. They look to their "religion" as the single remaining force for stability. But they must use discrimination in what they take to themselves as absolute in their spiritual heritage, or they will likely find that they have unwittingly created an idol for themselves. Hence our difficult age offers this advantage: it has unmasked our idols to the extent that only the untutored or the undiscriminating can have serious recourse to them. This puts us on alert that meeting the spiritual demand, which is the very purpose of our life, will require considerable responsibility and effort on our part. Yet this has always been the case, for, if I may repeat just one more time, "Only the violent shall bear it away!"

In sharing my reflections on important elements of the Christian heritage, my intention even in the more critical remarks has been positive, to purge and quicken the soul of Christianity. Or to repeat the phraseology I chose, to help awaken others to their spiritual responsibility and to encourage the necessary undertaking of an effective spiritual discipline. This alone is the spiritual life which Christian culture is to enable and nourish. To be sure, Christianity does possess a spiritual treasury, perhaps symbolized in an external way by the grandeur of St. Peter's. There might well be many persons associated with the Church who have scant interest, not to mention know-how, in drawing from this treasury in order to engage a spiritual discipline. For such ones, the institutional Church with its external forms and rituals *is* the only spirituality they know, so they become defensive of its well-being in its given form. Others, who also understand spirituality only in its outer institutional form, become critical of the present state of the Church with all its foibles, or they are apathetic to its apparent emptiness. This book has little to offer any of these people and does not wish to engage them in dispute.

There is another kind of person, though, already possessed of an innate sense of what Jesus meant in saying, "The Kingdom of God is within you." With sincere interest, hard work, and proper help these people will pass over the obstacles of the "all too human" elements of a burdensome tradition and discover the Heart of Christianity. Again, the words of Jesus are simply true: "Ask and you shall receive; Seek and you shall find; Knock and it shall be opened to you."

Such is the *radical reform* I am encouraging. We can expect in the Church the emergence of appropriate institutional forms that, in Thomas Jefferson's words, "must go hand in hand with the progress of the human mind." And yes, a theology that instructs us along the spiritual path will arise spontaneously as the Spirit is regenerated in the lives of Christians.

SELECT ANNOTATED BIBLIOGRAPHY

There are innumerable writings on the themes discussed in the chapters of this book. In selecting a relatively few titles that I feel are relevant to these issues, I cannot promise that they are the best or the most interesting books. But they may prove to be a good starting point in meeting the interest of one or another reader. These works are trustworthy, interesting, and, in varying degrees, readable.

I. JIMMY

- *The Untouched Key: Tracing Childhood Trauma in Creativity and Destructiveness*, Alice Miller, (Doubleday, 1991).

While some knowledge of the language of psychoanalysis is necessary for understanding much of Alice Miller's work, this particular reflection on the childhood experience of   certain famous personalities can be read for the simple stories they recount. They are stories that throw considerable light on the deadening effect that the intrusion of "Jimmy" into a young life can have.

II. AUTHENTIC CHRISTIANITY AND THE HISTORICAL CHURCH

- *The First Coming: How the Kingdom of God Became Christianity*, Thomas Sheehan, (Random House, 1986).

This is a clear historical account of how the spiritual community that gathered around the person and teaching of Jesus developed into the institution of Christianity in the early centuries of our era.

- *Bare Ruined Choirs: Doubt, Prophecy, and Radical Religion*, Garry Wills, (Dell Publishing Company, 1971), and *Trojan Horse in the City of God: The Catholic Crisis Explained*,   Dietrich von Hildebrand, (Sophia Institute Press, 1993).

These two works, both written shortly after the completion of the Second Vatican Council [although here I cite the recently revised edition of von Hildebrand's book], can be juxtaposed as contending responses to the meaning of *aggiornamento* as Vatican II enabled Roman Catholicism to finally face the modern world. The one-time conservative Wills reckons with the radical openness [dare I say *glosnost?*] that necessarily accompanied Pope John's call.The conservative von Hildebrand interprets *aggiornamento* as no more than a call to express the eternal verities in a language more accessible to "modern man."

III. THE CATHOLIC EXPERIENCE

- *The Catholic Moment*, Richard John Neuhaus, (Harper & Row, 1987).

A well-argued appreciation of the positive potential of Catholicism in the contemporary world, this work does not undertake the criticism that I see to be necessary for the Catholic Church to fulfill its spiritual potential.

- *Tomorrow's Catholics - Yesterday's Church: The Two Cultures of American Catholicism*, Eugene Kennedy, (Harper & Row, 1988).

This inspection of today's Catholicism by a noted psychologist and former priest helps explain some of the well-known disparities in "the Catholic experience" in the contemporary world.

- *The Catholic Myth: The Behavior and Beliefs of American Catholics*, Andrew M. Greeley, (Charles Scribner's Sons, 1990)

Father Greeley, a noted American priest-sociologist,presents us with certain cold facts of the American Catholic experience that simply must be accounted for.

- *A Flock of Shepherds: The National Conference of Catholic Bishops*, Thomas J. Reese, S.J., (Sheed & Ward, 1992).

Although this body of Catholic bishops no longer enjoys the authority over the American Catholic mind it once held, it is still an important facet of "the Catholic experience." Father Reese's meticulous research offers invaluable insight both into the major issues addressed by this religious body and into its workings—in particular its relations with the Vatican. Reese's companion volume, *Archbishop: Inside the Power Structure of the American Catholic Church* (Harper & Row, 1989) invites an interesting comparison with Paul Blanshard's long-standing criticism of this same "power structure" in his *American Freedom and Catholic Power* (Beacon Press, 1958). Certain practical implications of Pope John XXIII's *aggiornamento* are easily discernible.

IV. THE CULT OF THIS WORLD

- *The Anatomy of the Catholic Church: Roman Catholicism in an Age of Revolution*, Gerard Noel, (Doubleday & Company, Inc.,1980).

This engaging book describes the distortions that worldly influences worked on the Church during its long history as well as the problems such influences create in today's Church.

- *The Subversion of Christianity*, Jacques Ellul, (William B. Eerdmans Publishing Company, 1986).

This brief work is a biting criticism of the worldliness that has insinuated itself into the recesses of Christianity.

- *Kierkegaard's Attack Upon "Christendom" 1854-1855*, tr.Walter Lowrie, (Princeton University Press, 1944).

While much of this penetrating thinker's work requires philosophical training on the part of the reader, his "Attack" is as clear as a bell and may, beware, have a similar wakening effect on the reader.

V. OUR SPIRITUAL RESPONSIBILITY

- *Habits of the Heart*, Robert N. Bellah et al., (Harper & Row, 1985).

This is a probing study of individual Americans who seek to find meaning and purpose in their lives as defined and, in crucial ways, limited by "American cultural traditions."

- *Care of the Soul: A Guide for Cultivating Depth and Sacredness in Everyday Life*, Thomas Moore, (HarperCollins, 1992).

This valuable bestseller explores often bypassed regions of our psyche and unabashedly highlights the darker sides. It rightly envisions the nature of spiritual work not only as beyond a divine con-game of "do-goodism," but as attending to the full range of our psyches, including dimensions we might prefer to ignore, suppress, or eliminate.

VI. FAITH OR BELIEF

- *Fear and Trembling: A Dialectical Lyric*, Soren Kierkegaard, (Princeton University Press, 1941).

The only useful work I know that will support a profound pondering of the core spiritual reality of faith is this work of the nineteenth century's foremost religious *thinker*   [not sage, not mystic, not saint]. Kierkegaard's work probes the nature of faith through an extended reflection on the story of the Father of Faith, Abraham.

- For a more intellectually, in contrast to "thoughtfully," demanding consideration of faith, aside from the works by Tillich already cited, namely *Dynamics of Faith* and *Courage To Be*, I can recommend Gerhard Ebeling's *The Nature of Faith*, (Muhlenberg Press, 1961). Some familiarity with theological language and approaches is almost prerequisite for reading Ebeling.

VII. DOGMA OR INSTRUCTION

- *Beyond Ideology*, Ninian Smart, (Harper & Row, 1981).

This learned yet readable volume, while acknowledging the necessity and therefore validity of particular beliefs, highlights their cultural limitations in view of the diverse thinking and religious practices that shape the spiritual experience of the whole of humankind.

- My Search For Absolutes, Paul Tillich, (Simon and Schuster, 1967).

Without denying our need to think in ways that are limited, the discriminating thought of this major Protestant theologian identifies the error in attributing absoluteness to anything whatsoever that is not God, indeed to anything less than the "Godhead" even beyond God.

- Forgotten Truth: The Primordial Tradition, Huston Smith, (Harper & Row, 1976).

With his customary gift for clarity and readability, Dr.Smith discusses the profound religious symbolism that reaches across cultures to instruct us concerning our human place and purpose in the great scheme of existence.

VIII. ORIGINAL SIN OR ORIGINAL PURITY

- The Dogma of Original Sin, Alfred Vanneste, (Vander, Publisher, 1969).

Vanneste attempts to "update" the dogma of Original Sin by putting to rest the numerous intellectual difficulties that are associated with it, while he nonetheless maintains a basic "truth" to this teaching.

- Original Blessing: A Primer in Creation Spirituality, Matthew Fox, (Bear & Company, Inc., 1983).

Father Fox, a Dominican priest whose ministry has recently become estranged in respect to the official Church, seeks here to convey the Heart of Christianity as a positive spirituality, a way of life founded upon the inherent goodness of all creation, including humankind. Fox sets forth clearly "...the very shaky biblical grounds on which original sin doctrine is based" in order to supplant "...the exclusively fall/redemption model of spirituality" with the non-dualistic orientation of "Creation Spirituality."

IX. JESUS CHAUVINISM OR CHRIST UNIVERSALISM

- *The Myth of God Incarnate*, John Hick, ed., (The Westminster Press, 1977).

This collection of writings challenges naive thinking about an "incarnation of God" in Jesus of Nazareth which is based on a simplistic acceptance of the New Testament as a divine dictation and combines this with a traditional, Greek-centered philosophy that is, at best, inadequate to modern thought.

- *Incarnation in Hinduism and Christianity: the Myth of the God-Man*, Daniel E. Bassuk, (Humanities Press International, Inc., 1987).

Among the major world religions Christianity and Hinduism have developed the notion of "God-man" most explicitly. With responsible scholarship this work places the traditional Christian doctrine of Jesus of Nazareth as the Incarnation of God in a grander and less chauvinistic context, which has always been true of the Hindu idea of Incarnation.

X. MAGIC OR MYSTERY

- *Man and His Symbols*, Carl G. Jung, (Dell Publishing Co., Inc., 1964).

For the reader who is not professionally trained this work can be a sound basis for raising the mind's understanding above mere fact and literalism to the world of meaning and value, where *sacrament* dwells, albeit housed in its "outward signs," particular symbols empowered by usage.

- *The Power of Myth*, Joseph Campbell, (Doubleday, 1988).

This work can help us understand how the power that dwells in myth might be ennobled and raised to the sacred realm in those "outward signs" [persons, places, events, *rites, etc.*] that usage has, over time, made sacramental.

XI. THE POLITICS OF SPIRITUAL EXISTENCE

- *Caesar's Coin: Religion and Politics in America*, Richard P.McBrien, (Macmillan Publishing Company, 1987).

The intricacies of the relationship between religion and world, to speak most generally, is analyzed here in great detail as it has worked itself out in the American experience. This book is highly useful for defining central concepts and identifying many of the issues in the unavoidably complex relationship between religion and world.

- *Why We Need the Pope: the necessity and limitations of papal primacy*, Karl-Heinz Ohlig, (Abbey Press, 1975).

This is a clear, brief recount of the history of the development of the papacy in the West which over time presumed an absolute primacy that is not historically defensible.

- *Vicars of Christ: The Dark Side of the Papacy*, Peter De Rosa, (Crown Publishers, Inc., 1988).

A delightfully readable book, former Jesuit De Rosa's volume delivers exactly what it promises, a careful, historically knowledgeable look at the *dark side* of the papacy through the ages.

- *In the Vatican: How the Church is run—its personalities, traditions and conflicts*, Peter Hebblethwaite, (Adler & Adler, 1986).

A former Jesuit priest, the late Peter Hebblethwaite was perhaps the foremost "vaticanologist" of recent times. Here he offers a fascinating inside look—"amusingly fleshed out with gossip and scholarly asides" [*The Telegraph* of London]—at the actual workings of the Vatican. Particularly relevant to the book in hand is perhaps his chapter, "Watchdogs of Orthodoxy," which among other matters highlights the highhanded treatment of certain high-profile modern theologians by the Vatican's *Congregation for the Doctrine of Faith*, the one-time *Holy Office of the Inquisition*.

- *St. Peter's Banker: Michele Sindona*, Luigi DiFonzo,(Franklin Watts, 1983), *God's Banker*, Rupert Cornwell,(Dodd, Mead & Company, 1983), and *The Vatican Connection: The Astonishing Account of a Billion-dollar Counterfeit Stock Deal Between the Mafia and the Church*, Richard Hammer,(Holt, Rinehart and Winston, 1982).

These volumes detail the modern scandal, stupendous in extent, of Vatican financial dealings with nearly every unsavory element and dimension of mammon imaginable. Notwithstanding their sad factuality, these works read with the fascination of an early Ludlum novel.

- *Opus Dei: An Investigation into the Secret Society Struggling for Power within the Roman Catholic Church.* Michael Walsh, (Grafton Books, 1989).

While this book is clearly antagonistic to the organization *Opus Dei*, the facts it relates are startling and, for the most part, not easily disputed.

XII. DEMYSTIFYING THEOLOGY

- *Message and Existence: An Introduction to Christian Theology*, Langdon Gilkey, (The Seabury Press, 1979).

This noted theologian's attempt to relate theology to the needs and concerns of ordinary folk exemplifies some of the problems I critique in conventional theology.

- *Songs of the Avadhut*, Rang Avadhut Maharaj, (Avadhut Parivar, 1972).

This short spiritual classic can confront every religiously serious person with the question whether s/he is prepared to actually embrace a spiritual discipline or will be content to continue to "think about it," *theologically* so to speak.

INDEX